"This book makes an important contribution to our understanding of how participatory governance can produce improvements in social well-being and public goods allocations. Donaghy's work is a welcome addition to a growing body of work on citizen participation and participatory democracy, because it is the first book that combines large-N and case study analyses to demonstrate that these new democratic institutions generate public policies that have beneficial impacts on the lives of poor citizens."

—**Brian Wampler**, Boise State University

"This is an empirically rich and innovative 'mixed-method' study of participatory institutions in Brazil. Donaghy does more than tell us that civic participation makes for good social policy. She presents a nuanced analysis of why that is so, breaking with commonly accepted hypotheses such as that a preexisting history of civil society mobilization determines the success of government sponsored efforts to include citizens in decision making."

—**Rebecca Abers**, University of Brasília

Civil Society and Participatory Governance

Democratic institutions should promote accountability of government officials to the needs of citizens. Civil society plays a role in exposing corruption
as well as in communicating the needs of low-income residents to officials.
Neither the institutions of representative democracy nor the presence of civil
society, however, appear to automatically guarantee adoption of social benefits for the poor. Can democratic institutions be created to address social
challenges?

Scholars, development practitioners, donors, and activists propose participatory governance institutions as mechanisms to create accountability
and responsiveness through a public forum incorporating civil society. To
date, however, little comparative research exists to confirm whether these
institutions do influence adoption of social policies. Maureen M. Donaghy
remedies this gap by combining data from Brazil's 5,564 municipalities with
extensive fieldwork from five Brazilian cities to test whether participatory
municipal housing councils are associated with an increase in adoption of
social housing programs to benefit the poor. Housing represents an issue
of critical importance in Brazil and other developing countries where large
populations reside in informal settlements in unsafe and insecure conditions.

Civil Society and Participatory Governance is the first book of its kind
to move the conversation beyond budgeting to other social policy areas,
providing fresh theoretical and empirical insights to demonstrate that participatory governance institutions are effective mechanisms to coordinate
government officials and civil society to alter policy making.

Maureen M. Donaghy is Assistant Professor at Rutgers University–Camden.
Her research and teaching interests focus on development and civil society
with an emphasis on participatory governance, urban politics, and Latin
America.

Routledge Studies in Latin American Politics

Civil Society and Participatory Governance

Municipal Councils and Social Housing Programs in Brazil

Maureen M. Donaghy

Routledge
Taylor & Francis Group

NEW YORK AND LONDON

First published 2013
by Routledge
711 Third Avenue, New York, NY 10017

Simultaneously published in the UK
by Routledge
2 Park Square, Milton Park, Abingdon, Oxfordshire OX14 4RN

First issued in paperback 2014

Routledge is an imprint of the Taylor and Francis Group,
an informa business

Library of Congress Cataloging-in-Publication Data

Donaghy, Maureen M.

Civil society and participatory governance : municipal councils and social
   housing programs in Brazil / Maureen M. Donaghy.
     p. cm. — (Routledge studies in Latin American politics ; 5)
  1. Housing policy—Brazil—Citizen participation. 2. Public housing—
Brazil. 3. City councils—Brazil. 4. Municipal government—
Brazil 5. Civil society—Brazil. I. Title.
   HD7323.A3D66 2013
   320.8'54—dc23
   2012035701

ISBN 978-0-415-62958-4 (hbk)
ISBN 978-1-138-91574-9 (pbk)
ISBN 978-0-203-09801-1 (ebk)

Typeset in Sabon
by Apex CoVantage, LLC

This book is dedicated to Rob, with love always.

Contents

Tables and Figures

Tables

Figures

Acknowledgments

I owe a tremendous debt of gratitude to numerous people who contributed to the success of this project. First, I wish to acknowledge the financial support of the National Security Education Program, the University of Colorado, and Rutgers University, which allowed me to complete fieldwork in Brazil related to this project.

In Brazil, I would first and foremost like to thank my hosts in each of the cities I visited. Specifically, I would like to thank Benedito Barbosa, Evaniza Rodrigues, Maria das Graças, Luiz Herlein, Rev. Marcos Cosmo, and Marli Carrara for all their hospitality and generosity of time and spirit. This project would not have been possible without their patience and willingness to explain the housing situation and participatory process in each city. In addition, while in Brazil I had the privilege to be affiliated with the Fundação Getulío Vargas in São Paulo, and I sincerely appreciate the kindness and support of George Avelino during my stay.

At the University of Colorado at Boulder, my sincerest appreciation goes to David S. Brown for all his hard work, encouragement, and patience. His sound advice and incredible energy made this book a much better project, though any errors are of course still my own. I would also like to thank Lee Alston, Krister Andersson, Andy Baker, and Susan Clarke for all their invaluable comments and support.

Finally, I would like to thank all of my friends and family for their seemingly never-ending encouragement. In particular, I am forever grateful to my parents, Jim and Linda Donaghy, for providing me with a firm foundation, sound counsel, and an appreciation for lifelong learning. My brother, Jimi, and my sister-in-law, Bonnie, have also been a constant source of support and advice. In addition, I have been incredibly fortunate to have the encouragement of my grandparents, Mary and Tony Alberti; the extended Alberti and Donaghy families; and the whole Naranjo family. Though he is too young to know it, my son, Miles, also pushed me to finish this project while providing me with smiles and hope for the future at every turn. Last, but certainly not least, I would like to acknowledge all the sacrifice and support of my husband, Rob Naranjo. I am forever grateful to be on this journey with you.

1   Introduction

Democracy does not serve as an automatic remedy of ailments as
quinine works to remedy malaria. The opportunity it opens up has
to be positively grabbed in order to achieve the desired effect.

—Amartya Sen[1]

Can democracy remedy social challenges? As Amartya Sen makes clear
above, democracy on its own cannot solve all problems. While democracy
presents an opening for representation, more is required to capture the benefits of democratic governance to meet the needs of citizens. The question
is how the benefits of democracy may be capitalized on to create progress
in solving deep-rooted social problems. The traditional institutions of representative democracy—executives, legislatures, and courts—bring order to
policy making and may provide accountability and responsiveness through
elections and laws. But, despite the impressive growth of democracy in developing countries over the last two decades, poverty, inequality, and continued cynicism about democracy provide reasons to think that elections
and associated democratic institutions fail to engage important segments
of the population. While democratic institutions seem to be thoroughly entrenched, more work lies ahead if democratic governance is to address long-
standing social challenges.

Scholars have suggested that a strong civil society is the key for enabling
social development in a democracy. Alexis de Tocqueville argued that associations of citizens create a more informed citizenry, which in turn is able to
better hold governments accountable for their actions. Robert Putnam then
famously argued that social capital, generated within or outside of formal
associations, leads citizens to make greater demands of their leaders.[2] Fundamentally, in order for governments to act, they must feel pressure from
citizens. Democracy's ability to foster social development, then, may depend
on the strength of civil society to collectively make demands on government
officials. The question is how.

In this book I seek to answer whether democratic institutions can be
created to incorporate civil society interests into policy making in order to

address social challenges. To that end, I examine the impact newly formed participatory councils have on housing policy in Brazil. Housing is a critical policy area, particularly in developing countries with exploding urban populations, that affects the quality of life, safety, and economic potential of poor citizens worldwide. To date, however, little research has focused on the political motivations behind housing policy adoption. Given the growth of private sector real estate markets in developing countries, the voices of the poor demanding government assistance to attain safe and secure living conditions often become muffled. The goal of this study is to understand whether institutional innovation produces change for the poor as a subset of society often left at a political disadvantage. The following story from Curitiba, Brazil, motivates my study.

On a rainy Saturday I was invited by leaders of two housing rights organizations to visit a recent land occupation not far from the city center. Plywood shelters and plastic-sheeted tents housing 1,400 families lined the street and extended far back into the woods. It was the day before municipal elections, and Luiz, a longtime activist in the urban reform movement, was campaigning for city council on a platform to create a municipal-level housing secretariat and extend special zones for social housing. Luiz trudged along with us in the mud, wearing a suit with only a laminated campaign poster for cover, occasionally handing out campaign material to residents. That day an overflowing creek flooded numerous shelters with raw sewage, and families scrambled to keep their children and limited possessions dry. Seeing the situation, Luiz called the local Ministério Público[3] (Public Ministry) office and a local media outlet to alert them to the health emergency. Several hours later we left the occupation without any government official or media member arriving on the scene. In the interim, however, we did witness several other candidates for city council delivering soda and food supplies to the community. The next day Luiz came in in 553rd place out of 797 candidates for city council. Several weeks later, all the residents of the occupation were evicted in a violent clash with police, during which one person was killed.

In this instance neither the mechanism of elections nor the presence of civil society organizations (CSOs) served to hold the local government accountable to this community's needs. Clientelism, in which politicians promise favors in exchange for votes, often prevents candidates with ideas for broad policy reform from winning elections. In an atmosphere of intense electoral competition, short-term promises and gifts win votes from the poor, but long-term solutions to entrenched problems, such as homelessness and property rights, may remain unaddressed. In addition, even where an active civil society exists to represent the interests of the poor, there is no guarantee that those organizations have any influence with government officials. Though scholars often cite the media and the judicial system as mechanisms for civil society influence, this case demonstrates that neither mechanism necessarily guarantees civil society access to redress. A free media may promote transparency of government, but the media may find everyday instances of poverty mundane and be unresponsive to calls from CSOs looking to publicize perceived injustices. CSOs may also lack the capacity and the time to access the judicial system. Moreover, the judiciary cannot enact social programs to assist large segments of the population. These institutions of democracy are necessary to promote transparency and accountability, but they are not sufficient to generate lasting solutions to poverty.

Can institutional solutions be designed to address these problems? Political scientists and development scholars are still working to identify the kinds of democratic institutions that best promote accountability to the poor. In addition, though civil society may be a critical part of democracy, existing literature does not concretely identify how civil society best holds governments accountable for the provision of social welfare. In this book I evaluate participatory governance institutions as a particular type of democratic institution that incorporates civil society into policy making to promote accountability to the poor. In addition to accountability, participatory governance institutions should also ensure greater responsiveness to heterogeneous needs at the local level based on the direct input of civil society into policy making. Participatory governance institutions should fill the gap between democracy and CSOs by guaranteeing regular access to government officials, providing a forum for debate among actors, increasing transparency, and regulating social programs, in the end creating policies that better reflect the interests of the poor.

Through the case of Brazil's municipal housing councils, I analyze the effect of participatory governance institutions on pro-poor policy adoption and ask an important question: Can governments create institutions to promote greater responsiveness and accountability to the poor? Are participatory governance institutions effective democratic institutions to incorporate civil society demands and elicit action from governments? Here I test whether civil society incorporation in decision making through municipal housing councils affects the provision of resources. If municipal housing councils are associated with an increase in social housing programs, participatory governance institutions may in fact provide an answer to how democratic institutions and civil society may encourage adoption of social benefits.

POLITICAL INSTITUTIONS, CIVIL SOCIETY, AND THE POOR

Over the past few decades we have learned several important lessons about the role of democracy in addressing the challenges of poverty. Primarily, previous studies find that democracies produce more benefits for the poor than nondemocracies.[4] Quantitative evidence also supports the claim that democracies spend more than nondemocracies on social programs, particularly for education and health care.[5] Further, recent evidence suggests that where nondemocracies do have high levels of social spending, programs may be targeted at narrow groups of citizens whose support aids in maintaining the status quo.[6] In sum, democratic institutions appear to strongly influence the depth of social spending, and most likely the subsequent quality of life for citizens.

Scholars then suggest several mechanisms by which democracy benefits the poor. First, because elections allow citizens to punish officials for governance failures, politicians act strategically to prevent these failures from occurring. For instance, Amartya Sen finds that famines are less likely to occur in democracies because officials have strategic incentives to prevent famines from ever happening in the first place.[7] When failures do occur, freedom of the press in democracies aids in spreading information among citizens.[8] Competition among candidates should also lead to increasing promises for social programs.[9] Future elections then compel politicians to spend more on public goods once in office in order to retain support.[10]

These studies all point to electoral competition as the key to governmental accountability. Elections, however, appear to only go so far in producing benefits for the poor. Several scholars challenge the fundamental usefulness of elections as mechanisms for translating the interests of voters into policy action.[11] As mentioned in the story from Curitiba, clientelism may actually lead the poor to vote for candidates who provide immediate relief, prioritizing the present over potential future benefits. Moreover, once in office officials may have little contact with citizens and may not be directly concerned with the needs of low-income residents until it is time to campaign again. Elections may be a loose mechanism for accountability, thereby conferring broad benefits to the poor across countries and across time, but in the near term, the poor need action by governments to resolve pressing problems. In addition, as democracies experience higher economic growth rates, providing social assistance to the poor may become less broadly politically popular, decreasing the electoral incentive to enact social programs. While elections are certainly important for accountability, they are not perfect mechanisms for securing benefits for the poor.

Beyond elections, scholars cite the roles of legislatures, executives, and courts, and the inclusion of subnational governments in shaping political struggles and resource allocation.[12] For example, where more veto players exist, such as in federalist systems with strong separation of powers, the possibilities for welfare state development may be limited.[13] However, other scholars have called into question the effectiveness of controls over public officials, including courts and oversight bodies, which are supposed to ensure the functioning of representative democracy.[14] Neither the separation of powers nor specific mechanisms set up to promote accountability of politicians appears to effectively engender responsiveness to low-income citizens.

Recent research from the developing world, in particular, is beginning to uncover how federalism and decentralization may affect social policy. As Judith Tendler sums up the argument for decentralization, "greater proximity makes government more vulnerable to citizen pressures, and makes it easier for citizens to become more informed and hence more demanding of good service."[15] Research shows, however, that decentralization does not automatically lead to better outcomes for the poor.[16] But, when local stakeholders are involved and sufficient resources and power are given to the local level, decentralization does show promise for increasing accountability.[17] These studies suggest the need for further research into when decentralization leads to policies benefiting the poor and the type of decentralized institutions that enable inclusion of stakeholders.

Finally, as mentioned, civil society is also thought to be crucial to promoting accountability of the government to its citizens. Civil society, sometimes referred to as the third sector, can be broadly defined as the actors that operate between the state and the market. In reality, the lines between these three sectors are often blurred as actors move between government, the private sector, and civil society in both professional and personal capacities. Interactions with government and private sector actors may strengthen the organizational capacity of civil society. Though the lines between actors may sometimes be blurred, however, civil society remains an important categorization of actors representing neither the state's interests nor the private sector's primary quest for profits. The types of organizations that make up civil society vary tremendously across contexts, but in general CSOs include nongovernmental organizations (NGOs), social movements, community-based organizations (CBOs), religious organizations, and professional associations.

As mentioned, the causal relationship between CSOs, democracy, and policy outcomes is often framed by the classic work of Alexis de Tocqueville. Based on his experience in the United States, Tocqueville recognized the importance of a vibrant culture of associationalism to form a counterbalance to the weight of the state.[18] Through associationalism citizens would build connections with each other to help in times of crisis. Similar to Tocqueville's notion of associationalism, Robert Putnam found that social capital unifies citizens to make claims on the government and demand a response.[19] Putnam argued that a strong civil society is needed to counter the tendency of the state to protect elite interests and ensure that institutions function in the interests of residents. This ideal of civil society as protector of citizens' interests continues to drive much of the research on government accountability. As John Gaventa writes,

> Based on long standing ideas of the importance of "associationalism" in democracy, a robust civil society can serve as an additional check and balance on government behaviour [*sic*], through mobilizing [*sic*] claims, advocating for special interests, playing a watchdog role, and generally exercising countervailing power against the state.[20]

In general, however, the literature on social capital and associationalism lacks specific details about how civil society actually reaches governments to enforce accountability. We still know very little about which strategies and tactics work best under certain circumstances to produce policy change.

To some extent, scholars of social movements have picked up this question. Though by definition civil society includes a broader network of actors than social movements alone, as collections of citizens organized for a specific purpose, social movements make up an important part of the whole of civil society. Scholars on social movements cite shifts in the political opportunity structure as explaining when social movements are able to influence policy change.[21] The mechanisms by which social movements, and CSOs more broadly, traditionally influence policy making are through direct action such as protest, public campaigns, and bilateral negotiations with government officials. Public officials respond to demands made through direct action often out of fear of the economic and political impact of disruption.[22] This type of contentious politics, however, is difficult to maintain over the course of time.[23] Distribution of social benefits in response to these demands may then be targeted to specific claims rather than broad social policies. Second, public campaigns—either in support of or in opposition to public officials and their activities—may lead to policy changes where electoral fortunes are at stake. Social movements, and more broadly CSOs, use the media and their own networks to spread information, which may lead to public shame or to swaying voters' decisions. For instance, in South Korea, the growth in NGOs led to awareness of the inequities in coverage, which ultimately led to more universal programs.[24] Finally, social movements and CSOs are often invited by government officials to meet, or they request meetings in order to inform officials of specific citizen needs. Government officials may respond to requests once they are made aware of the need to act and are offered specific solutions. One claim against civil society is that these types of activities lead organizations to act in the interests of their own members without considering the broader social impact of their demands.

To date, more comparative research is needed to evaluate the contexts in which CSOs most effectively persuade governments to adopt social programs in their own interests and in the interests of the poor more broadly. We still need systematic research to understand exactly how CSOs are able to hold governments accountable to the needs of the poor.[25]

In sum, though we have good evidence that democracies produce better outcomes for the poor than authoritarian regimes, particularly in terms of social spending, we still need more information about how democratic institutions and civil society within democracies best hold governments accountable for improving the lives of citizens. Elections and decentralized institutions do produce some level of accountability to the needs of low-income citizens, but these two factors alone do not appear to solve entrenched social problems. Civil society may also be key for making democracy work for the poor, but the means by which scholars have identified civil society influence over government decision making are vague. We need to further identify the institutions through which civil society reaches government officials to affect change.

PARTICIPATORY GOVERNANCE INSTITUTIONS

Participatory governance institutions are innovative democratic mechanisms, capturing the benefits of decentralization and civil society. Simply put, participatory governance involves the inclusion of civil society to work with the state in managing resources and directing policies, programs, and/ or planning processes. These institutions theoretically provide an answer to questions of how to increase accountability to the poor and incorporate civil society more closely into policy making. The principal aim in terms of outcomes should be to change the redistribution of benefits to attend to the needs of those not previously engaged in policy making. The problem is that we still know very little about how these institutions work across contexts and whether they achieve the ultimate goal of shaping policies to benefit a broad array of citizens. We still need to understand whether participatory governance institutions can create responsiveness and accountability where other democratic mechanisms and civil society involvement alone have failed.

Participatory governance institutions are said to cement the role of civil society as "co-governor" with the state.[26] They are forums in which citizens and government officials discuss problems and deliberate together to generate solutions.[27] No longer can government officials selectively listen to certain civil society groups or individuals. Instead, both sides enter into a more formal, and ideally inclusive, mechanism for cooperation. Participatory governance institutions include a broad range of approaches, involving budgeting, policy making, service delivery, development planning, monitoring of public services, and oversight bodies.[28] All of these approaches undertake a different mode of incorporating civil society and the state based on different objectives, permanency of the process, and rules governing cooperation of actors. But all participatory governance institutions emerge based on the idea that traditional institutions of representative democracy do not adequately include the voices of the poor or respond to their needs.[29]

Participatory governance institutions expand decision making beyond the bureaucracy with the aim of balancing elite interests with the demands of civil society. CSOs involved in participatory governance institutions include NGOs and private sector associations, which may not traditionally represent the poor, in addition to social movements and neighborhood associations, which more typically represent low-income residents. Participatory governance institutions, therefore, represent a variety of interests from civil society, and may not automatically favor the poor. In this book I seek to assess whether participatory governance institutions, formally incorporating the diverse voices of civil society, make a difference in policy outcomes. While in some cases the complex dynamics between actors representing different parts of civil society make a difference to the outcomes, in others,

CSOs are more united in their efforts to create policies and programs to benefit the poor, specifically.

Over the last two decades, scholars, governmental entities, and NGOs have repopularized the notion of participatory democracy. Political theorists refer to "deliberative democracy" as a form of citizen participation often used interchangeably with participatory democracy. Deliberative institutions, however, differ from participatory governance institutions in that while citizens have a voice, policy makers are not bound to their decisions.[30] Participatory governance institutions are meant to allow citizens to shape policy through an ongoing, routine process in which participants should have the opportunity to vote on outcomes. These institutions are also meant to improve the linkages between the state and society. As Gianpaolo Baiocchi, Patrick Heller, and Marcelo Kunrath Silva theorize, participatory governance institutions address the Weberian problematic of how representative institutions translate popular interests into outcomes.[31] Greater participation by previously marginalized actors should create outcomes that respond more efficiently to the will of the people.

Support for participatory governance institutions also derives from the notion that various participatory approaches promote "good governance." The World Bank defines governance as the way in which states exercise power to manage economic and social resources.[32] Good governance is measured by the capacity of governments to provide public services, ensure transparency, promote well-being, and enable economic development.[33] Participatory institutions should enable good governance by mitigating the control of the state over resources and shining a light on budgeting and administrative planning, which are traditionally closed-door processes.

But, why would elites voluntarily give up control by implementing participatory governance institutions? Not only do participatory governance institutions decrease officials' relative power, but it can also be expensive to set up the financial, operational, and legal capacity to implement the results.[34] The most common explanation for creation of these institutions involves the influence of left-leaning parties, particularly in Latin America, which adopted participatory governance into their party platforms and seek now to implement participatory institutions since they have gained office.[35] A second argument involves modernization and a changing political culture: as citizens become wealthier, they become more politically aware and favor greater civic engagement.[36] Though these scholars do not argue that modernization directly leads to participatory governance institutions specifically, contemporary leaders may view participatory institutions as one answer to calls for deeper incorporation of citizen's voices. Third, greater decentralization of resources and power also facilitates the creation of participatory governance institutions. Once subnational governments have control over local policy decisions, governments may create participatory institutions to direct the implementation of policies and programs. If decision making remains concentrated at the national level, local-level participatory institutions are not necessary. Lastly, government officials create participatory governance institutions when it suits their social, political, and financial interests. Demand by civil society to establish participatory governance processes should increase the positive incentives for local officials to create these institutions.[37] By creating participatory institutions, elected officials win the confidence and votes of the members of CSOs calling for their creation.

But, once created, do participatory governance institutions in reality act as effective democratic institutions to benefit the poor? In this book, I argue throughout that participatory governance institutions should lead to increasing social benefits for the poor based on the basic mechanisms of responsiveness and accountability. Studies by development scholars find that decentralization of responsibilities and resources to local officials often leads to improved responsiveness and accountability of local governments to citizens' concerns.[38] Participatory governance institutions formally involve civil society in the process of decentralization. Further, when civil society has the opportunity to present the specific needs of the community, governments may respond directly to those needs rather than implementing programs that do not address the real problems. By increasing information sharing among and between CSOs, government officials, and the public at large, other scholars have argued that CSOs hold governments accountable within the forum and within the municipality by generating public scrutiny.[39]

Accountability has also been defined in terms of reduction in corruption and clientelism. Ackerman claims that participatory governance institutions reduce possibilities and incentives for corruption, the political use of funds, and the capture of state institutions by elites.[40] Participatory institutions that allow civil society to scrutinize public spending should reduce corruption where governments are held liable through elections.[41] Participatory governance institutions, therefore, complement the institutions of representative democracy in eliciting accountability.

Previous research on participatory governance institutions worldwide also identifies a number of areas of impact, which may contribute to a shift in policy outcomes.[42] First, individuals gain from the transfer of information and the empowerment from being heard by government officials in a public forum. Individuals, particularly low-income citizens, may never have felt their voices mattered in government decision making. Participatory governance institutions are meant to ensure that policy makers hear the voices of previously marginalized sectors within democracies. CSOs that participate may also gain from the networking opportunities involved in the institutions while strengthening their relationships with government officials. Sitting in meetings together should create a sense of common purpose and build common understanding. Participating in a public forum rather than negotiating benefits with government officials behind closed doors also democratizes the repertoires of CSOs.[43] CSOs, themselves, are reinvented through the participatory process. Finally, the creation of participatory governance institutions necessitates a change in government structures to accommodate new arenas of decision making and the flow of resources. For instance, new government agencies and leadership positions may need to be created to facilitate the implementation of these institutions.

Though current evidence suggests that participatory governance institutions do generate responsiveness and accountability,[44] little comparative research exists to confirm whether these institutions produce benefits to the poor in terms of programs and policies. Where scholars have focused on the question of outcomes, studies have been limited by empirical evidence and comparison across contexts. Those studies that do present comparative cases for study tend to focus on one type of institution: participatory budgeting processes.[45] To date scholars have focused very heavily on participatory budgeting and have not conducted broadly comparative studies to judge the impact of diverse institutions across contexts. Participatory governance institutions may promote responsiveness and accountability, but we need to know when and how they make a difference rather than making blanket proclamations regarding the broad benefits of participation for the poor.

If participatory governance institutions do lead to increasing benefits to the poor, this suggests that institutions may be created to enhance the performance of governments in responding to the needs of citizens. In this book, I test this claim based on the following broad hypothesis: *where participatory governance institutions exist, municipal governments will adopt a greater number of social programs to address the needs of the poor.* Municipal housing councils specifically make decisions related to social housing policy, directly related to the needs of the poor. If participatory governance institutions matter for policy outcomes that affect the poor, we should see that municipalities with these types of institutions are more likely to adopt social housing programs. By analyzing this particular institution for which decisions affect the lives of a great number of citizens across Brazil, I hope to speak to the broader question of whether institutions can be created to better address the needs of low-income citizens around the world.

THE BRAZILIAN CASE

Brazil presents an important test case for assessing whether participatory governance institutions can enhance the benefits of democracy. Though Brazil has experienced fast-paced economic growth and international praise, domestically the government must address social challenges in order to alleviate persistent poverty and inequality. Brazil has been classified as a "social democracy" based on its ability to manage economic growth while expanding social, political, and economic rights.[46] Former president Luiz Inacio Lula da Silva from the Worker's Party promised redistribution and economic growth within the market economy. The current president, Dilma Rousseff, has largely continued Lula's economic and social policies. However, though growth in Brazil as a whole has been robust, poverty, inequality, and social spending are still far from uniform across Brazil's 5,564 municipalities. This leads to the question, then, of whether democracy functions differently across this one country to produce such large variation.

Taken as a whole, poverty in Brazil is falling. In 2009, the official poverty rate stood at 21.4%, down from 30% just four years earlier.[47] In fact, the World Bank now classifies Brazil as an upper-middle-income country. Not only is the middle class growing, but the percentage of people living in extreme poverty is decreasing. Infant mortality fell 30% from 1998 to 2008 while the percentage of youth entering higher education doubled.[48] The improvement in development indicators is largely attributed to overall economic growth and the widespread use of the Bolsa Família program. Consolidated under President Lula, Bolsa Família is a conditional cash transfer program that addresses challenges to health, education, nutrition, and income by tying receipt of a monthly stipend to children's school attendance and regular health check-ups. In 2009, approximately 11 million families or 46 million people received Bolsa Família.[49]

Although national statistics indicate an improvement in extreme poverty across the country, regional statistics still tell a story of vast disparities in living standards. The North and Northeast regions of the country still experience the highest rates of poverty, while the Center West, South, and Southeast regions enjoy relatively high levels of development. Though poverty fell in all of Brazil's five regions between 1998 and 2008, the poverty rate in the Northeast region in 2008 stood at 41% versus 13% in the Southeast region.[50] Further, in the Northeast, 66.7% of children and youth still live below the national poverty line, compared to 44.7% of children and youth in the country as a whole. In addition, in 2010, 32% of households in the North lived with open sewage while only 4.2% of homes in the Southeast and 2.9% of homes in the Center-West lacked basic sanitation.[51]

These statistics demonstrate the importance of subnational research in Brazil. The study of local government has received increasing attention due to the recognition that democratic practice and levels of development vary widely not only across countries but within countries.[52] The size of the nation and the wide disparity in development indicators makes Brazil a prime location for study of subnational politics. High levels of urbanization also pose challenges to governance, making it an important case for urban planners, political scientists, and sociologists. According to the 2010 Census, over 84% of the Brazilian population lives in urban centers.[53]

Moreover, municipalities in Brazil enjoy almost unparalleled levels of responsibility and authority, especially as compared to other developing nations, which contributes to the significant variation in living standards, policies, and politics.[54] The Brazilian Constitution of 1988 established significant independence for municipalities. Each of the 5,564 municipalities is designated as part of the Brazilian federation, with an autonomous municipal government. Mayors and members of the municipal legislature (câmara municipal) are directly elected for four-year terms. Each municipality has the power to collect taxes, while also receiving transfers from the federal and state-level governments.

Scholars traditionally characterize Brazilian politics by its dysfunctional institutions. Since democratization, a large number of parties have developed, party switching among elected officials is common, and voters do not generally maintain strong party allegiances.[55] A weak party system leads to individualistic politics. At the national level, Barry Ames argues that a clientelist tradition leads legislators to favor pork-barrel politics over institutional reforms.[56] Without strong legislative majorities by party, mayors, state governors, and presidents, often must make deals with individual legislators to pass legislation. Legislators, then, are able to act in the interests of their narrow constituencies rather than in the interests of their parties. Without top-down direction by party leadership, distribution of benefits by elected officials among constituents is then often based on the tradition of clientelism, or the exchange of private goods between two unequal parties. High levels of inequality exacerbate the tendency toward clientelism. With a Gini coefficient of .57, Brazil is considered one of the most unequal countries in the world.[57] As mentioned previously, the poor who need immediate relief often willingly accept the gifts of politicians as the best the system can provide, and politicians capitalize on residents' vulnerability in order to win votes.

Dysfunction in Brazil's democratic institutions is both a symptom and a cause of poverty and inequality. Participatory governance institutions are meant to address some of the failings of representative institutions by limiting the influence of elite and wealthy interests. Channeling the demands of the poor through participatory institutions should limit the need and desire to accept clientelistic benefits and therefore reduce the votes for candidates promising particularistic benefits rather than broad change. By enabling greater impersonalization of politics, participatory institutions in Brazil should lead to more equitable distribution of resources, thereby breaking the cycle of poverty, inequality, and clientelism. In Brazil, and around the world, participatory governance institutions should address long-recognized problems of representative democracy, including a bias in favor of wealthier citizens, coordination between government agencies, and low participation of citizens.[58]

Civil society in Brazil has evolved since the days of state corporatism from the 1930s to the 1970s. Under state corporatism, CSOs operated at the will of government officials and negotiated directly with the bureaucracy. The corporatist tradition still manifests itself in the close relationships between CSOs and government officials, though today CSOs form independently of the government and do not have the same level of incorporation into the bureaucracy. In between corporatism and the present, a military regime disrupted the modern development of CSOs. In the 1970s and 1980s, a slow opening by the military government (1964–1985) provided citizens again with the opportunity to organize.[59] The Catholic Church in Brazil supported democratic organizing through the promotion of liberation theology and the creation of Christian base communities.[60] At the same time, industrial strikes propelled leaders, including eventual President Luiz Inacio Lula da Silva, to new recognition. In the 1980s, labor and social movements in Brazil coalesced to form the Worker's Party (Partido dos Trabalhadores [PT]). CSOs united around calls for democracy in the 1980s and subsequently grew to challenge the nascent democratic government to address various social challenges, including education, health care, land rights, and housing. As explained to me by Benedito Barbosa, a longtime activist and attorney, social movements in the 1980s were linked through three major national agendas: (1) strengthening the PT, (2) re-democratizing the unions, and (3) organizing rural workers into the Commissão Pastoral da Terra (CPT) and the Movimento dos Trabalhadores Rurais Sem Terra (MST) and organizing urban movements around public policy issues, including health and housing.[61] These three objectives shaped the transition to democracy alongside the organizations of the Catholic Church. These movements were then very active in pressing for specific provisions for democratic rights and social benefits in the 1988 constitution.

The PT, which has now controlled politics at the federal level for a decade, began as a leftist opposition party committed to socialist goals of redistribution and internal principles of democratic governance.[62] Since its founding, the PT has been closely associated with a broad range of social movements calling for a more equitable society, less political corruption, and more effective service delivery. They have also traditionally promoted the idea of new institutions to allow greater participation.[63] The PT calls for the creation of participatory processes as a means of using formal democracy to create new opportunities for inclusion.[64] The development and professionalization of CSOs associated with the PT has paralleled the party's evolution from an opposition party to the party in power. Though CSOs involved in participatory governance institutions are by no means all affiliated with the PT, the demand for participatory governance institutions has traditionally been associated with the PT and leftist social movements.

In addition to the consolidation of the PT and the space for associationalism created by democratization, urbanization also contributed to the development of civil society in Brazil. As James Holston argues, migrants arriving in Brazilian cities in search of the benefits of industrialization had to construct their own homes and infrastructure without assistance from the state. Creating communities through this autonomous process often went hand and hand with the development of social movements and a desire to claim the rights of citizenship.[65] The claim to social benefits as a right of citizenship permeates the language of urban CSOs today.

The process of developing participatory governance institutions in Brazil coincided with the progression toward democracy in the country. Much like in other new democracies, CSOs lobbied for the inclusion of participatory governance institutions as part of the democratic transition.[66] During the drafting of the new constitution in 1988, Brazilian scholars Vera Schattan Coelho, Barbara Pozzoni, and Mariana Cifuentes explain,

> Hundreds of thousands of interest groups worked throughout the country as the constitution was being drafted and collected half a million signatures to demand the creation of participatory democratic mechanisms. Underpinning such demand was the belief that by opening spaces for citizens to participate, the policymaking process would become more transparent and accountable and social policies would better reflect the needs of citizens.[67]

Participatory governance institutions in Brazil have been at the heart of civil society strategy to press the federal, state, and municipal governments to address the needs of the poor. CSOs, including NGOs and social movements, continue now to demand the implementation of participatory governance institutions and the release of resources from the federal to the municipal level.

The most well-known example of participatory governance in Brazil is the participatory budgeting process in Porto Alegre, a city in the South of the country. When the PT won the municipal elections in Porto Alegre in 1988, one of their primary initiatives was the introduction of participatory budgeting. According to Pedro Jacobi, the impetus for focusing on the budget specifically was that "the budget becomes the incentive for all popular debates, and the definition of priorities is an extremely important instrument in mobilizing community practices."[68] The process of negotiating the budget, therefore, becomes a mechanism for collectivizing preferences across a range of actors and a means for both sides to understand more about the other's needs and restrictions. In Porto Alegre, the participatory budgeting process is open to all residents. In regional assemblies, citizens first debate and vote on budget priorities before electing representatives to a citywide council that eventually forwards a budget proposal to the mayor for approval. As of 2008, approximately 20% of the city's residents had participated in the budgeting process.[69] The participatory budgeting process demonstrates that ordinary citizens can effectively participate in technical and complex decision making. Further, evidence shows that in Porto Alegre and in other sites of participatory budgeting, resources tend to be more greatly redistributed to poor areas.[70] Evidence on participatory budgeting in Porto Alegre also suggests that the process generates social capital, efficacy, and deliberative capacity among participants.[71] Participatory budgeting processes have been widely replicated across Brazil, and as of 2005, about 25% of the Brazilian population lived in a city that had some type of participatory budgeting process.[72]

Though participatory budgeting initiatives, particularly those in Porto Alegre, have received the most international attention as examples of institutions demonstrating the potential benefits of collaboration between citizens and government, numerous other types of municipal-level councils exist throughout Brazil, tasked with both policy and programmatic responsibilities. An important distinction between participatory budgeting processes and other types of councils, though, is the nature of representation. In participatory budgeting processes, individual citizens participate as they choose, at least in the beginning citywide assembly phase of the process. In many of Brazil's municipal councils, representatives from CSOs are appointed or elected to participate for predetermined terms. These types of councils generally allocate half of the seats for government officials and half for representatives of civil society. Brazilian scholars estimate the number of policy and program councils to be around 20,000, with several hundred thousand citizens participating.[73] In general, these councils have the power to debate the direction of policy, propose new programs, make budgetary decisions, define program criteria, and provide oversight during program implementation.

While informative case study research exists to suggest these municipal councils and other types of participatory governance institutions provide a voice for previously marginalized citizens, questions remain regarding the extent of resulting benefits for the poor and the context in which these institutions have the greatest impact.[74] Brazil's municipal councils for housing offer an opportunity to assess whether participatory governance institutions, as democratic institutions incorporating civil society into decision making, matter for the variation in social policy across the country.

HOUSING POLICY AND PARTICIPATION

In this study I assess the effect of municipal housing councils on social housing policy. Housing is an issue of vital importance to the poor in developing countries, particularly in urban areas. It presents a key social benefit for which governments provide direct assistance, financing, and indirect support through community improvements. Across Brazil the need for housing continues to rise as indicated by the increasing percentage of the population living in favelas.[75] Between 2000 and 2010 the population in the favelas grew by 75% while the overall population grew by only 12.3%.[76] In 2008, according to the national statistics agency, there were 15 million homes deemed to be "inadequate." Homes are deemed "inadequate" if they lack basic infrastructure or property title or are overcrowded with residents. Approximately 6.2 million more houses are also needed to reduce the "quantitative" housing deficit. The quantitative housing deficit refers to the need to house families who cannot afford to live independently or who currently live in precarious conditions, including areas of environmental risk and favelas without adequate shelter. Of these 6.2 million families, 89.4% earn less than three minimum salaries, or the estimated salary needed to rent or purchase decent accommodations in the market.

The Brazilian Constitution of 1988, which guarantees the right to housing along with many other social rights, provides the legal basis for CSOs to call on the government to urgently address the severe lack of housing throughout the country. In fact, the Brazilian government has a long history of investing in housing, though not on the scale needed or to the lowest-income citizens. Since the 1930s the government has provided financing through the Caixa Econômica Federal (Federal Savings Bank) and state-level banks. In 1964 the government established the Banco Nacional de Habitação (National Housing Bank [BNH]), which established financing for low-income residents to purchase individual homes. However, according to the Centro Gaspar Garcia de Direitos Humanos, a Brazilian NGO, by 1980 only 8% of the 4.5 million homes financed through the BNH went to families earning less than five minimum salaries.[77] In other words, the majority of government financing did not benefit the lowest-income citizens. In 1982 the government closed the BNH, leaving the country without a clear national housing policy or large-scale programs until 2004, when the Lula administration created the Ministry of Cities. In the past decade, national programs, such as the Program for Accelerated Growth (PAC) and the Minha Casa Minha Vida Program, have provided significant funding for housing projects. Municipalities, however, are still primarily responsible for devising local housing policy and implementing housing projects.

Civil society oriented toward housing in Brazil includes a diverse collection of organizations, ranging from professionalized NGOs to social movements and neighborhood associations. Many CSOs in Brazil grew out of the movement for democratization in the 1980s. The goals of CSOs working on housing issues in Brazil and other developing countries revolve primarily around government provision of resources and land claims. CSOs dedicated to housing respond to the challenges in cities, peri-urban areas, and rural communities. The main housing CSOs, however, are oriented toward urban reform. The four main entities for housing are the União Nacional dos Movimentos por Moradia Popular (UNMP), the Central de Movimentos Populares (CMP), the Confederação Nacional dos Associações da Moradia (CONAM), and the Movimento Nacional de Luta por Moradia (MNLM). These four organizations then work together under the network of the Fórum Nacional da Reforma Urbana (National Forum for Urban Reform [FNRU]).[78] Of the four main organizations, the UNMP is most closely aligned with the PT and has been the most vocal in demanding participatory institutions for housing policy. The CMP is also strongly linked to the PT and the UNMP, though the CMP also addresses issues outside of housing policy. CONAM tends to concentrate their efforts at the community level while the MNLM adopts the most radical tactics of the four. All of the organizations have affiliates throughout the country, though the UNMP appears to have the broadest reach, with members in 21 of Brazil's 27 states.

Both nationally and locally, organizations in Brazil have been particularly vocal about the need for strong participatory institutions to which they can direct their demands.[79] But, at the same time many CSOs also continue to undertake a number of different strategies calling for policy change and increasing housing assistance. For instance, social movements concerned with housing in urban areas, such as the Movimento dos Trabalhadores Sem-Teto (Roofless Worker's Movement [MTST]), which began in São Paulo and now operates around the country, carry out occupations of city buildings. CSOs also engage in direct lobbying, arranging personal meetings with municipal housing officials, or, if they cannot secure a meeting, protesting outside of the housing secretariat until their demands for negotiation are met. In rural areas, workers' organizations and social movements, such as the MST, also struggle for benefits from the municipal, state, and federal levels. While urban CSOs are concerned with improvement of favelas, rehabilitation of city centers, and construction of new units, in rural areas CSOs are more likely to petition for programs to provide construction materials, plots of land, and flexible financing options.

CSOs of all kinds involved in housing developed strength in the 1980s under democratization, waned in the 1990s under structural reforms, and then reemerged in the late 1990s under worsening economic conditions.[80] The four major social movements for housing in Brazil lead policy demands at the federal, state, and municipal levels. Though São Paulo remains the centers of activity for movement leaders, each of the four main movements has strong networks of members throughout the country. Their demands can be traced from federal legislation and spending priorities to municipal-level housing councils and increasingly diverse programs at the local level. Alongside social movements, professional NGOs, such as the Instituto Pólis, are engaged in research, advocacy, and capacity building for smaller organizations, and often participate in the councils themselves.

Municipal housing councils in Brazil incorporate members from civil society and local government officials to deliberate on programs and policies to benefit low-income residents. Many municipal housing councils formed in the early 2000s at the initiative of mayors from the PT. Since then, however, municipal housing councils have been created by mayors from diverse parties and in response to the creation of the National System for Housing in the Social Interest (Sìstema Nacional de Habitação de Interesse Social [SNHIS]). Under this new decentralized housing system, every municipality wishing to receive funds for social housing from the federal level should have created a municipal housing council by the end of 2009. The variation in municipalities adopting housing councils both before and after the mandate provides for comparison across the country.

Municipal housing councils have the opportunity to shape the housing environment for the poor through the approval of new programs, by directing resources to certain programs or citizens and by speaking up when the government fails to follow through on promises or misuses state resources. For the analysis in this book, I use data on the types of housing programs adopted by each municipality to assess whether the existence of a municipal housing council increases the likelihood of social housing program adoption. All housing programs reported in this data set can be considered "pro-poor" in that through a variety of mechanisms they seek to allow low-income residents the opportunity to live in more secure housing arrangements. Housing programs, as categorized by the Brazilian government's MUNIC survey (Pesquisa de Informações Básicas Municipais), involve construction of new units, offering plots of land, providing construction materials, regularizing land titles, urbanization of the community, acquiring units, and improving existing units.[81] As will be discussed throughout the book, not all programs respond equally to the types of initiatives demanded by CSOs nor do CSO demands remain constant across contexts, but this list of programs generally contains the menu of options from which municipalities choose to provide housing benefits to the poor.

My goal in this study is to assess whether municipal housing councils are associated with an increase in social housing benefits as measured by the adoption of housing programs. Further, I seek to determine *when* and *how* these participatory governance institutions lead to policy and program change. My hypothesis is that municipal housing councils may be key to the variation in housing policy across municipalities. Where participatory governance institutions exist, municipal governments should be more responsive and accountable to citizens' needs. Here I seek to provide concrete evidence to an important question for Brazil and other developing countries: Can participatory governance institutions generate responsiveness and accountability to social needs across diverse contexts?

RESEARCH DESIGN

For this study I employ a mixed-method approach. I use both case studies and large-N quantitative methods to test the hypotheses and to understand the causal mechanisms by which municipal housing councils influence housing policy in Brazil. The benefit to this type of mixed-method approach is that the two parts inform each other to strengthen overall confidence in the findings.[82] I begin with a survey of Brazilian municipalities, which contained questions regarding housing programs and institutions in both 2005 and 2008.[83] I use these data first to evaluate the claim that municipal housing councils are associated with an increase in adoption of housing programs. In conjunction with several other Brazilian government sources, I also use these data to test whether a strong civil society enhances the effect of municipal housing councils in eliciting social housing programs.

Based on a review of the data, out of the 20 largest cities in the country I selected my initial case studies based on the density of civil society and whether a council for housing existed in the municipality. From this I selected four cases in diverse regions of the country. Table 1.1 displays the results of this analysis.[84]

Table 1.1   Initial Case Study Selection Criteria

	No Housing Council	Housing Council
Low Civil Society	Curitiba – South	Salvador – Northeast
High Civil Society	Recife – Northeast	São Paulo – Southeast

Like most field studies, however, the picture became more complex once I landed on the ground and began talking to government officials and civil society leaders in each city. While according to the survey data and online information Recife and Curitiba did not have municipal housing councils, in the fall of 2008 it turned out that both had recently passed laws to create housing councils in response to the federal mandate, requiring that all municipalities receiving federal funds create a council by the end of 2009. This enabled me to look more closely into the question of how the reason behind creation of participatory governance institutions influences the commitment of actors and the eventual outcomes. But, because the housing councils in these two cities were not yet really functioning, I do not include them in my analysis of how civil society–state dynamics influences outcomes in participatory institutions. In addition, once on the ground I decided to investigate the case of Santo André on the outskirts of São Paulo because I heard repeatedly that they had a model municipal housing council operated by a long-term PT government. I wanted to see how the presence of a stable, leftist administration affected the participatory governance process in Santo André, as opposed to the cases of São Paulo and Salvador, in which changing political administrations seemed to shift the dynamics of the municipal housing councils.

Within each of the five case cities, to the extent possible, I interviewed all government officials involved with the housing councils. In Santo André and Salvador, which have relatively small housing departments, this involved interviews with a few key officials. In São Paulo, where an extensive bureaucracy exists to manage social housing programs, I interviewed approximately 10 relevant officials. In Curitiba and Recife I interviewed the few officials who were involved in the initial creation of the housing councils. To find my interviewees, I called or emailed housing departments and requested meetings or made contact with officials during housing council meetings I attended.

I also spoke with leaders from all four of Brazil's major housing organizations, in addition to the FNRU, to gauge their perceptions of the councils and their effectiveness in bringing about greater prioritization of housing interventions at the municipal level. My contact with CSOs began in São Paulo and snowballed across the country. By attending several meetings of the UNMP I met many of the most influential leaders in the Brazilian housing movement. From these meetings, I received contacts from the UNMP and the other three major movements for housing around the country. In each city I was hosted by affiliates of the UNMP, though I also met with leaders from the other major movements, NGOs, and locally based associations. Through these interviews I gained an enormous respect for the daily struggles of these activists and lengthy process they have gone through to negotiate the creation of participatory governance institutions. Their immense dedication to securing better living conditions for their fellow citizens is truly remarkable. In addition, I also interviewed private sector interests in each city, though with a particular emphasis on the real estate sector in São Paulo. By speaking with a diverse group of actors, I hope to have received a well-rounded view of the municipal councils, including the benefits and pitfalls of participatory governance.

Throughout this book, information from the case studies informs the hypotheses and interpretation of results. Based on the results from the preliminary statistical analysis in Chapters 3 and 4, in Chapter 5 I review the case studies to provide evidence as to how the policy-making process works in municipal housing councils. This review informs the statistical analysis regarding how the policy process affects outcomes in municipal housing councils. When the statistical analysis provides results contrary to my expectations, another look at the case studies helps to explain why. Chapter 6 then relies on the case studies and quantitative evidence to assess how the reason behind creation of municipal housing councils leads to variance in outcomes. Finally, in Chapter 7 I revisit the case of the Municipal Council for Housing in São Paulo to assess what leads to changes in participatory governance institutions, and how shifts in actors and agendas impact institutional longevity. Though the findings from case studies and quantitative analysis do not always agree as much as I would like, the combination of methods allows me to be more confident in my ultimate conclusions.

OVERVIEW OF CHAPTERS

In this study I test a general theoretical proposition regarding participatory governance institutions as mechanisms for responsiveness and accountability while also exploring the current civil society and policy environment for housing in Brazil. I begin with a discussion of housing policy as a critical issue for democracy and development both in developing countries worldwide and in Brazil. I then turn to the basic empirical question regarding the effect of participatory governance institutions on the adoption of social programs. In addition, based on existing literature and my observations in the field, I identify several variables, which may alter the effect of participatory governance institutions on policy outcomes: the density of civil society, civil society–state dynamics, institutional rules, and the reason for creation. The following provides an outline for each chapter of the book.

Chapter 2: Housing Policy

Scholars of democracy and social policy often overlook housing policy. However, housing as an issue of physical shelter, community development, and infrastructure provision, is increasingly important in developing countries where large slum populations and underserved rural communities demand benefits from the state to improve their basic quality of life. In defining housing policy, I follow the logic of Brazilian scholars Renato Cymbalista and Paula Freire Santoro: "A housing policy assumes a wide variety of objectives—from provision of new units, slum reurbanization, emission of ownership waivers, intervention in tenements, to rent subsidies."[85] The objectives of housing policy aim to reduce homelessness and provide more secure shelter for citizens. These objectives translate into locally and nationally devised programs to provide individual families with units in which to live and programs to improve existing communities. In Chapter 2 I discuss housing policy in more detail, illustrating the similarities and differences between Brazil and developing countries around the world.

Chapter 3: The Effect of Municipal Housing Councils

In Chapter 3 I present the main theoretical argument for the effect of participatory governance institutions on policy outcomes. I then test the hypothesis that municipal housing councils should increase the probability of municipalities adopting social housing programs. Positive findings suggest that governments can create democratic institutions to improve responsiveness and accountability to the needs of the poor. This chapter sets the stage for subsequent chapters in which I assess the variables that influence the policy process and outcomes of municipal housing councils.

Chapter 4: Civil Society Density

In Chapter 4 I test the claim that the density of civil society matters for the outcomes participatory governance institutions produce. Building on Putnam, scholars studying participatory governance institutions argue specifically that low levels of social capital impede the impact of participatory institutions.[86] In a cross-municipal study of participatory budgeting councils in Brazil, Leonardo Avritzer found that the councils did not provide the intended forum for deliberation where there was not already a significant community of organizations to participate.[87] Participation may be predicated on whether organized networks of civil society exist, and further, outcomes may be a product of how those networks are able to control the discussion.[88] Without considerable mobilization of demands, participatory institutions may be easily co-opted by elites and have no effect on democratic deepening or policy outcomes.[89] Using statistical analysis, I initially hypothesize that the greater the number of CSOs per capita in a municipality, the stronger the effect of participatory governance institutions in eliciting social policies. Contrary to my expectations, however, the data do not provide evidence to support this hypothesis.

Chapter 5: Civil Society–State Dynamics and Institutional Rules

In Chapter 5 I evaluate the effect of civil society–state dynamics and institutional rules on the policy process before turning to the effect of these variables on policy outcomes of municipal housing councils. The relationship between civil society and the state should influence the policy process in participatory governance institutions.[90] I argue that the party of the administration in power, the strength of the private sector, and the strategies of CSOs influence the dynamic between civil society and the local government. Baiocchi, Heller, and Silva find that participatory governance institutions expand the traditional political opportunity structure through which civil society influences government action.[91] The ideological predisposition of the government leadership makes a difference for their enthusiasm for participatory institutions and their inclination to include civil society in decision making. Previous research shows that the political context in which CSOs operate either encourages or impedes their ability to reach policy makers throughout the stages of the policy process.[92] Whether policy makers' ideological predispositions and interests align with CSOs leads to strained or mutually beneficial relationships and communication between CSOs and policy makers.[93]

Participatory governance institutions may either exacerbate tensions among actors or facilitate cooperation. In addition, the strength of private sector interests and their alliances with government officials and civil society also matter for the direction of policy making. Government officials have to balance demands for economic opportunities with the demands of CSOs to provide benefits to the poor. Finally, the strategies by which local CSOs traditionally reach government officials matter for whether CSOs are viewed as partners or adversaries. If CSOs continue to rely on direct action, including land occupations, or bilateral negotiations with government officials, participatory governance institutions may have little effect on policy.

But, as Avritzer argues, institutional design is also critical to how citizens and government engage in decision making.[94] How participatory institutions are devised should matter for whose voices are included and the outcomes they produce.[95] The structure of the institution, in terms of rules governing composition and responsibilities afforded to members, may then determine the policy process and outcomes of participatory governance institutions. In order to create the synergistic process that scholars and development practitioners have idealized, institutional design must be taken into account.[96]

Chapter 6: The Reason for Creation

Whether participatory governance institutions are created by ideologically inclined mayors or imposed by federal mandate may matter for the commitment of government officials and CSOs to the process. Scholars have found that the commitment of the local and central governments to the process is critical for the effectiveness of participatory governance institutions.[97] Inclusion of civil society and the responsibilities accorded to participatory governance institutions demonstrate the commitment of the government to making the process work. In addition, the commitment of civil society is also critical to the effectiveness of institutions, which by definition rely on the input of community members outside of government. In Chapter 6 I assess how the reason for creation affects the commitment of government officials and civil society members, and further how this commitment affects the outcomes of participatory governance institutions.

Chapter 7: Longevity in Participatory Governance Institutions

In Chapter 7 I review the case of São Paulo, Brazil, to assess how participatory governance institutions change over time. Based on interviews and documents related to the housing council in São Paulo, I review the changes in actors and agenda over the 10 years of the council's existence. Shifts in the membership of participatory institutions, due to changes in municipal administration and civil society's commitment to participation, shift the institution's agenda. The long- and short-term agenda of these institutions also responds to changes in needs, resource transfers from the federal level, the role of the private sector, and changes in the perception of housing needs. I find that though changes in the commitment of the municipal administration are critical for shifts in actors, agendas, and outcomes of the housing council, the fortitude of leftist-oriented social movements keeps the institution relevant to policy making. During a critical time of crisis for the housing council in São Paulo, the institutional rules and government commitment were put to the test, but social movements used the institutions of representative democracy—courts and the legislature—to hold the government to its obligation to operate the Municipal Council for Housing. The case presents lessons for other participatory governance institutions to ensure that all actors have incentives to participate and maintain committed to the process.

MAIN FINDINGS

The main finding of this book is that participatory governance institutions do matter for adoption of policies benefiting the poor. Where municipal councils for housing exist, municipalities are more likely to adopt a variety of social housing programs. Participatory governance institutions can create greater responsiveness and accountability to citizens' needs. More than the depth of civil society, these institutions have the ability to shift government decision making. In fact, I find that municipal housing councils are associated with greater adoption of social housing programs regardless of the density of civil society within a municipality. This suggests that the institution is more important than the density of civil society and that the institution may have a strong effect on redistribution across contexts in Brazil.

Second, I find that the rules of participatory governance institutions matter for the outcomes they produce. In the case studies, civil society–state dynamics significantly alter the policy-making process within municipal housing councils, but in the aggregate the institutional rules appear to strongly influence program adoption. Civil society–state dynamics, including the party in power, the role of the private sector, and the strategies of civil society, do determine the level of transparency, the scope of who is involved, and the nature of deliberation within municipal housing councils. All these factors influence the details of housing programs, where projects are located, and the depth of municipal resources allocated to housing. Across cases, however, the transparency generated by oversight responsibilities allocated to municipal housing councils appears to significantly alter program adoption.

Third, I find that the impetus for creation matters for the commitment of actors to participatory governance institutions. Whether municipal housing councils are initiated from the bottom-up rather than the top-down plays a role in how committed government officials and CSOs are to the process. In turn, the commitment of government officials and civil society matters for the outcomes municipal housing councils produce. Participatory governance institutions mandated at the municipal level by the federal level, therefore, may not have the same impact on generating benefits for the poor.

Finally, through the case of the Municipal Council for Housing in São Paulo, I find that shifts in actors and agendas of participatory institutions are inevitable. Not surprisingly, the depth of commitment of social movements ensures the longevity of participatory institutions. Policy makers and CSOs should have realistic expectations about what participatory governance institutions can change and what they cannot, due to capacity constraints or conflicting interests. Institutional rules should be clearly defined to prevent conflict and regular resource contributions ensure long-term relevance of the institution.

CONCLUSIONS

In a democracy everyone should have the opportunity to have his or her voice heard. But the institutions of representative democracy—elections in particular—may not be enough to hold governments accountable to the needs of the poor and promote adoption of social benefit regimes. Traditional tactics of civil society—protest, bilateral negotiation, advocacy campaigns, and so on—may also not be enough for civil society to change the priorities of government officials to respond to the needs of low-income residents. Instead, the formal incorporation of civil society into decision making through participatory governance institutions may provide a critical seat at the table leading to changing policy outcomes that benefit the poor. Rather than the depth of civil society alone, the institutionalization of participation is pivotal to generating responsiveness and accountability.

Scholars, development practitioners, and donors hail participatory governance institutions as a means toward achieving "good governance," in which civil society provides an active voice in managing state resources. These institutions incorporate civil society into policy making in a new way, providing CSOs with unprecedented information, access, and opportunities for input. When civil society is involved in decision making, outcomes should better reflect the interests of the poor. While this appears to be a reasonable proposition, little comparative evidence exists to support this claim. This study remedies this gap by testing whether one type of participatory governance institution—municipal housing councils—are associated with greater adoption of benefits to assist the poor. That housing represents a key social challenge in the developing world adds to our understanding of what leads to the provision of social benefits in the developing country context.

The findings of this study have implications for designing institutions that meet redistributive goals and for the strategies of social policy advocates. Statistical evidence demonstrates that there are broad patterns in policy outcomes, while highlighting the contextual nature of the impact of participatory governance institutions. This has implications for whether policy makers—both domestic and international—continue to call for participatory governance institutions to be implemented broadly as a means of bringing about greater redistribution of resources. Most of the studies on participatory democracy have come from a few cases—Brazil, the Philippines, India, and South Africa. While this study continues the trend by focusing on Brazil, the results are more generalizable through the comparisons of contexts across the country, helping to pinpoint representative cases for replication of results.

Housing is representative of poverty in the conception outlined by Amartya Sen in his landmark study of the deprivations that impede individuals in enjoying basic opportunities and developing capabilities.[98] Though Sen and others theorize that democracy is vital to the creation of good governance and pro-poor policy, this study provides empirical evidence to the debate about how a new kind of democratic institution influences policy adoption through careful, systematic comparison. It also offers evidence as to whether participatory governance institutions are worth further investment to meet goals of poverty reduction.

Democracy may be better for the poor than authoritarian regimes, but traditional representative institutions may not provide sufficient channels for the voices of the poor to translate into policy outcomes that specifically address their needs. This study provides an answer to the question of whether a new type of institution can generate responsiveness and accountability to enhance the benefits of democracy.

2   Housing Policy as Critical Challenge for Development and Democracy

> The quality of the [council] process is very important for the creation of an idea of citizenship. Most people believe that there is quite a difference between being a city dweller and being a citizen. People living in the periphery and in favelas are not seen as having full rights, first of all because they are illegal and informal. Having the councils is a matter of having inclusion and creating citizenship.
>
> —Raquel Rolnik, Special Rapporteur for Housing to the United Nations[1]

Housing policy presents a test for how democratic governance may address social challenges. In developing countries, governments face enormous challenges in fast-growing cities and in rural areas where millions of residents reside in informal and often unsafe and unsanitary conditions. Citizens need shelter to live productive and healthy lives, improving their own quality of life while also contributing to local and national development. In Brazil and elsewhere housing is about more than the provision of shelter. In Brazil, civil society organizations (CSOs) involved in housing policy generally use the term "moradia" to define their claims. Though "moradia" does not have a precise translation in English, it generally refers more to a quality living space than solely a physical structure.[2] The use of "moradia" instead of the more directly translatable term "habitação" (housing) emphasizes the importance of not just having a roof and four walls to call one's own, but the need for safety, security, and dignity associated with a home.

Housing involves the improvement of communities and quality of life as well as the benefits of citizenship and inclusion within democratic institutions. The opening quote from Raquel Rolnik illustrates the difficulty that low-income residents face in demanding citizenship and inclusion. Municipal councils for housing provide the poor with unprecedented access to policy making, but the challenges remain daunting in Brazil and developing countries around the world. Traditionally politicians who need to provide tangible benefits to voters use housing as a political symbol. As such, housing often falls prey to clientelistic behavior between elected officials and the poor.

In this chapter I examine the importance of housing as a policy issue in developing countries. Housing is an important issue for democracy and development as a human right and as a means to reducing poverty and inequality. In addition, housing is critical to improving security and promoting environmental sustainability. As a tangible political issue, politicians are also motivated by elections to address housing needs. Policy makers, scholars, and donors throughout the world struggle to create policies and programs to address the diverse needs of the poor in terms of creating new housing, improving existing shelter, upgrading infrastructure, and providing land titles. Though housing is not always part of the traditional definition of welfare policies, in the developing world where a significant portion of the population lives in informal settlements without proper infrastructure or property rights, the importance of housing to citizens' welfare cannot be denied. While participatory institutions are a critical part to democratizing the process of decision making and implementation of housing policy, other civil society strategies and outside forces clearly also impact policy outcomes.

In Brazil, housing policy has evolved since democratization into a decentralized system of resources and policy control. Civil society struggles to define the needs of the poor and maintain pressure on policy makers and donors to meet these needs. Housing policy is also perceived by civil society as key to asserting the right to participatory governance. Civil society has been heavily involved in creating the new system, which seeks to decentralize resources and more closely integrate the poor and all levels of government into policy planning. I argue that Brazil is both an outlier and representative of developing countries around the world. Given the high level of decentralization, Brazil is an outlier in terms of the structure of policy making and the diversity of programs adopted by municipalities across the country. However, Brazil has followed similar trends in approaches to housing policy compared with other developing countries. The challenges in Brazil are representative of those faced by governments, civil society, and the poor living in undignified conditions throughout the world.

POLICY CHALLENGES IN DEVELOPING COUNTRIES

The scope of housing challenges around the world remains staggering. According to the United Nations (UN), one in three people in the world will live in "slums" by 2030.[3] Currently, 940 million people or one in six people on the planet live in areas without access to basic services or land security. A "slum" household, according to UN Habitat, is lacking in at least one of the following: access to improved water, access to improved sanitation, sufficient living area, structural quality, or security of tenure or title. "Housing" challenges worldwide, therefore, include much more than the quality of a single physical shelter, but rather involve the entire surroundings in which people live.

Scholars and policy makers often link housing challenges to urban development and politics. For the first time in history, more than half of the world's population now lives in urban areas.[4] Rapid increases in the urban population—over 5% per year in parts of Sub-Saharan Africa and Asia—place stress on the urban infrastructure and lead to increasing number of residents living in slums across the globe. In developing countries, 36.5% of the urban population lives in slums. In Sub-Saharan Africa 62.2% of urban residents live in slums, while in Latin American and Caribbean cities 27% of residents live in slums.[5] Density is a particular problem in urban areas where people flock to central areas of the city in search of work.[6] In their volume on squatter settlements, Satterthwaite and Mitlin justify focusing on urban areas in Africa, Asia, and Latin America and the Caribbean by the immense scale of urban populations, the scale of deprivation among these populations, and the potential for urban poverty reduction due to the presence of local civil society organizations.[7] For housing, specifically, the UN estimates the needs in urban areas of developing countries as the following:

> The annual need for housing in urban areas of developing countries alone is estimated at around 35 million units (during 2000–2010). The bulk of these, some 21 million units, are required to cater for the needs of the increasing number of households. The rest is needed to meet the requirements of people who are homeless or living in inadequate housing. In other words, some 95,000 new urban housing units have to be constructed each day in developing countries to improve housing conditions to acceptable levels.[8]

While these figures are astounding, they more than likely vastly underestimate the problem given that by the Brazilian government's calculation, the housing deficit for Brazil alone is approximately 5.6 million, or a little over one-seventh of the UN's world total. Differences in how the housing deficit is calculated vary by country, leading to some disparities in the exact worldwide numbers of those living without housing or residing in substandard housing.

In looking at trends for the future, the growth of cities indicates growth in the slum population as well. The UN predicts that all of the population growth in the next 25–30 years will be in urban areas. Already in 2000, three-quarters of the population in Latin America and the Caribbean lived in urban areas and two-fifths of the population in Africa and Asia lived in urban areas.[9] In 2007, the top four cities by population were Tokyo, Mexico City, New York, and São Paulo, respectively.[10] But by 2025, the UN predicts that the top four cities by population will be Tokyo, Mumbai, Delhi, and Dhaka, with São Paulo in fifth place. This shows the changing demographics of megacities around the world, which underscores the importance of tackling urban challenges, including housing, in the coming years.

This is not to say that housing is purely an urban issue. The need for adequate housing and infrastructure exists in both rural and urban areas. Regardless of population density, citizens face resource constraints to building and purchasing shelter with secure land tenure. The nature of the intervention to housing challenges, however, may differ across rural and urban areas. Housing programs in urban areas are generally defined by construction of large public housing units, subsidies for financing, land titling, and slum improvement schemes, while in rural areas residents may prefer construction materials to build their own homes in addition to land titling programs for security.

The problems of informality exist across the rural-urban divide. Residents of informal settlements risk eviction and the government can legitimize not providing services to areas that are not legally registered.[11] Collective action may then be important for attaining land security and public investments in infrastructure. Addressing the need for additional housing units, basic infrastructure, sanitary conditions, and land titles in developing countries worldwide poses a tremendous challenge to governments and international donors for the foreseeable future.

HOUSING CHALLENGES IN BRAZIL

Housing statistics in Brazil are divided by the "housing deficit," or the gap between people who need housing and the existing stock, and "inadequate" housing, characterized by lack of access to basic services, land titles, and sufficient infrastructure. In 2008, the official housing deficit in Brazil, according to the Ministry of Cities, stood at 5.6 million, down from 6.3 million in 2007.[12] The good news in Brazil, then, is that the official number of housing units needed throughout the country is falling.

Still, significant challenges remain. Across years, 83% of the housing deficit was located in urban areas, and 90% of those in need of housing earned between zero and three minimum salaries.[13] The majority of those in search of housing, therefore, are extremely poor and urban, as in much of the world. For all of Brazil, 39.3% of the deficit is attributed to citizens forced to live with family, 32.2% to excessive rent burden, 23% to precarious housing, and 5.5% to excessive density in rental housing. The averages belie the differences between rural and urban areas. In rural areas, 60% of the deficit is for precarious housing, while in urban areas it is only around 10%. The reasons behind the housing deficit, therefore, differ across the rural-urban divide. In urban areas people are forced to cram themselves together in tight, often unsanitary and insecure conditions, while in rural areas people are more likely to live in unsafe and perilous circumstances.

In addition, about 10.5 million homes across the country are counted as "inadequate."[14] Of these, 1 million houses did not have a bathroom and 2 million did not have proper land titles. Two million more are located in "subnormal settlements," in which residents may have land title but do not have access to basic services, such as electricity, piped water, sewage, or trash collection. Of the 80% of the population living in urban areas, about 40% are counted as living in inadequate and/or insecure housing.[15] In Brazil, and in other growing cities in the developing world, rising incomes have improved affordability of housing, but speculative investment and density have also increased prices in many cities.[16] Though the housing stock is growing, significant numbers of people still cannot afford to purchase or rent units in the market. Government interventions to improve inadequate housing units and provide new units to decrease the deficit are therefore still critical to addressing Brazil's housing challenges.

The very poor in Brazil—defined as those earning below three minimum salaries—generally have three options: (1) occupy unused land; (2) rent accommodation, which may consume a disproportionate share of their incomes and require sharing with other families; or (3) purchase land on an illegal subdivision, which generally does not have basic infrastructure and sanitation.[17] Brazil's favelas are mainly the result of land occupations by citizens squatting on any piece of land available. In addition, social movements often organize members to occupy land before negotiating with the municipal government either to build on the land or to be relocated to government-subsidized housing elsewhere. Cortiços, or tenement buildings, in which multiple families live together in often crowded and unsanitary conditions, are a particular phenomenon in the country's largest city, São Paulo. Though the city passed a law to hold landlords responsible for the miserable conditions in the cortiços, many city residents who desire to live close to employment in the city center continue to pay high rents for substandard living conditions. Finally, residents who can afford it often purchase land in subdivisions, called loteamentos, in which owners sell off plots of land without respecting city codes to provide sidewalks, roads, electricity, and other basic infrastructure. According to civil society leaders, housing policy in Brazil has never responded adequately to the needs of the very poor currently living in these three types of situations, either with subsidized financing, public housing, or infrastructure investment. Civil society demands, therefore, often focus on meeting the needs of the lowest-income citizens.

In sum, closing the housing deficit in Brazil requires significant interventions in both rural and urban areas. Across the country, residents need safer living conditions with greater access to basic infrastructure and security of tenure. In Brazil, as in poor communities across the globe, citizens have been resourceful in making home wherever they are able. But this type of informal building may not be sustainable as the economy grows, land becomes more valuable, and people—rich and poor—demand greater attention from the government to the problems of informality, inequality, and poverty. Given the scale of housing needs, it is clear that greater investment and innovation in housing policy is needed to improve the lives of a large segment of the population.

HOUSING AS A POLICY PRIORITY

Though statistics indicate the severity of housing problems, given competing social challenges, it is crucial to understand the benefits governments may gain by prioritizing housing interventions. First, the right to adequate housing is enshrined in international law as a basic human right of all citizens. Governments concerned with reputational effects and pleasing their own citizens may be concerned with fulfilling the promises of human rights. Second, addressing housing needs is a critical part of economic growth: when people have access to housing as an asset, they may be able to invest in their businesses. In addition, the real estate and construction industries in the developing world are increasingly viewed as engines for growth. Further, improving communities through physical shelter and infrastructure may reduce violence and crime within poor neighborhoods and improve environmental sustainability in cities and in rural areas. Finally, as I argue throughout this book, governments make housing a priority because it is politically popular. Governments respond to citizen demands through a variety of incentives, which generally boil down to a desire to win at election time.

The Right to Adequate Housing

The right to housing is enshrined in international law along with other basic rights to ensure a decent quality of life. The Covenant for Economic, Social and Cultural Rights (CESCR) calls for state parties to "recognize the right of everyone to an adequate standard of living for himself and his family, including adequate food, clothing and housing, and to the continuous improvement of living conditions."[18] The right to adequate housing is conceived of as central to the enjoyment of economic, social, and cultural rights and is both a positive and a negative human right: governments are responsible for both ensuring acquisition of adequate housing and removing obstacles to its attainment. "Adequate" housing is defined by legal security of tenure, availability of services, affordability, habitability, accessibility, location, and cultural adequacy.

The right to adequate housing is also reflected in the Millennium Development Goals, which call for "significant improvement in the lives of at least 100 million slum dwellers." Toward the goal of ensuring the right to adequate housing, UN Habitat and the Office of the United Nations High Commissioner for Human Rights (OHCHR) began the UN Housing Rights Programme (UNHRP) in 2002. The UNHRP focuses on issues of forced evictions and the rights of indigenous peoples, in particular. Though the force of international law may be disputed, the fact that adequate housing is viewed as a basic human right by the UN and governments around the world provides legitimacy to the claims made by CSOs for housing interventions and places some degree of opprobrium on those governments unwilling to respond.

In fact, to bring violations of housing rights to light, the UN appoints a special rapporteur on housing. Citizens may contact the rapporteur directly to report housing rights abuses. The current special rapporteur, Raquel Rolnik, hails from São Paulo and has focused directly on human rights violations associated with displacement of people as a result of infrastructure development for the 2014 FIFA World Cup and 2016 Olympic Games to be held in Brazil.

In addition, social movements throughout Brazil use the language of rights as justification for their demands. For example, following the occupation of several buildings in São Paulo's city center, in an open letter to municipal, state, and federal government officials, the Frente de Luta Moradia (Front for Housing Struggles [FLM]), called on the government to renovate three buildings for low-income residents. The movement stated that the government "has the obligation to provide dignified housing to those that have none, as they should guarantee health, education, transportation, security."[19] When negotiations with the municipal government broke down, the movement sought to file a petition with the Ministério Público (Public Ministry) claiming that the human rights of protestors had been violated because they were forced to live in subhuman conditions.[20] This is just one instance of a long list of incidents in which social movements use the force of law to address the legality of evictions. Moreover, CSOs not only use the constitution to hold the government accountable for abuses of the law, but they also press for the government to comply with their responsibility to provide housing.

In addition, CSOs use the language of human rights to encourage their members to take action. In São Paulo, during a meeting to engage new members, a leader of the União dos Movimentos da Moradia (Union of Housing Movements [UMM-SP]) urged a packed room of attendees to fight for the fundamental right to dignified housing. In his words, housing is a right of democracy, but citizens must be informed and continuously pressure the government to secure their rights. The National Forum for Urban Reform (FNRU) in Brazil also calls on citizens to challenge the government to ensure the right to dignified housing. In March 2010, the right to adequate housing was reaffirmed in the final declaration of the UN-sponsored World Urban Forum in Rio de Janeiro, in which CSOs, including the FNRU, successfully lobbied for a strong statement defining the goals of the conference theme, "the right to the city."[21]

Across the world, the UN and other nongovernmental organizations (NGOs) use the language and force of human rights to engender action from state governments. In Brazil, civil society calls on the federal, state, and municipal governments to comply with human rights principles guaranteeing the right to "adequate" housing. To the extent that all governments comply with human rights principles, they gain reputational benefits and may face fewer challenges from civil society.

Housing as Source of Economic Growth

Housing may be a source of capital and an engine of private sector development, both of which enable broad national economic development. In his highly acclaimed book *Mystery of Capital*, Hernando de Soto argues that the poor's homes are significant assets, but without formal titles these houses are "dead capital."[22] Based on a study in Peru, his work led international and domestic leaders to call for increasing property rights in developing countries worldwide. With secure property rights, the poor can use their homes as collateral in order to access business loans, which may enable incorporation into the formal market and increase the size of small enterprises. Property rights, then, are key to economic growth: if the poor have the means to access loans, businesses should be more productive and add to overall economic gains. Governments have a stake in formalizing tenure arrangements to enable residents to use their homes as assets.

Furthermore, the construction and real estate industry are drivers of economic growth in the developing and industrialized world. Investment in housing not only benefits individual households, but provides employment for construction and profits from sales. Broader benefits from infrastructure investment also contribute to economic growth. Research has found a positive association between infrastructure investment and economic growth in developing countries.[23] To increase profits in the construction and real estate industries, governments often enter into public-private partnerships for building or upgrading of communities. Rather than managing construction themselves, private contracts enable market growth with externalities beyond the families who benefit from new homes and basic service provision.

In 2009, the Brazilian government announced the creation of the Minha Casa Minha Vida program. Part of the aim of this program was to provide construction and real estate companies with needed investment in the wake of the global financial crisis beginning in 2008. In the first phase of the program, from 2009 to 2012, the Caixa Econômica Federal contracted to build 1 million housing units.[24] In the second phase of the program, the government aims to build 1 million additional units by 2014. The benefits of this large-scale building program accrue not only to the families that occupy the homes, but also to the developers and construction workers involved in their development.

As a means to improving overall economic growth, therefore, governments should take investment in housing seriously. Granting security of tenure to people currently living in informal or illegal situations may foster capital investment in communities and businesses. Land titling, or regularization of tenure, in which residents are given the right to stay where they are, may be low-cost opportunities for governments to improve economic growth. Providing more money for building and construction also enables economic growth through investment in the private sector. As all governments wish to spur or continue economic growth, housing represents a valuable sector to increase expenditures.

Improving Security

Governments may also be incentivized to respond to housing challenges based on the real and perceived benefits to security. Much has been written about the dangers of favelas in Rio de Janeiro and São Paulo.[25] Several theories offer explanations linking insecurity in housing to violence, particularly in urban communities. First, informal communities create a feeling of inferiority among residents and a stigma of crime.[26] Regardless of the actual level of violence within an informal settlement, wealthier residents stereotype favelados, as they are known in Brazil, as criminals. This perception of the favelas as dangerous places leads to isolation and further marginalization of residents.[27] Second, slums may embody low levels of social capital. Though studies find that people living in cities have high levels of community participation, residents in slums tend to have very low levels of trust.[28] Very generally, with low levels of social trust, residents may be less likely to look after one another and more likely to engage in criminal acts against their neighbors. In Latin America, Luis Rosero-Bixby also finds that existing crime and fighting over scarce resources lead to lack of trust among low-income residents.[29]

James Holston offers an extensive critique of democracy in Brazil, arguing that violence in Brazilian cities separates the poor from the elite within public spaces and erodes the rights of citizenship.[30] Corruption in the police and judicial institutions further weakens the right to redress. Within this setting in which citizens have been forced into a process of auto-construction, Holston argues that insurgent citizenships developed to make demands of the state. To create more inclusive and productive cities, the government should understand the need to work with communities to root out violence and attend to their demands. Without mutual cooperation, the cycle of government neglect and violence continues to produce vacuums of power and disaffection among citizens.

Beyond the local effects, for cities around the world looking to improve their image on the world stage, improving security through housing interventions serves to attract investment and tourism. As Brazil prepares to host the 2014 World Cup and 2016 Olympic Games, decreasing violence through community engagement, but also through improving housing and infrastructure, takes center stage. In Rio de Janeiro, an increased police presence in several key favelas has reduced the level of drug-related violence.[31] Improvements in housing within these communities goes hand in hand with progress in community-police relations, changing the perception and reality of favelas as separate from the rest of the city.

Deprivation and urban crowding may be sources of insecurity to residents and a challenge to government officials to improve community relations. In order to prevent violence, crime, and disaffection, governments may then prioritize housing interventions. As cities increasingly rely on international financing, investment, and tourism for revenue, increasing security through improving housing conditions further serves as an enticement for governments to take action.

Environmental Sustainability

In the list of UN Millennium Development Goals, improving the lives of slum dwellers is situated within broader goals of environmental sustainability, clearly linking the two. Environmental problems resulting from informal housing conditions include poor air quality, water contamination, waste dumping, and negative impacts on fragile ecosystems.[32] Improving the living conditions for slum dwellers should reduce pollution and overuse of natural resources. Constructing housing, but also providing slum dwellers with basic services and infrastructure, may improve environmental conditions within slums and in the region. As environmental degradation takes a greater toll on cities and rural areas, governments may be persuaded to act. Combined with the other benefits to economic growth and security, housing interventions and urbanization programs may generate large payoffs for minimal investments.

In the Rio+20 United Nations Conference on Sustainable Development, held in June 2012, CSOs strongly campaigned to make sure urban development and housing issues were explicitly linked to environmental sustainability. The final document from the meeting called for states to provide greater access to affordable housing and better infrastructure.[33] To the extent that countries may be seen as global leaders in protecting the environment through housing interventions, they may also gain added reputational benefits.

Compared to large-scale, global interventions to prevent environmental damage, improving local housing and infrastructure to promote environmental sustainability presents many fewer challenges to coordination. Though metropolitan governance poses some problems for protecting common resources, as the entities responsible for managing zoning and city planning, to some extent municipalities can generate their own independent solutions to rehouse people living in areas of environmental risk, such as waterways, and building housing and infrastructure on municipally controlled land. As environmental problems, such as water contamination, continue to mount, municipal governments are incentivized to take decisive action.

Political Popularity

Finally, the motivation for prioritizing housing policy comes back to the fact that housing interventions are generally politically popular. Politicians can easily point to physical improvements in slums and to new, brightly colored housing complexes as signs of progress. Both democratic and authoritarian regimes traditionally use housing to capture political support. For example, in both Chile and Peru, under authoritarian regimes leaders used housing to maintain popularity.[34] Fragile democracies, including South Africa, India, Thailand, Mexico, and Brazil, have also adopted new housing schemes in recent years.[35] Housing interventions to gain political support may be clientelistic in nature—direct benefits to one community in exchange for loyalty—or they may more broadly respond to citizen demands, both rich and poor. Wealthier citizens often desire to improve the landscape of cities as much as the poor desire decent homes and communities in which to live. Both rich and poor voters, then, may make their electoral decisions based on policy expectations or on evidence of housing interventions.

In addition, as this book argues, in Brazil and other developing countries, large civil societies oriented toward housing and other issues of urban planning and property rights play a direct role in policy making. The NGO Slum Dwellers International unites local associations from 34 developing countries, demonstrating the scale and associational reach of housing organizations around the world. Though the tactics for influencing policy range according to local context, in general, CSOs occupy lands, stage protests, file legal actions, demand meetings with government officials, and field candidates for office. In Brazil and in other parts of the world where participatory institutions are established, their influence is felt through voting in participatory mechanisms, including municipal housing councils, and indirectly through the transparency generated by a public space for discussing resource allocation. Armed with information regarding the government's contributions, or lack thereof, CSOs can negotiate with government officials and publicize the shortfalls to their members and fellow citizens. Though all the tactics of CSOs may have some influence on the political popularity of housing interventions, I argue that participatory institutions in particular enable CSOs to publicize the actions of the government, thereby giving CSOs added political weight.

Particularly in urban areas where large numbers of voters live in slums, what the government does for housing matters at election time. Though clientelism in terms of politicians securing votes through promises of new housing construction for the poor or community upgrades still exists, with increased transparency of information from participatory governance institutions, voters may also hold government officials accountable for addressing housing challenges more broadly.

PAST AND CURRENT HOUSING POLICIES
IN DEVELOPING COUNTRIES

Worldwide, the housing policy environment has changed in light of increasing democratization, a move toward decentralization in policy making, adoption of market-oriented economic approaches, and emerging housing finance systems.[36] More housing needs today are in urban areas, and in many cases families living in informal settlements or in need of housing options are second-generation migrants to cities.[37] Trends in housing policy have also coincided with theories regarding the role of the state in the economy. From the 1950s to the 1970s, state planning dictated the construction of large public housing complexes and destruction of slums.[38] From the 1970s forward, the norm shifted toward market-based solutions, mainly involving subsidy or voucher programs and site-and-service programs to improve informal settlements and provide land titles. In the 1990s, reliance on market-based reforms increased while donors and scholars also began to promote the idea that community groups and NGOs should be consulted on poverty alleviation projects.[39]

The trend away from state involvement in large public housing complexes from the 1970s followed economists' warnings that state intervention in real estate can only be market distorting and managing public housing was an inefficient use of state resources. Traditionally, once slums had been cleared, residents were transferred to public housing units, most often in the peripheries of cities. Jenkins, Smith, and Wang argue that public housing in the developing world failed for much of the same reasons it failed elsewhere: "remote, un-serviced locations, inadequate dwelling space, lack of opportunities for income generation, high costs and lack of accessibility to the lowest income brackets."[40] Public spending alone could neither meet the demand for housing nor respond to the needs of poor residents. Starting in the 1970s, therefore, many countries shied away from constructing large public housing complexes in favor of "site and service" programs and slum upgrading of informal settlements.[41] Site and service programs were developed in recognition that the single, modern housing unit was out of reach for most of the poor. Instead of emphasizing the illegality of informal settlements, governments aimed to provide some basic services and infrastructure to existing communities. As Mitlin argues, however, site and service programs alone have failed to significantly alter housing problems because of lack of supply, bad locations, unregulated buildings, and issues in targeting beneficiaries.[42]

The Inter-American Development Bank (IADB) labels market-based approaches the "enabling approach," which includes removing regulations, improving land titling, and encouraging the private sector to produce low-income housing. Expanding the market for mortgage finance to low-income citizens has enabled the poor to purchase homes in a number of countries, including Indonesia, India, and the Philippines.[43] In these countries, and in Brazil, fast-paced economic growth has increased available finance and raised incomes to allow residents the opportunity to purchase homes. Community investment funds, savings schemes, and lending by microfinance institutions for incremental improvements are also current interventions implemented around the world based on the enabling approach.

Still, according to the IADB, while a number of countries in Latin America and the Caribbean have made some strides in reducing the quantitative housing deficit, the qualitative deficit is slow to change.[44] In a pivotal report on the housing sector in the region, the IADB found that the private sector failed to produce enough affordable housing to meet low-income residents' needs for several reasons: (1) building for wealthier residents is still more profitable, (2) land and construction costs are high, (3) excessive regulations increase the cost of building, and (4) many people would still prefer to live in informal arrangements. They found that upper-lower income and middle-income residents tend to benefit the most from new construction with the lowest-income residents still locked out of the formal housing market. The result is that most of the poor continue to live in slums without access to basic infrastructure.

In recognition that the market cannot solve all problems, most developing countries today do appear to implement a mix of state construction, site-and-service projects, and market-based approaches. In addition, increasing incorporation of the poor and civil society representatives into policy making has been key to initiating settlement upgrading projects and self-build projects. According to Diana Mitlin,

> Neighborhood upgrading requires building a relationship between low-income communities and the state. The state has to engage with low-income communities through issues related to both the legalization of land tenure and the regularization of plots, so that they comply with regulations and other legislation. The provision of subsidies (for infrastructure improvements and, sometimes, other investments) also requires involvement with the state to establish beneficiary rights and entitlements. The growth of participatory planning mechanisms has helped to consolidate positive relationships between the residents of low-income settlements and their local government.[45]

Mitlin argues that improving informal settlements requires direct communication and negotiation between residents and the state. Neighborhood associations, often working under the umbrella of a larger social movement or in consultation with professional NGOs, need to be integrated into government planning processes in order for citizens' needs to be met. Participatory mechanisms, including municipal housing councils in Brazil, directly respond to this need for a space where civil society and the state meet and generate guidelines for housing interventions.

In addition, in Brazil and elsewhere, governments promote "self-build projects" as a means to capitalize on informal strategies the poor already use. The majority of the poor already live in housing they have built themselves working in associations.[46] In many self-build projects the poor apply for resources from the state to carry out their own community improvement projects or construction of individual or collective dwellings. From Nigeria and Spain to Afghanistan, self-build projects are increasingly seen as "best practice" interventions because they promote community involvement and require far less resources than typical large-scale public housing complexes.[47] This type of intervention clearly involves close collaboration between association and the state to generate project proposals and to ensure that resources are used effectively.

In sum, housing policy worldwide has evolved from large-scale state interventions to market-based approaches with civil society involvement. Though construction of individual housing units by the government still exists, private contractors and housing associations of residents are now more involved than in the past. Evidence from around the world suggests that the trend in housing policy is toward programs that are more pro-poor in terms of collective finance solutions, inclusion of the poor in program design, and upgrading of slums rather than evictions.[48] Though problems certainly persist, as evidenced by the daunting statistics on housing challenges, innovations in housing interventions indicate promising improvements for the future.

HOUSING POLICY HISTORY IN BRAZIL

To a large extent, housing policy in Brazil reflects the trends in policy through-out the developing world, evolving alongside trends in macroeconomic ap-proaches. In the 1970s, city governments in Brazil were overwhelmed by the influx of migrants from the countryside. Under the authoritarian govern-ment (1964–1985), the norm was to clear informal settlements and relocate residents to large public housing complexes in the periphery. The National Bank for Housing (Banco Nacional de Habitação [BNH]) also provided fi-nancing to low-income residents to purchase individual units. According to longtime activist Benedito Barbosa, owning an individual home rather than renting is the dream for most Brazilians.[49] Financing through the BNH, how-ever, was only available to families earning over three minimum salaries and did very little to limit growth of the housing deficit.[50] By 1990, the BNH col-lapsed due to corruption.[51] According to civil society leaders, the collapse of the BNH left a void in housing policy at the national level for over a decade.

Since democratization, housing policy has been heavily influenced by trends toward decentralization. As opposed to national or local political elites, in Brazil civil society has been the impetus for decentralization of policy making.[52] Civil society has fought to ensure access to social rights through the implementation of decentralization reforms. For instance, the 1988 Constitution established universal access to health care through a con-solidated national system (Sistema Única de Saude [SUS]). Under the system, each municipality is required to have a participatory council, composed of providers, users, and government officials, that controls funds transferred from the federal level. The health councils must reach consensus on an an-nual budget in order for the municipality to receive federal funds. The SUS was the basis for the construction of the system for housing policy today.[53] In the late 1980s and early 1990s, housing movements began to call for a national fund for housing to dispense resources from the federal to the state and municipal levels. As Benedito Barbosa explains, "The fight began with the call for a national fund for popular housing, but ended with a discussion of the system." In the meantime, the FNRU achieved several victories, in-cluding creation of the national Ministry of Cities and passage of the Statute of the City in 2001. President Fernando Henrique Cardoso signed into law the Statute of the City (Estatuto da Cidade), which provides interpretation for the constitutional chapter on urban planning, including legal require-ments for property rights based on land use for social purposes. It is used as an example worldwide for land use policies and city master planning.

Housing movements collected over 1 million signatures for the original proposal for a national fund for housing, which leaders presented to the Brazilian Congress as proof of support for new legislation.[54] However, the final law to create the Fundo Nacional de Habitação de Interesse Social (Na-tional Fund for Housing in the Social Interest [FNHIS]) was not approved until 2005, during Lula's first term. In the same year, federal law created the Sistema Nacional de Habitação de Interesse Social (National System for Housing in the Social Interest [SNHIS]) with the aim of "implementing policies and programs that promote access to dignified housing for the low income population."[55] SNHIS is meant to organize the direction of all housing programs, funding agencies, and governmental departments involved in housing at the federal, state, and municipal levels. It also provides the structure for the federal, state, and municipal participatory councils for housing across the country. The FNHIS centralizes funding sources for urbanization of subnormal settlements and social housing. Funding for the FNHIS comes from the federal budget as well as international and national donors and receipts from past loans. In 2009, the budget for FNHIS was R$1.5 billion, which sought to benefit approximately 90,000 families.[56] According to Marta Arretche, a Brazilian decentralization scholar, the innovation of FNHIS is really the reach of subsidies to the poor.[57] Prior to the creation of the fund, people earning under three minimum salaries were essentially left out of the housing finance system.

SNHIS provides some degree of civil society control over federal resources and policy planning. According to Brazilian scholar Patricia Cardoso, the objective is for diverse actors to work together to formulate housing interventions.[58] Municipal housing councils connect the state and federal levels to local program implementation. Though this study analyzes municipal housing councils, it is also critical to view these institutions as part of a much larger national system of decentralized power and resources. Construction of the SNHIS has been the long-term strategy of civil society for housing and urban reform in Brazil. From the constitutional process, according to Raquel Rolnik, "the bet was that [the state] should radically democratize in order to have their voices heard in the decision-making of policies. This way the policies would naturally open themselves towards the demands, the needs and the propositions of the poor, or the excluded."[59] Though the system is continuously in construction, this study attempts to identify whether at least part of this bet has paid off.

CURRENT BRAZILIAN GOVERNMENT PROGRAMS

The Brazilian Constitution specifies that the municipality is the entity responsible for housing program implementation. Much of the program direction and resources, however, flow from the federal level. President Lula's administration used a mix of grants and financing for production and acquisition of housing, urbanization of precarious settlements, provision of construction materials, improvement in housing units, urbanization of plots of land, and renovation of buildings for housing use.[60] President Dilma Rousseff has largely continued these programs. Through these programs the government claims to have benefited approximately 2 million families, 75% of whom earn less than five minimum salaries. As a result, the percentage of families without housing fell from 16.1% to 14.9% from 2000 to 2005.

By the end of the decade, two of the administration's most popular programs were PAC (Programa de Aceleração do Crescimento) and Crédito Solidário. PAC began during the second Lula administration to improve basic infrastructure in the country.[61] It contains three areas for infrastructural projects: logistic (including roads and railways), energy, and "social and urban." Within the "social and urban" category, the program provided R$8.2 billion for housing projects in 2008. According to the regulations, 12 metropolitan regions and capitals and municipalities with more than 150,000 residents get priority in funding decisions. To be considered, municipalities must submit a proposal to the Ministry of Cities. In 2008, the Ministry chose 192 projects in 157 municipalities. One of these projects is the Abençoada por Deus housing complex in the city of Recife, in which residents were moved from precarious shacks on a riverbank to apartment units constructed under the direction of the municipal government. Municipal housing councils often work with the municipal housing secretariat to develop and send forward proposals under PAC to the federal level. PAC, then, provides resources for both construction and urbanization projects. This type of program corresponds closely to housing interventions in many developing countries in which the federal government invests directly in constructing units or improving existing informal settlements to avoid relocating residents.

The Crédito Solidário program includes the type of civil society collaboration promoted by international donors and scholars. The program provides financing for housing projects organized by "associations, cooperatives, unions, and other civil society entities."[62] The Ministry of Cities manages the project, but the Caixa Econômica Federal operates the financing. Organizations are responsible for formulating their own proposals for projects and for securing technical assistance once they have received funding. Resources are generally used for land, construction materials, and labor to build new housing complexes. Many of the projects are built through the process of *mutirão*, in which residents themselves construct the units, while the majority is built through the process of *auto-construção*, in which laborers are hired by the association to do the work. According to Regina Ferreira from the FNRU, mutirão projects, which were the direct result of civil society pressure under São Paulo Mayor Luiza Erundina (Worker's Party [PT]) in the late 1980s, largely influenced the creation of the Crédito Solidário program. Since the project provides financing rather than direct grants to the associations, over the course of 20 years each family must then pay back their loan in monthly installments. The National Secretary for Housing under the Ministry of Cities selects final projects to fund based on the prioritization given by the state and municipal councils for the project and by their location in urban areas with sizable housing deficits.

As mentioned earlier, in March 2009, the federal government announced a program called Minha Casa Minha Vida (My House My Life) to build 1 million housing units in the country by the end of 2010. Civil society groups, including the FNRU, praised the government for making an effort to reduce the enormous housing deficit in the country as long as "in practice it represented a response to the demands of the Brazilian urban reform movement."[63] To avoid further "peripheralization" of the poor they called on the government to utilize a combination of methods to make sure they attended to the needs of the poorest segments of society. In June 2009, the Brazilian government announced that a portion of the funding for the program would go to cooperatives, associations, or nonprofit organizations to provide subsidized credit toward low-income housing. CSOs worked with the Lula administration to formulate regulations for eligibility and projects. Funding goes toward purchasing lands, construction, and/or acquisition of existing buildings. Now in its second phase, the government aims to construct 1 million more housing units by 2014.[64]

Under the federal fund for housing, FNHIS, the federal government established the Program for the Production of Social Housing (Programa de Produção Social de Moradia). This program provides funding to associations or nonprofit entities in urban or rural areas to assist families earning below three minimum salaries (R$1,125 a month). Regulations specify that entities may use the money for "construction or acquisition of housing units, construction or acquisition of urbanized plots of land, and renovation of buildings."[65] In order to access this money and other funding from FNHIS, by the end of 2009, each municipality should have created a housing council to manage a fund for housing. Further, municipalities were required to create a master plan for housing, documenting the extent of the problems in their municipality and outlining programmatic solutions.

From the previously mentioned programs, it becomes clear that the government of Brazil and municipal governments increasingly reject the role of manager of public housing complexes in favor of forwarding money to associations or private sector actors. For example, in São Paulo, the municipal government under PT mayor Marta Suplicy constructed two public housing communities in 2004. The current government, led by PSD (Partido Social Democrático) Mayor Gilberto Kassab, criticizes the project for near complete default by tenants and the need for the government to provide continuing maintenance in the community.[66] The Kassab administration has sworn that they will not undertake any more projects that make them managers. Instead, in São Paulo and other municipalities, governments prefer to assist housing associations with proposals for projects, which provide federal, state, and municipal resources. In addition, the Kassab administration and administrations throughout the country increasingly rely on private contractors for construction and management of public housing projects. In fact, the Minha Casa Minha Vida program specifically mandates that all buildings constructed with the funds be no more than four stories, thereby eliminating the need for an elevator. This is in direct response to the complaint by municipal administrators that maintaining elevators in public housing buildings is costly and time-consuming.

Finally, since municipalities in Brazil control local land use, regularization programs, under which residents receive land titles, are by law municipal responsibilities. The Statute of the City provides legal categories for land titles, including land that is to be used for social housing production. Though the chapter in the constitution for urban policy specified that unused land must be used for social purposes, the Statute of the City clarified under what circumstances land could be titled to individuals. Out of 5,564 municipalities, 1,133 had regularization programs in 2008.[67] Municipal officials often view regularization programs as low-cost alternatives to housing interventions, because they require less government investment than construction programs.

Brazil today has a diverse array of housing interventions, with financial resources and program direction flowing from the federal level. However, the municipality is still responsible for direct program implementation and for applying for funds from the federal level. In this way, municipalities control the types of programs within their jurisdiction. The implementation of programs is also still dependent on the motivation of the municipality to forward proposals to the state and federal levels and to contribute their own resources of land and money toward projects. Municipal housing councils often coordinate proposals to the federal level and encourage municipal governments to seek federal resources.

CIVIL SOCIETY ORGANIZATIONS FIGHTING FOR REFORM AND BENEFITS

Participatory governance institutions make up one part of civil society's strategy to demand greater government investment in housing for low-income residents. CSOs oriented toward housing encompass a broad range of actors, but at the core they are interested in improving slums and producing low-cost, secure housing for the poor. The four major housing movements in Brazil largely present a unified front at the federal level. The União Nacional dos Movimentos por Moradia Popular (UNMP), the Central de Movimentos Populares (CMP), the Confederação Nacional dos Associações da Moradia (CONAM), and the Movimento Nacional de Luta por Moradia (MNLM) all coordinate activities under the National Forum for Urban Reform. All of the movements call for urbanization of favelas, provision of low-income housing in the city centers, and construction of new units. In more rural areas, movements including the Movimento dos Trabalhadores sem Terra (Landless Worker's Movement [MST]) call for programs to provide materials to enable residents to build their own homes and secure loans on a schedule congruent with the seasonal nature of agricultural work. As Brazil is over 80% urbanized, I mainly focus here on the demands for urban housing interventions, though the statistical analysis in the following chapters includes municipalities of all sizes.

In the five case studies I surveyed for this study, the demands of CSOs varied somewhat according to the geographic configuration of the city and the government's past and current interventions in housing. But in each case the basic demands were the same: more investment by the municipal government in social housing for the poorest of residents. In all of the cities, social movements called on the municipal government to renovate abandoned buildings in the city center, though the calls for this type of intervention were perhaps the strongest in São Paulo, where the size of the city and the expense of transportation made commuting long distances from the periphery difficult. In Curitiba, Salvador, and Recife, construction of small houses predominated over large apartment buildings as in Santo André and São Paulo, though construction of new units is a critical demand across cases. In all cities, too, social movements demanded the regularization of land claims and urbanization of existing communities over removal. In Recife, in particular, the government had responded to calls to improve the infrastructure and safety of housing for residents living along waterways. In sum, though the types of programs vary across cases to some extent, overall CSOs seek the full complement of programs to address the large-scale needs of the poor. For this study, I evaluate the impact that municipal councils for housing have on the adoption of each type of program as well as the diversity of programs municipal governments choose to adopt.

CONCLUSION

Housing policy in Brazil reflects the trends in developing countries throughout the world, but Brazil has also been a trendsetter with its decentralized system for housing and the inclusion of civil society in policy making. The challenges to provide safe, secure, and affordable housing for the poor in developing countries remain overwhelming. But the benefits to addressing these challenges lie beyond the provision of physical shelter.

Governments prioritize housing policy to protect human rights, promote economic growth, prevent violence, and advance environmental sustainability. In addition, housing interventions continue to be politically popular, particularly in dense urban centers where both rich and poor residents demand that politicians address the problems of informal settlements and basic infrastructure. The diverse array of policies, legal instruments, and decentralized housing systems in Brazil are models for other developing countries struggling with the same challenges. Before this model is exported to other countries, however, it is critical to assess whether inclusion of civil society in policy making as part of the larger housing policy environment matters in practice for producing pro-poor policy outcomes.

3 The Effect of Municipal Housing Councils on Policy Outcomes

> Our role is to manage the resources and put forward our priorities. It is very important for civil society to participate directly in the [council] process. There is more transparency and legitimacy for the actions of the government, and the responses are more significant.
>
> —Social movement leader in Salvador, Brazil
> regarding the role of civil society in
> the municipal council for housing[1]

Civil society organizations (CSOs) in Brazil and elsewhere call for the implementation of participatory governance institutions because they believe they can influence policy by having a seat at the table with government officials.[2] As the leader quoted here states, the role of CSOs is to present their demands and manage the resources governments make available to them. Through this process the government gains legitimacy and CSOs gain social benefits for the citizens they represent. But, does the participatory process live up to its promise? Are participatory governance mechanisms effective democratic institutions for creating accountability and responsiveness to the needs of the poor? The answers to these questions are critical as development scholars, donors, and governments continue to recommend participatory institutions as a means of generating greater redistribution of resources toward addressing social challenges.

Through empirical analysis I test whether in fact participatory governance institutions are associated with pro-poor policy outcomes. Toward that end I examine one central question: does incorporation of civil society through participatory governance institutions have an impact on the provision of social programs? At this stage in the research on participatory governance institutions it is critical to compare participatory governance institutions across contexts and concretely define policy outcomes as measures of effectiveness. I hypothesize that the existence of participatory governance institutions has an independent effect on increasing program adoption. A public forum for communication and debate should encourage responsiveness and accountability of government officials. Officials are presented directly with information regarding the needs of the community and are more likely to act on CSO demands made in public, particularly if they are concerned with reelection.

For this analysis I use Brazilian government data, supported by evidence from the field, to assess the impact of municipal housing councils on social housing programs. Across Brazilian municipalities, I find significant evidence to support the hypothesis that municipal housing councils lead to more resources dedicated to housing provision for the poor. Formal incorporation of civil society does appear to be important for redistribution of resources.

This chapter serves to establish that the presence of municipal housing councils is associated with the adoption of social housing programs across Brazilian municipalities. I first review the background of municipal housing councils and the civil society environment for housing before turning to the theoretical reasons for expecting that civil society and municipal councils will have substantial effects on whether programs are adopted. I then present the data and model used for the analysis, followed by the results and discussion of the findings. The model and findings from this analysis motivate the subsequent chapters, which analyze when and how municipal housing councils matter for policy outcomes.

MUNICIPAL COUNCILS FOR HOUSING IN BRAZIL

Municipal councils in Brazil, which incorporate elected members from civil society and appointed government officials to deliberate on policy direction, program implementation, and the allocation of resources, are one type of participatory governance institution.[3] As mentioned in the Introduction, Brazil's 1988 Constitution established municipal-level councils for health care, education, social assistance, and child/adolescent rights. Many other types of councils, including those for housing, emerged later, either through the demands of civil society or by ideologically driven municipal officials.[4] Municipal policy councils, such as those for health, are directly involved in the formation of national legislation. Programmatic municipal councils, such as housing, are directed more toward developing government programs for a well-defined population.[5] Different councils are given varying degrees of responsibility. For example, health councils have the power to veto the plans of the Health Secretariat, which leads to funding being withheld from the Health Ministry.[6] Where municipalities have established a specific fund for housing, municipal housing councils are generally responsible for allocating those funds.[7] Each policy, programmatic, and thematic council operates autonomously from the other, though overlapping membership is possible.

The Brazilian Constitution specifies that the municipality is the entity responsible for implementing housing policy.[8] As such, municipal housing councils would seem well placed to make a large impact on policy and program decisions. In 2005, municipal housing councils existed in 18% of Brazilian municipalities, while by 2008 the percentage had risen to 31.[9] Across years, councils are created either by legislation passed by the city council or by decree from the mayor. Both mechanisms generally establish rules for the composition of the council, how often the council will meet, and the scope of the council's decision-making authority. The great majority of councils mandate that at least half of the council's membership come from civil society, with municipal and state government officials making up the other half.[10] During interviews in cities across Brazil, council members from various types of CSOs told me their role on the councils is both to propose new programs and policies and to respond to government proposals and information provided on current programs. In this way civil society plays both a proactive and reactive role in establishing social housing policy.

As mentioned in the previous chapter, until 2005 when federal law created the National System for Housing in the Social Interest (SNHIS), Brazil had not had an established national housing policy since democratization.[11] Even with the new federal agency, Renato Cymbalista argues that resources have been slow in reaching municipalities. Municipal housing policies consist of the provision of new units, upgrading of favelas, distribution of titles of possession, allocation of construction materials, and intervention in slum disputes. Though these types of housing policies are common throughout the developing world, and to some extent in industrialized countries, scholars argue that Brazil has an especially diverse array of housing policies and programs as a result of the decentralized policy-making process.[12] The tendency in Brazil has been toward recognition of informal settlements and improvement of settlements through technical, social, and legal intervention. However, more traditional programs to construct new units for the poor—either through rental or ownership mechanisms—are still the most common types of programs across Brazil.

Municipal housing councils present a unique opportunity to study the effect of participatory governance institutions in a policy arena in which the problems and solutions are broadly similar across municipalities. While the scale of the housing deficit varies across municipalities, the challenges of a shortage of affordable units and lack of basic infrastructure remain fairly constant. In addition, the details of program implementation may change across the country, but the categories of possible interventions—constructing new units, providing infrastructure, regularizing land titles—are sufficiently broad to enable comparison of program adoption in different contexts. Though CSOs' demands do vary across contexts, to some extent, all forms of social housing programs respond to their demands for increasing interventions to address housing needs. Case studies in subsequent chapters will draw out the differences in CSO demands further, but the analysis here seeks to provide a baseline to show that municipal housing councils are generally associated with greater adoption of social housing programs.

THEORETICAL BACKGROUND

Whether democratic institutions can be devised to remedy social challenges remains a critical question in political science. In addition, answers to when and how CSOs affect policy outcomes requires further research. Previous literature suggests that CSOs on their own and working through participatory governance institutions influence policy outcomes based on the dynamics of responsiveness and accountability.[13] CSOs present information to government officials regarding the depth and intricacies of the problem in an effort to provoke satisfactory responses. Once government officials make promises to act on this information, councils then offer transparency and a public forum to encourage accountability.[14] This accountability should induce governments to implement programs that address diverse local needs. Rather than continue to ignore social problems, withhold investment, or provide selective benefits to a few groups of supporters, governments should respond by increasing the number of social programs within their jurisdiction.

Contrary to this claim, other scholars argue that participatory governance institutions may perpetuate clientelistic relationships between CSO members and government officials where CSOs are primarily concerned with securing benefits for their members.[15] In other words, CSOs may use their power in decision making to make deals with government officials that benefit their own members without concern for wide-ranging problems. Municipal councils, then, would serve the needs of CSOs without generating an increase in social housing programs to benefit the population more broadly. I argue that contrary to these claims, municipal councils will produce social housing programs to benefit the poor due to the existence of a formal space for airing demands and the public nature of deliberation.

RESPONSIVENESS AND ACCOUNTABILITY

In municipal housing councils and other participatory governance institutions, government officials and civil society leaders meet in open forums to discuss ongoing problems and debate government responses.[16] CSOs make their preferences known to government officials, who in turn present both the limitations and promises of potential interventions. With specific information about local problems, though, government officials can more effectively respond to the needs of the community.[17] Given the locally specific nature of housing policy and programs, municipal councils ensure attention is given to the precise needs of the community.

As a public forum, participatory governance institutions also expose governments to scrutiny. Government officials may be required to present budgetary information or at the least they are challenged by CSOs to defend their actions or inaction in addressing what CSOs believe to be severe social problems. CSOs can then pass on this information to their members and to the public at large. When the public has access to greater information and CSOs communicate issues to their members, both appointed and directly elected officials are persuaded to act out of self-interest to maintain their positions. Without the councils there is not a formal space for civil society to air grievances and for the government to transmit information about its activities to civil society. Armed with information about government actions, civil society should be better equipped to publicize shortfalls in the government's response to housing needs, including to residents within favelas for whom housing weighs heavily in voting decisions.

Participatory governance institutions may also reduce possibilities and incentives for corruption, the political use of funds, and the capture of state institutions by elites.[18] The incentives of CSOs to hold governments accountable, however, should not be taken as given. For instance, Merilee Grindle finds that in municipal participatory institutions in Mexico, organizations were more concerned with gaining benefits for their members than exposing governments' corrupt or clientelistic behavior.[19] In these cases CSO members of participatory governance institutions appear to be acting in their rational self-interest to provide selective benefits to their bases, along the lines suggested by Mancur Olson in his classic *Logic of Collective Action*.[20]

In Brazilian municipal housing councils, the opportunity to promote self-interests certainly exists, but there are several reasons to expect that municipal councils still offer an opportunity for promoting broad benefits. First, as other scholars have argued, participatory governance institutions offer spaces for negotiating between groups, which leads to a breakdown in bilateral CSO-government ties.[21] As an activist in Recife, Brazil, argues, municipal councils level the playing field in terms of CSO access to government officials, leading to negotiation among groups for benefits rather than local government officials selectively choosing which groups should receive access.[22] Second, not all CSOs elected to councils are social movements or neighborhood associations responsible to their members. Professional nongovernmental organizations without membership bases also participate in the councils and are likely to steer program decisions toward a broader pro-poor agenda. Third, particularly since municipal councils for housing in Brazil are increasingly adopted in response to the new federal system instead of by ideologically driven mayors, municipal officials and CSOs are often from different parties and lack strong ties. This may make the councils even more relevant as spaces for negotiation between sides not apt to cooperate otherwise.

As developing countries move forward with decentralization and participatory democracy, it is crucial to assess when participatory governance institutions actually lead to policies and programs to reduce poverty and inequality. Municipal councils for housing in Brazil offer an opportunity for systematic comparison of the outputs of participatory governance institutions and the impact of civil society on policies benefiting the poor in developing countries. Here I evaluate whether municipal councils make a difference in policy outcomes.

DATA

For this analysis, I use data collected by Brazilian government agencies. Currently in Brazil there are 5,564 municipalities, providing a high degree of variation. An annual survey of municipal governments conducted by Instituto Brasileiro de Geografia e Estatística (IBGE), the national statistical agency (Pesquisa de informações básicas municipais: Perfil dos municípios Brasileiros, gestão publica [MUNIC]), yields considerable data on the structure of municipal governments, with thematic questions varying by year. The survey is sent to municipal officials annually and is mandatory to complete. In most years of the survey, since it began in 1999, there are questions relating to housing needs, institutions, and programs. For this analysis I use data from both 2005 and 2008 to increase the reliability of the findings.[23]

HOUSING PROGRAMS AS DEPENDENT VARIABLES

The existence of various types of social housing programs indicates the commitment of the municipality to addressing housing needs. In the MUNIC survey, municipal government officials check "yes" or "no" to indicate whether each type of housing program exists in their municipality. Federal, state, or municipal governments may finance housing programs, though municipal governments are responsible for program implementation, and the decision to adopt programs is left solely to the municipality. Table 3.1 illustrates the distribution of programs in Brazilian municipalities. These programs exist across municipalities of various size and region throughout Brazil (see Appendix A for details).

The construction of new units, provision of construction materials, regularization of land titles, and awarding of plots of land are all programs that

Table 3.1   Percentage of Brazilian Municipalities with Each Type of Housing Program

	2005	2008
Construction of New Units	48%	61%
Construction Materials	35%	36%
Offering Plots of Land	19%	25%
Regularizing Land Titles	9%	20%
Other Programs	25%	N/A
Acquisition of New Units	N/A	16%
Improvement of Units	N/A	46%
Urbanization of Settlements	N/A	14%

address the demands of CSOs representing the needs of the poor. These needs include affordable, safe housing on land they can occupy without the threat of seizure by the state or private entities. In 2008, the survey included three additional types of programs: those to acquire housing units, improve units, and urbanize neighborhoods. These programs represent the shifting priorities in housing policy, influenced by national housing movements, trickling down from the federal to the municipal level, often through federal government funding.

Programs to construct new units have been the most common type of intervention. These types of programs generate jobs for the real estate and construction industries and alleviate much of the quantitative housing deficit, comprised of people who simply cannot find adequate, affordable housing on their own. CSOs have criticized construction programs in the past for relocating residents to distant areas lacking infrastructure and job opportunities. Construction programs also tend to appeal to politicians who can point to new buildings as tangible signs of government investment. Despite some criticisms, CSOs do continue to call for increasing construction as one part of housing policy to deal with the large deficits.

Programs that provide construction materials to low-income citizens present opportunities for both rural and urban residents. Across Brazil, 34% of the smallest municipalities (those with fewer than 20,000 residents) and 41% of the largest municipalities (those with more than 500,000 residents) have programs to provide construction materials. In rural and urban areas, these programs enable residents to improve existing structures or build new ones, capitalizing on the tradition of auto-construction that Holston deftly identifies in his work on insurgent citizenship.[24] In urban areas, in particular, CSOs have called upon governments to provide construction materials for collectively built houses constructed through the process of "mutirão." Social movements like these types of programs, which have been a significant part of housing policy in the city of São Paulo, because they perceive them as mechanisms to build community bonds rather than just generic housing units.

Programs to offer plots of land and provide regularization of land title respond to the need for security of tenure. The distribution of programs to offer plots of land is relatively similar across municipalities regardless of population size. Regularization programs, in which municipal governments grant temporary or permanent right to residents to live on the land they occupy, exist across municipalities of all sizes, but are particularly prevalent in high-density areas. It makes sense that people living in crowded urban conditions are at greater risk of losing the space they occupy, and CSOs have focused on ensuring that large cities implement regularization programs. As Hernando de Soto found, providing the poor with property rights incentivizes them to invest in their homes and use them as collateral for entrepreneurial activities.

Lastly, CSOs have fought for additional programs that stop short of removing residents from their existing communities. Improving favelas through paving streets, supplying electricity, and rehabilitating houses, or acquiring units for renovation often in urban centers, provide alternatives for reducing the qualitative housing deficit. CSOs promote the use of urban centers for mixed-income renewal rather than creating ghettos of poverty in the peripheries of cities. Programs to improve units, however, also existed in 46% of the smallest municipalities in 2008, signifying that housing improvement is not only an urban phenomenon.

For this analysis I assess the determinants of individual types of programs as well as the number of programs in a municipality using a housing program index. Adopting multiple housing programs represents the government's willingness to address diverse needs of citizens and demands of CSOs. The greater the number of programs adopted by a municipality, the greater their commitment to alleviating housing issues.

MUNICIPAL HOUSING COUNCILS

The key independent variable of interest for this analysis is the existence of a municipal council for housing. Participation through a municipal housing council should put pressure on the municipality to enact housing programs and may also lead to a search for more resources from the federal level. There is significant variation in the existence of councils by region and population levels in both 2005 and 2008 (see Table 3.2). The data show that these participatory institutions are not limited to one region or to urban areas.

Table 3.2 Municipal Housing Councils by Region and Population

Region	Number of Municipalities	2005 Housing Council	2008 Housing Council
In Brazil	5563	18%	31%
North	449	5%	18%
Northeast	1793	8%	19%
Center-West	466	26%	34%
South	1187	38%	51%
Southeast	1668	14%	31%
Population			
Under 20,000	3965	16%	25%
20,001 to 50,000	1026	15%	36%
50,001 to 100,000	313	24%	52%
100,001 to 500,000	220	39%	67%
500,001 and up	39	56%	74%

Hypothesis: Municipalities with housing councils are significantly more
likely to adopt individual programs and a diverse array of programs as
measured by a housing program index.

ADDITIONAL FACTORS INFLUENCING
HOUSING PROGRAM ADOPTION

In general, local governments choose to adopt social programs of any
type based on need, access to resources, and political will. Though housing councils are theoretically important to determining program adoption, here I also control for and assess the independent effects of other
variables.

Civil Society

Through a range of activities, CSOs may influence government policy regardless of the presence of a municipal housing council. By conducting advocacy campaigns, engaging in direct negotiations, staging protests, and
setting up occupations, housing organizations seek to influence housing
policy. I argue that municipal housing councils give civil society a greater
voice in policy making, but to allow for the outside influence of CSOs I also
control for variation in civil society across contexts.

While broad data on CSOs at the municipal level is limited, the registry
of businesses in Brazil coordinated by IBGE offers a section of data on nonprofits and foundations from 2005.[25] These data allow me to capture a measure of the density of civil society. For each municipality I divide the number
of nonprofits and foundations by the total population to find a proxy for
the density of civil society: the number of nonprofits and foundations per
capita.[26] Though nonprofits and foundations do not comprise the entirety
of civil society, they are an important part of the whole. It is important to
note, however, that this measure accounts only for registered CSOs, which
may not include less formalized housing movements and neighborhood associations. The average number of nonprofits and foundations per 1,000
residents in a municipality is 2.6, with a standard deviation of 2.4 and a
range from .043 to 32.

Ideology of the Administration

In both 2005 and 2008, the ideology of the administration is measured by
the existence of a PT (Worker's Party) mayor. Since municipal elections were
held in 2004 and October 2008, the mayor remained the same across these
four years. Previous research from Europe and Latin America finds that
leftist parties are associated with higher levels of social spending.[27] In this

study I expect that the PT may have a positive effect on housing programs as a party to the left.

Availability of Resources

Where there are more resources available there will likely be a greater number of housing programs. An established fund dedicated to housing programs illustrates the commitment of the municipality to expend resources on low-income housing programs.[28] Municipalities with housing funds should be more likely to adopt multiple housing programs. Also, in both years I include a measure of the municipal budget per capita. Municipalities with higher budgetary resources should be more willing and able to allocate funding for housing programs. Finally, I use state dummy variables to control for variation in state resource transfers for housing programs.

Inequality

Within any setting, inequality may lead to less governmental accountability by limiting participation of the poor.[29] I use a municipal-level Gini coefficient from 2000 to measure inequality. Where inequality is highest, I expect that elites may be less inclined to implement social welfare programs for housing. The Gini coefficient among Brazilian municipalities ranges from a low of .358 to a high of .819, with .56 as the average.

Urbanization and Population Size

Urbanization is measured by the 2000 census, provided by IPEA (Instituto de Pesquisa Econômica Aplicada) and population size is measured by the 2005 estimate by IBGE. According to the data, as the population increases, municipalities are significantly more likely to adopt all types of housing programs, with the exception of programs to provide construction materials, for which the marginal difference is small. I use both percentage of the population living in urban areas as well as population size since, theoretically, population size represents the size of the municipality whereas the percentage urban represents clustering in the administrative center of the municipality. Perhaps surprisingly, these two measures are only correlated at .165. Since the federal government often uses population and urbanization as criteria for program eligibility, both of these measures should control for the federal impact on program adoption.

Need

Income per capita is also provided by the 2000 census. In wealthier municipalities, there should be less need for housing programs. Therefore, I expect income per capita to have a negative relationship with housing programs. Income per capita varies widely among Brazilian municipalities: from a low of R$28 to a high of R$955, with R$171 as the average. In addition, a variable indicating the presence of favelas is available from the MUNIC survey. Clearly, where there are favelas registered by the municipal government, there is a need for some type of housing program to address the quantitative and qualitative housing deficit.

ADDRESSING ENDOGENEITY

Before proceeding with the statistical analysis, it is useful to clarify the role endogeneity may play in biasing the estimates. First, one might expect that housing councils were created in municipalities in which government officials were already more interested in addressing housing needs. These municipalities would also then be more likely to have previously adopted multiple housing programs, creating endogeneity between housing councils and housing programs. To address this concern, I evaluated whether municipalities with each type of housing program in 2005 were more likely than average to create a housing council by 2008. About 21% of municipalities across Brazil adopted a housing council between 2005 and 2008. As Table 3.3 illustrates, municipalities with existing programs in 2005 were only slightly more likely to adopt housing councils. The exception are municipalities with regularization programs, which were about 16% more likely than average to adopt housing councils. I suspect this is because regularization programs and housing councils are both significantly more likely to be adopted in urban areas. In the full model, in which I include population and percentage of population in urban areas, this relationship should be mitigated. Correlations between programs in 2005 and housing councils in 2008, displayed in the last column of Table 3.3, further demonstrate a lack of strong association between existing programs and council creation.

Table 3.3 Associations between Program Adoption and Creation of Municipal Housing Councils

Program	Percentage of Municipalities with Each Type of Program in 2005 That Created a Housing Council by 2008	Correlation between Program in 2005 and Housing Council in 2008
Construction of Units	25%	0.09
Materials	24%	0.04
Plots of Land	22%	0.01
Regularization	37%	0.11
Other Programs	24%	0.03

Further, as the political party emerging from the labor movements of the 1970s, the PT has been the party most strongly associated with participatory governance institutions.[30] According to the data, however, municipalities with housing councils were only approximately 3.5% more likely to have a PT mayor in charge across years. Though this shows the odds are slightly higher that a municipality with a council has a PT mayor, the difference does not lead me to conclude that the PT is endogenous to the existence of a council.

MODEL

I estimate several probit models to assess the relationships between these independent variables and the adoption of individual housing programs. Probit is an appropriate regression model for dichotomous dependent variables and provides intuitive results regarding the probability of program adoption. I also use negative binomial regression models to measure the effects on the adoption of multiple housing programs using a housing program index.[31] The models are based on the hypothesis that municipal councils lead to housing program adoption.

RESULTS FROM THE STATISTICAL ANALYSIS

Municipal Councils

I find that the existence of municipal housing councils is associated with an increase in the adoption of all types of social housing programs across years (see Tables 3.4 and 3.5).[32] This provides evidence to confirm the primary hypothesis that participatory governance institutions lead to programs benefiting the poor.[33]

Table 3.6 illustrates the substantive effect of the municipal councils. Using the full probit model, the percentages reported in Table 3.6 represent the marginal effect of the existence of a municipal council on adoption of each type of housing program, holding all other variables at their means. In other words, the percentage reported in Table 3.6 indicates the change in the probability of adoption of each type of housing program (coded as 0–1) given a one-unit change in the dependent variable (the existence of a housing council coded as 0–1). In both years, the councils make a substantial difference in whether programs are adopted, holding all else constant. Councils have the greatest impact on programs to construct new units and improve existing units, such as in favelas or dilapidated buildings, while the councils only have a small effect on programs to acquire new units, often associated with renovating city centers, and urbanization of informal settlements or favelas.

To assess the impact of municipal housing councils on the diversity of programs adopted by a municipality, I also created an index of programs for

Table 3.4 Probit Results for the Impact on Housing Programs, 2005*

	Construction of Units	Offer Materials	Offer Plots of Land	Regularization	Other Programs
Municipal Housing Council	0.26***	0.10	0.24***	0.39***	0.34***
	(0.07)	(0.07)	(0.08)	(0.09)	(0.07)
Municipal Housing Fund	0.39***	0.31***	0.34***	0.25***	0.19***
	(0.07)	(0.07)	(0.08)	(0.09)	(0.07)
Population (log)	0.27***	0.13***	0.19***	0.44***	0.27***
	(0.03)	(0.03)	(0.04)	(0.05)	(0.04)
Percent Urban Population (log)	0.16***	0.12**	0.19***	0.08	0.12*
	(0.06)	(0.06)	(0.07)	(0.10)	(0.07)
Municipal Budget per Capita (log)	0.61***	0.46***	0.43***	0.36***	0.40***
	(0.08)	(0.08)	(0.08)	(0.10)	(0.08)
PT Mayor	0.05	-0.27***	-0.02	-0.11	0.20**
	(0.08)	(0.08)	(0.09)	(0.12)	(0.09)
Gini Coefficient	0.51	0.85**	0.08	0.87	0.77*
	(0.42)	(0.43)	(0.49)	(0.63)	(0.46)
Income per Capita (log)	-0.19**	-0.306***	-0.12	0.23*	-0.12
	(0.09)	(0.09)	(0.10)	(0.13)	(0.10)
Civil Society Density (log)	0.07*	0.00	0.03	-0.01	0.12***
	(0.04)	(0.04)	(0.04)	(0.06)	(0.04)
Existence of Favelas	0.07	-0.02	-0.20***	-0.01	0.08
	(0.06)	(0.06)	(0.07)	(0.08)	(0.06)
Constant	-5.66***	-4.06***	-5.20***	-9.99***	-5.11***
	(0.81)	(0.80)	(0.88)	(1.10)	(0.84)
Observations	3869	3864	3878	3869	3878

*State dummies also included in the model.
Standard errors in parentheses. *** $p < 0.01$, ** $p < 0.05$, * $p < 0.1$.

Table 3.5 Probit Results for the Impact on Housing Programs, 2008*

	Construction of Units	Offer Materials	Offer Plots of Land	Regularization	Acquire Units	Improve Units	Urbanization
Municipal Housing Council	0.29***	0.14**	0.16**	0.24***	0.16**	0.28***	0.18**
	(0.07)	(0.06)	(0.07)	(0.07)	(0.07)	(0.06)	(0.08)
Municipal Housing Fund	0.25***	0.09	0.19***	0.14**	0.09	0.03	0.16**
	(0.06)	(0.06)	(0.07)	(0.07)	(0.07)	(0.06)	(0.08)
Population (log)	0.20***	0.08**	0.10***	0.35***	0.13***	0.06*	0.43***
	(0.04)	(0.03)	(0.03)	(0.04)	(0.04)	(0.03)	(0.04)
Percent Urban Population (log)	0.14**	0.20***	0.26***	0.03	0.03	0.18***	0.03
	(0.06)	(0.06)	(0.06)	(0.07)	(0.07)	(0.06)	(0.08)
Municipal Budget per Capita (log)	0.49***	0.37***	0.27***	0.34***	0.18**	0.19**	0.46***
	(0.08)	(0.07)	(0.08)	(0.08)	(0.08)	(0.07)	(0.09)
PT Mayor	0.05	0.10	-0.10	0.25***	0.07	0.12	0.06
	(0.08)	(0.08)	(0.09)	(0.09)	(0.09)	(0.08)	(0.10)
Gini Coefficient	1.25***	1.28***	0.01	-0.03	0.24	1.98***	0.98*
	(0.42)	(0.42)	(0.45)	(0.48)	(0.49)	(0.41)	(0.53)
Income per Capita (log)	0.07	-0.17*	0.03	0.17*	0.10	-0.11	0.04
	(0.09)	(0.08)	(0.09)	(0.10)	(0.10)	(0.08)	(0.11)
Civil Society Density (log)	-0.04	-0.07*	0.03	-0.09**	-0.01	0.13***	-0.11**
	(0.04)	(0.04)	(0.04)	(0.04)	(0.04)	(0.04)	(0.05)
Existence of Favelas	-0.00	-0.06	-0.00	0.30***	0.06	-0.04	0.38***
	(0.05)	(0.05)	(0.05)	(0.06)	(0.06)	(0.05)	(0.06)
Constant	-6.43***	-4.36***	-4.10***	-8.27***	-4.33***	-2.06***	-10.35***
	(0.83)	(0.77)	(0.82)	(0.88)	(0.87)	(0.76)	(0.98)
Observations	4093	4080	4093	4093	4093	4083	4083

*State dummies also included in the model.
Standard errors in parentheses. *** $p < 0.01$, ** $p < 0.05$, * $p < 0.1$.

Table 3.6   Percentage Change in the Probability that a Municipality Has Each Type of Program Given the Presence of a Municipal Housing Council, Holding All Other Variables Constant

Type of Program	2005	2008
Construction of Units	10%	11%
Construction Materials	4%	5%
Offering Plots of Land	7%	5%
Regularization of Land Titles	6%	6%
Other Programs	11%	
Acquisition of New Units		4%
Improvement of Units		11%
Urbanization of Settlements		3%

analysis in a negative binomial model (see Appendix B for results).[34] Using the index of housing programs, Figures 3.1 and 3.2 illustrate the predicted probabilities of municipalities adopting multiple housing programs given the presence of a municipal housing council in 2005 and 2008. All other independent variables were set to their means. In both years the mean number of predicted programs is significantly higher in municipalities with housing councils than in those without councils.

In sum, the presence of a municipal council is strongly associated with the adoption of each type of program as well as an increase in the number of programs in a municipality. Figures 3.1 and 3.2 demonstrate that between 2005 and 2008, the relationship between councils and the number of programs gained strength as the mean number of programs in municipalities with councils increased from around two to almost three programs.

The results also point to a number of secondary observations regarding the control variables. Each of these findings contributes to our understanding of the factors that influence local-level housing policy. First, the funding available is key for housing program adoption. Both the presence of a dedicated fund for housing and the size of the municipal budget matter for the adoption of housing programs. Second, the results demonstrate that the larger the population and the more urban the municipality, the greater the probability of program adoption.

Interestingly, two variables that political scientists would expect to have a significant effect on social policy—the presence of a leftist administration and the density of civil society—do not have a consistent effect on the adoption of housing programs. Subsequent chapters will explore the impact of these variables in the policy-making process within municipal housing councils and whether the density of civil society or the party in power changes the outcomes of participatory governance institutions.

Here the statistical results confirm the main hypothesis that municipalities with housing councils are more likely to adopt all types of housing

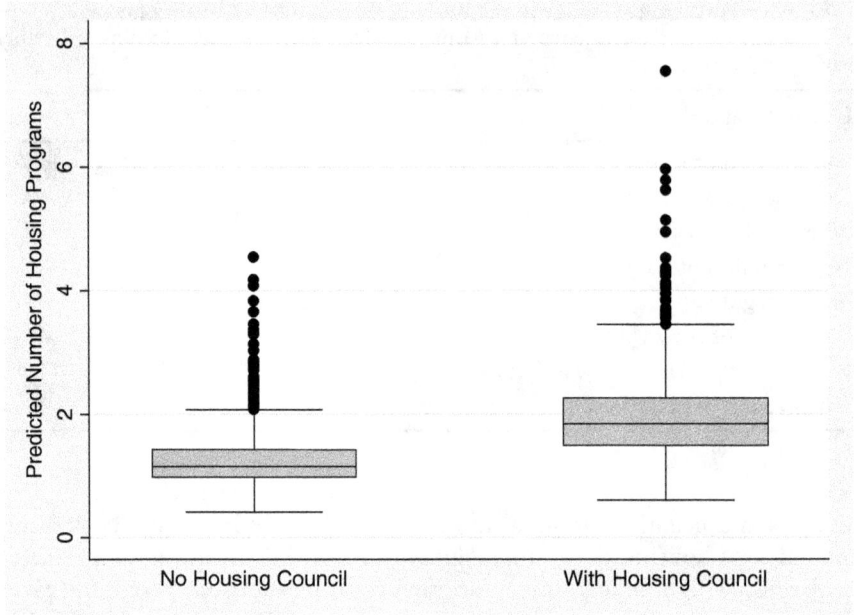

Figure 3.1 Predicted Number of Housing Programs Given the Presence of a Municipal Council for Housing, 2005

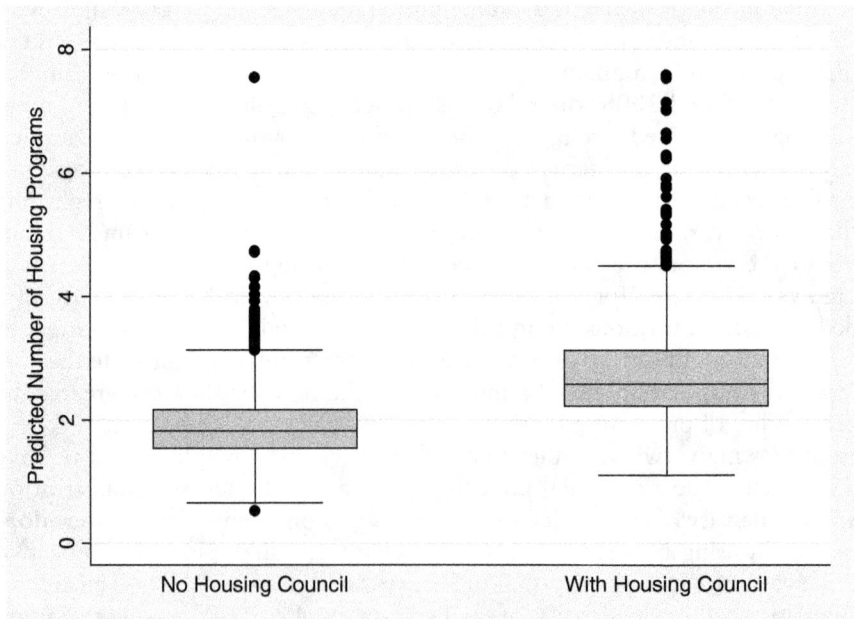

Figure 3.2 Predicted Number of Housing Programs Given the Presence of a Municipal Council for Housing, 2008

programs. Across years the existence of a municipal housing council is associated with an increased probability of adoption of each type of housing program and multiple housing programs.

Municipal Housing Councils Matter for Program Adoption

According to the results, overall municipal councils are effective mechanisms for incorporating civil society into decision making to bring about greater numbers of social programs and pro-poor policies. Municipal councils for housing do seem to be credible institutions for promoting accountability and responsiveness among governments at the municipal level. Municipal councils are associated with a greater probability of municipalities adopting each type of program and a broad range of programs, which may reflect the negotiation of CSOs and government officials to respond to calls for new units as well as renovation of existing favelas and renewal of city centers.

Municipal councils appear to alter the policy environment toward heterogeneous needs by increasing the probability of municipalities adopting each type of program. In large cities social movements have often criticized municipal governments for marginalizing the poor by building large public housing complexes in the periphery of the city, cut off from essential services and employment.[35] For example, in São Paulo, the União dos Movimentos da Moradia has fought against the continued construction of large public housing blocks on the periphery and instead calls for communally built projects and affordable housing in the city center. According to Raquel Rolnik, an urban policy expert in Brazil who is currently the Special Rapporteur on Housing Issues to the United Nations, in the 1970s and 1980s government officials were most concerned about removing residents from favelas and illegal occupations of land and placing them in public housing units. The participatory movement, including the councils, has changed the ways in which people view solutions to housing problems. Today, Rolnik says, "the dissemination of the idea that favelas must be urbanized and integrated, and that they have rights to stay, is something that changed the administrative culture and housing policies in this country."[36] Rural-based movements have also argued that housing policy in Brazil has not addressed the needs of seasonal laborers and geographical variation in the country. People living in rural areas prefer more freedom to construct houses that meet their needs and to be able to pay back loans on a more flexible schedule.[37] The MST encourages members to voice their demands for government support, including construction materials and mortgage subsidies.

The call for acknowledging the diversity of needs in urban and rural areas is underscored by the increase in adoption of an array of programs between 2005 and 2008 that is strongly affected by the presence of a municipal council for housing. For instance, programs to regularize land titles, in essence to legalize the occupation and dwelling of favela or rural residents to provide them with land security, increased from 9% of municipalities in 2005 to

20% in 2008. Holding all other variables constant, Table 3.6 shows that the probability of a municipality adopting a regularization program is 6% higher where municipal housing councils exist. Municipalities with housing councils are also significantly more likely than municipalities without councils to adopt a number of different types of housing programs in both years, indicating that councils appear to have an effect on the government's responsiveness to a diversity of demands. These results provide evidence to skeptics that municipal councils exist more than as institutions on paper.

In the end, participatory governance institutions, as demonstrated by the case of municipal housing councils in Brazil, are able to positively affect policy outcomes for the poor by increasing the transfer of information between citizens and government officials regarding needs and improving transparency to allow CSOs to hold the government accountable for their actions. As a social movement leader from the Northeastern city of Salvador explained, the councils are important forums for them to direct resources, but more broadly they use the councils to solicit information, demand responses, and follow up to make sure the government does what it says it will. Though the councils are not perfect mechanisms for accountability, they provide greater access to government and serve as a place for discussion that never existed before. Across Brazilian municipalities, incorporating civil society into decision making does appear to induce local governments to invest in social housing programs, while perhaps breaking some of the clientelistic relationships of the past.

CONCLUSIONS

The findings in this chapter contribute to the debate about whether participatory governance institutions bring about pro-poor policy outcomes. According to this analysis incorporation of civil society through participatory governance institutions does lead local governments to adopt social programs to benefit the poor. These types of institutions may then be innovative mechanisms for welfare provision, particularly in developing countries without a strong history of broad participation.

Answers regarding the effectiveness of civil society and participatory governance institutions hold important implications for developing countries seeking to address mounting social needs, particularly in urban areas where the poor seek housing solutions to overcome political, geographic, and economic marginalization. Though this analysis produced significant results regarding the effect of municipal councils on pro-poor outcomes, additional analysis will provide direct evidence of accountability. An assessment of the institutional rules and dynamics between civil society and state actors will further demonstrate the internal struggles that occur within municipal councils to clarify how and when participatory governance institutions make a difference for the poor.

4 Civil Society Density, Participatory Governance, and Policy Outcomes

> Our greatest challenge is to break the dictatorship in the city. We need to show that the people need participation and they have a right to it. It's not the job of the government to decide who can participate. The struggle is to mobilize people and overcome corruption from the government to win over the people.
>
> —Housing rights activist in Curitiba, Brazil[1]

In the previous chapter I find that though municipal housing councils are associated with an increase in social housing policy adoption, the density of civil society is not consistently related to the adoption of housing programs. The number of civil society organizations (CSOs), as measured by nonprofits and foundations per capita, does not appear to make a significant difference for municipal-level social policy outcomes. An organized civil society alone does not lead governments to make changes in housing program adoption. This finding would seem to make participatory governance institutions all the more important for including the voices of CSOs in policy making. Participatory governance institutions may be the missing link between the institutions of representative democracy and the vital role of civil society in promoting accountability and responsiveness.

But, scholars argue that a "strong" civil society is necessary for participatory governance institutions to function well.[2] Participatory governance institutions may be the critical connection between policy influence and civil society, but not without a significant presence of CSOs committed to the participatory process. Without strong CSOs, scholars argue that participatory institutions cannot function to overcome the will of the government or transmit information to their membership and the rest of the public as a means of promoting accountability. This claim, however, has not been thoroughly tested across contexts or by measuring the effect of civil society on outcomes of participatory governance institutions.

In this chapter I ask a key question: is the effectiveness of participatory governance institutions in bringing about program adoption contingent on a strong civil society? I hypothesize that a highly organized civil society increases the effectiveness of participatory governance institutions. Civil society needs the capacity to make proactive proposals while also presenting a united front to counteract the reticence of government officials to expend scarce resources on social programs. If this is true, I would expect to see a more significant association between housing program adoption and municipal housing councils as the density of civil society increases.

Contrary to my hypothesis, however, I find that a highly organized civil society does not appear to have a consistent impact on the adoption of housing programs where municipal councils exist. A strong civil society does not necessarily influence government officials to expend resources any more than CSOs in a weaker civil society environment. Though this contradicts the work of previous scholars, I argue that the findings signal good news in that this suggests that the effectiveness of participatory governance institutions is not contingent on a highly organized civil society: across contexts, incorporation of existing civil society in participatory governance institutions may still lead to pro-poor policy change.

THEORETICAL ARGUMENT

Does a particularly strong civil society have a different effect on the outcomes of participatory governance institutions?

Most scholars studying participatory governance institutions, building on Putnam and others, argue specifically that high levels of social capital are necessary for participatory governance institutions to have any significant impact.[3] In a cross-municipal study of participatory budgeting councils in Brazil, Avritzer found that an existing community of organizations was necessary to create the intended forum for deliberation.[4] Without considerable mobilization of demands, participatory governance institutions may be easily co-opted by elites and have no effect on democratic deepening or policy outcomes.[5] Without a strong civil society, scholars have argued, participatory governance institutions may be little more than rubber stamps for government proposals.[6] In addition, Brazilian researchers find that "effective" councils are dependent on CSOs' technical capacity to formulate and analyze public policy and their ability to make strategic alliances.[7]

The counterargument is that a stronger civil society environment could also lead established CSOs accustomed to competition for scarce resources to fight for selective benefits within the councils, thereby limiting the broad effectiveness of the councils for generating pro-poor benefits. Through fieldwork I witnessed professional CSOs, including NGOs (nongovernmental organizations) and social movements dedicated to housing, using strategies developed over time to gain access to government officials in private or public meetings. In these meetings, most of the discussions center on specific housing projects—which families will be included, and the contributions from the municipal, state, and federal levels—rather than broader allocation of resources across diverse programs.

As in the previous chapter, I argue that the introduction of participatory forums to debate programmatic decisions should mitigate the need for these types of bilateral strategies. Where civil society is particularly well established, the desire for CSOs to continue to seek particularistic benefits for their members, and for governments to appease CSO members by responding to their demands in exchange for political loyalty, may remain strong. However, based on my observations in the field, particularly in the cities of São Paulo and Salvador, CSOs have learned the value of working in a coordinated network to confront government proposals and business interests. Civil society representatives are still accountable to their membership bases, but they also recognize there is strength in numbers. An organized civil society working through municipal councils should therefore increase rather than decrease governmental responsiveness and accountability.

The stronger the community of CSOs, the greater impact they expect to have on the outcomes of participatory governance institutions. Where civil society is more highly organized, their capacity to work collaboratively should help to counteract business interests and government reluctance to allocate scarce resources to social programs. Civil society needs the capacity to express demands within the council in order to be proactive and form alliances to prepare responses to government proposals. Working in coordinated networks within the councils is likely to dilute the strength of bilateral relationships between CSOs and government officials, resulting in adoption of a broad range of programs.

ANALYSIS

To address the question of whether a strong civil society makes a difference in the outcomes of municipal housing councils, I conduct statistical analyses based on the statistical model developed in the previous chapter. The dependent variables are individual types of housing programs and a housing program index. The variable I use to indicate the strength of civil society is based on the density of civil society as measured by the number of nonprofits and foundations per capita.[8] The FASFIL survey (Pesquisa das Fundações Privadas e Associações Sem Fins Lucrativos) lists the number of nonprofits and foundations by municipality as recorded for the purposes of tracking the business environment in the country. To attain a civil society density score for each municipality, I divide the total number of nonprofits and foundations by the official population for the municipality.

Measuring civil society is a complex task, and given that the findings of this analysis hold important implications for future recommendations regarding participatory governance institutions, making sure the measure is representative of reality is critical. Three criticisms of the measure used in this analysis are important to address: (1) The measure only includes registered nonprofits and foundations, which leaves out more informal movements and neighborhood associations. (2) The measure does not indicate that the organizations have anything to do with housing. (3) *Density* of CSOs does not necessarily indicate the *strength* of civil society.

To address the first question regarding the validity of this measure of civil society I turn to my case studies for help. What kinds of CSOs does the measure actually represent? I find that the numbers listed in Table 4.1 largely reflect my perception of the depth of civil society in each city. Even though the official numbers only record registered nonprofits and foundations, the measure appears to capture the broader associational environment. While still not a perfect measure, I believe it to be a close proxy for the depth or density of civil society.

For instance, as the largest city in the country, struggling with a high degree of inequality and tremendous urban challenges, São Paulo has a thriving civil society, composed of professionalized NGOs, neighborhood associations, and social movements. A civil society density score of 0.0019, at the higher end of the case studies, matches my perception of civil society in São Paulo, which incorporates diverse interests and types of organizations. The numbers also reflect the more limited nature of civil society in Santo André, a smaller city on the outskirts of São Paulo long dominated by the PT (Worker's Party). That the civil society density measure lies in the middle of these cases captures the presence of strong labor unions. The Northeastern city of Salvador has the lowest civil society density score among the case studies. Again, this matches the reality I observed on the ground in which civil society appeared very fragmented in the wake of a long-standing notoriously conservative and corrupt government. In Salvador there are few professionalized NGOs and the associations that exist tend to center on preservation of the Afro-Brazilian culture or direct social service provision rather than policy change. Recife, also in the Northeast of the country, has a larger presence of NGOs than Salvador, though here again a history of clientelism has fragmented many of the housing associations and social movements. Neglect of housing issues by the municipal government has radicalized existing social movements in the way suggested by James Holston in *Insurgent Citizenships.*[9] Land occupations and protests remain the central

Table 4.1   Civil Society Density

City	Nonprofits and Foundations per Capita
São Paulo	0.0019
Santo André	0.0014
Salvador	0.0010
Recife	0.0015
Curitiba	0.0024

strategies of housing movements. A middle-range civil society density score appears to fit the reality on the ground in which civil society is growing, but still struggling to unify around common goals. Lastly, the high civil society density score for Curitiba reflects the large number of professionalized NGOs and associations in the city. Curitiba does have a strong community of housing rights movements, but is dominated by professional urban planning associations because of the long tradition of urban innovation in the city. This case, then, does reveal the bias of the measure toward registered organizations.

Overall, the case studies confirm the validity of the civil society density measure. The aim of the measure is to provide a picture of the associational atmosphere within the municipality. The case of Curitiba illustrates the bias of the measure toward professionalized NGOs, however, and the results of the analysis should be interpreted in this light.

The second potential criticism that this measure does not indicate whether the organizations recorded have anything to do with housing has some merit, but I do not believe this negates the findings of the analysis regarding the importance of a strong civil society for participatory governance institutions. The FASFIL survey does include a subcategory for organizations oriented toward housing. However, I choose not to use these data for two reasons. First, organizations oriented toward housing often focus on multiple policy areas and therefore may be categorized under the broader heading of social assistance or urban reform organizations rather than housing alone. Using the number of organizations listed under the "housing" subcategory, then, would underestimate the number of CSOs actually involved in activities related to housing. Second, the number of organizations recorded under the housing subcategory is very low across cases, and when divided by the population, provides a somewhat meaningless score. In my experience in the field, I found a number of NGOs, social movements, and professional associations participating in the housing councils, which would not have been categorized under the housing subcategory on the survey. By using the total number of CSOs in a municipality, I hope to capture a snapshot of the associational environment, which should relate to the overall concentration of social capital.

The third issue with this measure involves the definition of a "strong" civil society. Does the density of civil society indicate the strength of civil society? What exactly defines a "strong" civil society? In recent literature on civil society, a strong civil society is often characterized by its effect. For example, Michael Edwards asserts that "a strong civil society can prevent the agglomeration of power that threatens autonomy and choice, provide effective checks against the abuse of state authority, and protect a democratic public sphere in which citizens can debate the ends and means of governance."[10] Here, strength is equated with effectiveness. But this does not provide a picture of what a strong civil society might look like. The density of organizations provides one way to judge whether civil society is able to have the desired effects in a democracy. Carlos Waisman characterizes Latin American civil society as strong based on the existing dense web of associations. Waisman also defines a strong civil society by its autonomy from the state and capacity to use democratic institutions to solve conflicts.[11] But density forms the core for measuring the level of associational presence within a defined territory. According to Robert Putnam, the greater the density of CSOs, the higher the level of social capital.[12] For the purposes of this analysis, then, I use the civil society density score as a proxy for the strength of civil society.

In sum, based on the case studies I argue that the density score does reflect the overall associational environment in a municipality, which should impact advocacy efforts in the city and the ability of civil society to participate in participatory governance institutions. Theoretically, a more dense civil society should generate greater levels of social capital. With housing issues figuring prominently across Brazilian municipalities, CSOs of all kinds become involved in efforts to ameliorate the problems around them. As described previously, the civil society density scores largely coincide with my perception of CSOs oriented toward housing as well as the broader community of CSOs in the city.

The key question for the subsequent analysis is whether a strong civil society makes a difference in the outcomes of municipal housing councils. Though the analysis in the previous chapter did not find a significant relationship between the density of civil society and the adoption of social housing programs, I hypothesize that a strong civil society should enhance the effectiveness of municipal housing councils as mechanisms to increase the government's willingness to adopt programs. For this analysis I add an interaction term to the model established in the previous chapter: presence of a housing council × civil society density.

> Hypothesis: Where municipal councils exist, a higher number of CSOs per capita is associated with an increase in the probability of municipalities adopting all types of housing programs.

ENDOGENEITY

One final issue to be addressed before proceeding with the analysis is the question of endogeneity between civil society and housing councils. Particularly prior to 2005, when the federal government enacted the new National System for Housing in the Social Interest, requiring municipalities receiving federal funds to create municipal housing councils by the end of 2009, housing councils were largely created in response to the demands of CSOs or by ideologically committed mayors. Therefore, it might appear that the density of civil society is endogenous to the creation of municipal councils for housing. However, the data show that the average number of nonprofits and foundations per capita across municipalities (.0026) is not significantly different than the average in municipalities with housing councils (.0033 in 2005 and .0031 in 2008). For this reason I do not believe that this measure of civil society is endogenous to the existence of municipal housing councils.

STATISTICAL RESULTS

As shown in Tables 3.4 and 3.5 in the proceeding chapter, civil society density, as measured by the number of nonprofits and foundations per capita, does not have a strong, consistent effect on the adoption of housing programs across programs or across years. But does a strong civil society increase the probability of social program adoption where mechanisms for formal incorporation, in the form of municipal housing councils, exist? To shed light on this question, I add an interaction variable for civil society and housing councils to the original probit models (see Tables 4.2 and 4.3.)

The results show that the density of civil society is not consistently associated with adoption of housing programs across years, either where municipal councils do or do not exist. However, there are several exceptions depending on the type of program. In 2005, where municipal councils for housing exist, a strong civil society is positively associated with programs to offer families construction materials. This could indicate that CSOs, who often lobby for self-build (auto-construção) projects in which associations receive government funding for materials to build homes, are more successful when they are able to make these demands within municipal councils. By 2008, however, a stronger civil society is negatively associated with programs to offer construction materials, and the relationship is unchanged by the presence of a municipal council.

In 2005, civil society is positively associated with "other programs," though the presence of a municipal council does not enhance the effect. In 2008, interesting associations emerge for two programs that likely fall under the catchall category of "other programs" in the 2005 survey: programs to improve units and urbanization programs. A strong civil society increases the probability of municipalities adopting programs to improve units, and the presence of a municipal council amplifies this effect. This may mean that housing associations, particularly those working with more professional NGOs, which are more likely to be included in this measure of civil society, are reaching government officials to improve housing units, allowing residents to stay within their communities. Again, the presence of a municipal housing council may provide the forum for CSOs to negotiate these demands. The relationship between urbanization programs and civil society, however, contradicts the result for programs to improve units. Here, a strong civil society is negatively associated with urbanization programs, and the presence of a municipal housing council has no effect. Though

Table 4.2 Variables Associated with Housing Program Adoption, Including an Interaction Effect for Civil Society and Housing Councils, 2005*

	Construction of Units	Offer Materials	Offer Plots of Land	Regularization	Other Programs
Municipal Housing Council	0.64	1.13***	0.99**	0.04	0.71
	(0.44)	(0.43)	(0.49)	(0.64)	(0.45)
Municipal Housing Fund	0.39***	0.31***	0.34***	0.25***	0.19***
	(0.07)	(0.07)	(0.08)	(0.09)	(0.07)
Population (log)	0.27***	0.14***	0.19***	0.44***	0.27***
	(0.03)	(0.03)	(0.04)	(0.05)	(0.04)
Percent Urban Population (log)	0.16***	0.12*	0.19***	0.08	0.12*
	(0.06)	(0.06)	(0.07)	(0.10)	(0.07)
Municipal Budget per Capita (log)	0.61***	0.46***	0.43***	0.36***	0.40***
	(0.08)	(0.08)	(0.08)	(0.10)	(0.08)
PT Mayor	0.05	-0.26***	-0.02	-0.12	0.20**
	(0.08)	(0.08)	(0.09)	(0.12)	(0.09)
Gini Coefficient	0.50	0.83*	0.06	0.87	0.76*
	(0.42)	(0.43)	(0.49)	(0.63)	(0.46)
Income per Capita (log)	-0.19**	-0.31***	-0.12	0.23*	-0.12
	(0.09)	(0.09)	(0.10)	(0.13)	(0.10)
Civil Society Density (log)	0.05	-0.03	0.00	0.01	0.11**
	(0.04)	(0.04)	(0.05)	(0.07)	(0.04)
Existence of Favelas	0.07	-0.02	-0.21***	-0.01	0.08
	(0.06)	(0.06)	(0.07)	(0.08)	(0.06)
Housing Council × Civil Society Density (log)	0.06	0.17**	0.12	-0.06	0.06
	(0.07)	(0.07)	(0.08)	(0.10)	(0.07)
Constant	-5.76***	-4.35***	-5.41***	-9.85***	-5.22***
	(0.82)	(0.81)	(0.89)	(1.12)	(0.85)
Observations	3869	3864	3878	3869	3878

*Model includes state dummies.
Standard errors in parentheses. *** $p < 0.01$, ** $p < 0.05$, * $p < 0.1$.

Table 4.3 Variables Associated with Housing Program Adoption, Including an Interaction Effect for Civil Society and Housing Councils, 2008*

	Construction of Units	Offer Materials	Offer Plots of Land	Regularization	Acquire Units	Improve Units	Urbanization
Municipal Housing Council	0.16 (0.38)	0.17 (0.37)	0.58 (0.40)	-0.07 (0.43)	-0.38 (0.43)	0.92** (0.37)	0.20 (0.51)
Municipal Housing Fund	0.25*** (0.06)	0.09 (0.06)	0.19*** (0.07)	0.14** (0.07)	0.09 (0.07)	0.03 (0.06)	0.16** (0.08)
Population (log)	0.20*** (0.04)	0.08** (0.03)	0.10*** (0.03)	0.35*** (0.04)	0.12*** (0.04)	0.07** (0.03)	0.43*** (0.04)
Percent Urban Population (log)	0.14** (0.06)	0.20*** (0.06)	0.26*** (0.06)	0.03 (0.07)	0.03 (0.07)	0.18*** (0.06)	0.03 (0.08)
Municipal Budget per Capita (log)	0.49*** (0.08)	0.37*** (0.07)	0.28*** (0.08)	0.34*** (0.08)	0.18** (0.08)	0.19*** (0.07)	0.46*** (0.09)
PT Mayor	0.05 (0.08)	0.11 (0.08)	-0.10 (0.09)	0.24*** (0.09)	0.06 (0.09)	0.12 (0.08)	0.06 (0.10)
Gini Coefficient	1.25*** (0.42)	1.28*** (0.41)	-0.02 (0.45)	-0.02 (0.48)	0.28 (0.49)	1.93*** (0.41)	0.98* (0.53)
Income per Capita (log)	0.07 (0.09)	-0.17* (0.08)	0.03 (0.09)	0.17* (0.10)	0.10 (0.10)	-0.11 (0.08)	0.04 (0.11)
Civil Society Density (log)	-0.03 (0.04)	-0.07* (0.04)	0.00 (0.04)	-0.07 (0.05)	0.02 (0.05)	0.09** (0.04)	-0.11* (0.06)

(Continued)

Table 4.3 (Continued)

	Construction of Units	Offer Materials	Offer Plots of Land	Regularization	Acquire Units	Improve Units	Urbanization
Existence of Favelas	-0.00	-0.06	-0.00	0.30***	0.06	-0.04	0.38***
	(0.05)	(0.05)	(0.05)	(0.06)	(0.06)	(0.05)	(0.06)
Housing Council × Civil Society Density (log)	-0.02	0.00	0.07	-0.05	-0.09	0.11*	0.00
	(0.06)	(0.06)	(0.06)	(0.07)	(0.07)	(0.06)	(0.08)
Constant	-6.38***	-4.38***	-4.28***	-8.13***	-4.10***	-2.32***	-10.36***
	(0.84)	(0.79)	(0.84)	(0.90)	(0.89)	(0.78)	(0.99)
Observations	4093	4080	4093	4093	4093	4083	4083

*Model also includes state dummies.
Standard errors in parentheses. *** $p < 0.01$, ** $p < 0.05$, * $p < 0.1$.

speculative, this relationship could be a result of strong CSOs focusing on gaining selective benefits for their members in the form of improving individual units rather than demanding improvements in whole communities through urbanization programs. For instance, in Santo André, a large city outside of São Paulo, CSOs have fought for the improvement of individual run-down public housing units, rather than for infrastructure projects. Given limited resources, CSOs may focus on small victories rather than more expensive large-scale urbanization projects.

Using the housing program index as the dependent variable, in 2005, the depth of civil society appears to have a positive effect on the adoption of multiple programs where there is not a municipal council (see Appendix B for results). When a municipal housing council is in place, the positive relationship becomes even stronger. Incorporation of a strong civil society into formal decision making does seem to add to the impact of municipal councils. While these results are suggestive of a strong relationship between civil society, formal incorporation, and adoption of a broad array of housing programs, the pattern does not hold across years. In 2008, the relationship is not significant. Different results across years lead to further questions about the differences in civil society influence and the effectiveness of municipal councils after 2005. The results suggest that the beginning implementation of the new federal system for housing between 2005 and 2008 may affect the influence of civil society within and outside of municipal councils, a question that is in part addressed in Chapter 6.

DISCUSSION: LEVELING THE PLAYING FIELD

Previous claims that a strong civil society is a necessary condition for effective councils—however that is defined—do not hold true in this analysis defining effectiveness through program outcomes. The analysis suggests that municipal housing councils level the playing field for civil society to access government officials. Contrary to previous research and my own hypothesis, the results show that the density of civil society, which may indicate increased capacity, is not a prerequisite for effectiveness of participatory governance institutions.

The results do not confirm previous claims that a strong civil society is necessary for creating effective participatory governance institutions. Though the measure used here is an imperfect representation of all civil society, it provides a proxy for the density of civil society based on the number of registered organizations. One conclusion to be drawn from this result is that CSOs working through participatory governance institutions are able to collaborate and form alliances to make proactive proposals and counter government and business interests, regardless of the numbers of existing organizations. Municipal housing councils offer the space for cooperation against common "threats," which unite CSOs of all types to make common demands.

The results regarding programs to improve units and urbanization programs in 2008, however, insinuate that a strong civil society may have an opposing effect for different types of programs. A different process may be taking place in adoption of these two types of programs. Further case study research will serve to elucidate whether CSOs continue to pursue traditional bilateral relationships with government officials to gain selective benefits for their members as may be reflected in the finding that a stronger civil society tends to bring about programs to improve individual housing units rather than community-enhancing urbanization programs. Alternatively, the number of registered nonprofits and foundations tends to be higher in cities where real estate interests are also likely to be strong. In urban areas the value of land is higher, and it may be more difficult to convince municipal leaders to clean up the slums without any financial gain for construction companies. The councils may not be powerful enough mechanisms to overcome business interests, even where a strong civil society exists. The role of the private sector is further addressed in Chapter 5.

Finally, the finding that a strong civil society environment was associated with adoption of multiple housing programs where housing councils existed in 2005, but not 2008, implies there was a shift in the effect CSOs had on the policy process and municipal housing councils between these two years. As municipalities across Brazil adopted housing councils in response to the new federal system, the depth of civil society appeared to matter less than the act of formally incorporating voices from civil society in the decision-making process. Further examination of this relationship and the influence of funding from the federal level is needed to clarify the role of increasing resource transfers versus civil society.

CONCLUSIONS

The findings suggest the density of civil society is less important than the formal incorporation of CSOs in decision-making institutions. Though past research suggests strong capacity of civil society is necessary within participatory governance institutions to counter elite proposals and avoid cooptation, this analysis implies collaboration among CSOs is possible regardless of the density of formal organizations. I regard this as a positive finding in that it widens the possibilities for participatory governance institutions to function effectively across contexts.

Civil society encompasses a broad range of actors with diverse interests. That the density of CSOs does not appear to largely influence the outcomes of participatory governance institutions does not mean that the various strategies and demands of CSOs across contexts do not significantly shape the direction of policies and programs, particularly in the details of implementation. The next chapter seeks to understand how CSOs shape the policy process in participatory governance institutions, leading ultimately to important decisions.

5 Pathways to Participatory Governance
Civil Society–State Dynamics and Institutional Rules

> Brazil has very serious problems with our democracy, which is still very recent. Civil society is still dealing with how to have an impact on public policy given the problems of corruption. Therefore, the councils are very important for the influence movements are able to have on the allocation of resources for housing policies. We need to participate in the councils, ensure their consolidation, and guarantee the allocation of resources is more transparent.
>
> —Benedito Barbosa, housing movement activist, São Paulo, Brazil[1]

Municipal councils for housing will never be the only deciding factor in policy outcomes, but as the movement leader indicates in the opening quote, CSOs (civil society organizations) believe that the councils legitimize the policy process and affect change in the distribution of resources. In Chapter 3 I find that the existence of municipal housing councils does significantly increase the probability of municipalities adopting all types of programs. This effect is not dependent on a strong civil society, suggesting that the existence of the participatory institution matters more than the actual density of CSOs. But what does lead to differences in the policy process and outcomes of participatory institutions? Though scholars have begun to name potential variables that influence the policy-making process and outcomes of participatory governance institutions, this chapter undertakes a comparative analysis of Brazilian cities to provide evidence for how and when context matters.

In this chapter I seek to identify the factors that enhance both the policy-making process and outcomes in Brazil's municipal housing councils and participatory governance institutions more broadly. Though in the previous chapter I analyzed the statistical relationship between municipal housing councils and policy outcomes in the form of social housing programs, here I look more in depth at the policy process before turning again to the policy outcomes. Based on the work of previous scholars, Andrew Selee and Enrique Peruzzotti argue that participatory governance institutions should enhance representation in the policy process through three mechanisms: (1) by replacing clientelistic relationships with more transparent means of decision making,

(2) by leveling the playing field for previously unorganized or excluded sectors of society, and (3) by providing spaces for deliberative decision making to set public policy.[2] Here I attempt to narrow down the variables that shape each of these mechanisms. Decisions about public goods should then rely on the process in which those decisions are made. As such, I seek to assess how variables that influence the policy process in turn shape outcomes of municipal housing councils.

Previous research identifies two groups of variables, institutional rules and civil society–state dynamics, which influence the effectiveness of participatory governance institutions. First, scholars find that institutional design must be taken into account in order to assess accountability and responsiveness of participatory governance institutions.[3] This piece of the puzzle, however, has not been clearly defined or studied across contexts to a significant extent. Second, scholars argue that the dynamic between civil society and political society largely shapes participatory governance institutions.[4] Again, this dynamic needs further systematic study across cases.

Here I assess the role of institutional rules and civil society–state dynamics in influencing the policy process and outcomes in municipal housing councils. First I use a qualitative process-tracing method to analyze how transparency, a level playing field, and deliberative decision making are shaped by institutional and civil society–state dynamics in three Brazilian cities—São Paulo, Santo André, and Salvador. Based on case study analysis, I find that in practice the party in power strongly influences the policy-making process within municipal housing councils. Where a mayor from the Worker's Party (Partido dos Trabalhadores [PT]) holds power, the council's agenda, membership, and alliances may shift to privilege civil society voices in the policy-making process.

Across cases, I then test the role of institutional rules and civil society–state dynamics in increasing the probability that municipalities adopt social housing programs where housing councils exist. I hypothesize that across Brazil, where a PT administration is in charge the municipal council for housing will have a greater effect on bringing about housing programs and commitment of municipal resources. Contrary to expectations, however, I do not find a consistent effect for the presence of a PT mayor. Instead, the statistical results suggest the importance of institutional rules for determining outcomes of housing councils. What is true for the policy process does not appear to apply to the outcomes across cases. I conclude that the PT may display significant variation in commitment to participatory governance across the country, while institutional rules may be more generalizable in their effect. The importance of oversight responsibilities points to the need for transparency to engender responsiveness and accountability in participatory governance institutions.

I first begin with a review of the factors shaping the performance of participatory governance institutions. I then provide a background for the three case studies, including the creation and structure of each municipal housing council. Using the case studies I assess the impact the institutional rules and civil society–state dynamics on the policy process. Finally, I turn to quantitative analysis to determine whether institutional rules and the party in power change the effect of municipal housing councils on adoption of social housing programs.

WHAT AFFECTS THE PERFORMANCE OF PARTICIPATORY GOVERNANCE INSTITUTIONS?

In this chapter I seek to assess potential variables that explain variance in the policy process and outcomes of participatory governance institutions. Based on these three case studies and existing literature, I propose the institutional rules of the housing councils and civil society–state dynamics as intervening variables determining the policy-making process in Brazilian municipal housing councils.

Institutional Rules of Housing Councils

Scholars argue that institutional rules matter for how civil society is incorporated into decision making and the influence CSO members have on resource allocation.[5] This research builds on the tradition of "new institutionalism," in which scholars have developed tools to understand how institutional rules largely shape behaviors and outcomes through the incentives they produce.[6] Variation in institutional rules, therefore, should be partly responsible for the differences we see in the policy process and policy outcomes across municipalities. The creation of participatory governance institutions first changes the institutional environment within municipalities, while the rules that govern municipal housing councils further shape the incentives of actors to use the councils as spaces for policy making.

Institutional rules for municipal housing councils are decided by individual municipalities and written into the law or decree establishing the council. Among other rules, these municipal laws or decrees state the responsibilities afforded to each council. In 2008, the Brazilian government survey of municipalities asked questions about whether the municipal housing council was consultative, deliberative, or normative, or provided oversight, indicating the extent to which the council actually has power over housing planning decisions.[7]

In consultative councils the role of members is to study existing programs and suggest activities to be undertaken in the area of housing.[8] Deliberative councils then have the power to make decisions regarding the implementation of policies and the administration of resources. Though housing secretaries and mayors may still overrule the council's decisions, the council does at least have the authority to present final decisions for implementation. Normative councils are those in which members establish rules and direction for the administration of resources, and finally, oversight (fiscalização) councils oversee (fiscaliza) the implementation and functioning of policies and administration of resources. I expect that housing councils with designated oversight responsibilities will generate the most transparency in policy making because council members should be guaranteed access to financial documents and program reports on a regular basis.

The rules governing the distribution of council seats by civil society, private sector associations, and government officials should also be associated with the performance of municipal housing councils. According to the MUNIC survey (Pesquisa de Informações Básicas Municipais), in 2008, 86% of municipal housing councils had at least half civil society representation.[9] On the surface, then, there would appear to be very little variation in council make-up. In practice, however, councils vary in the definition of who is included in "civil society." Some councils reserve seats for civil society, defined as NGOs (nongovernmental organizations), business associations, social movements, academics, and neighborhood associations, while other councils separate the category of "civil society" from that of "social movements." Though the broad categorization from the MUNIC survey does not allow for comparison of the detailed make-up of councils across all cases, the three case studies discussed here present significant variation in council membership. I argue that distinctions made between civil society and social movement members and the inclusion of private sector associations increases conflict and may decrease the achievement of a level playing field.

In addition, institutional rules governing the frequency of meetings contribute to the prospects for deliberative decision making in municipal housing councils. Clearly, without scheduling meetings councils cannot be effective spaces for policy making. I argue, though, that the rule for meeting frequency may only exist on paper without an active civil society to hold governments accountable for conducting meetings. Though the institutional rule for meeting frequency may be important for determining deliberative decision making, it is not a sufficient condition to ensure meetings occur and are deliberative.

Finally, the institutional rules governing responsibilities, council make-up, and meeting frequency should have a combined effect on council outcomes. Oversight responsibilities, rules of representation that limit conflict, and frequent meetings should enable the benefits of participatory governance to achieve the principle goal of redistributing public goods to benefit broad sectors of society. In the case of municipal housing councils, given available data I test whether the rules governing responsibilities increase the likelihood of governments adopting an increasing number and variety of social housing programs to respond to civil society demands.

Civil Society–State Dynamics

Several scholars also suggest that the dynamic between civil society and the state is critical for determining the function and outcomes of participatory governance institutions.[10] Though Robert Putnam argues that the density of CSOs matters for institutional accountability, in the previous chapter I do not find that the density of civil society in Brazilian municipalities significantly alters the effect of municipal housing councils.[11] Perhaps, as several scholars have argued contrary to Putnam, the density of civil society is less important than the dynamic between civil society and political society.[12] If so, in order to understand when participatory governance institutions have an effect on the policy process and outcomes, we need to identify the factors that influence the dynamic between civil society and the state. Though scholars, such as Leonardo Avritzer and Brian Wampler, have begun to name these variables, questions remain regarding whether patterns of interaction exist across contexts and various types of participatory governance institutions. Based on the work of other scholars and through my own fieldwork I identify three variables, which appear to influence civil society–state dynamics in participatory governance institutions. Though not an exhaustive list, these three factors—the party in power, the role of the private sector, and the strategies of civil society— appear to make a difference across contexts in determining the policy-making process between civil society and government officials.[13]

Party in Power
How does the party in power affect the relationships between civil society and state actors in participatory governance institutions? Participatory governance institutions in Brazil, including housing councils, are considered a hallmark of the PT.[14] Therefore I expect that where the PT is in charge there is more cooperation between civil society and municipal government and less conflict, both within and outside of the housing council. Under PT administrations, incorporation of civil society into the housing secretariat—often as full-time "liaisons" hired to promote communication between government and civil society—should promote transparency through an increase in information sharing. Second, the party in power may determine which CSOs participate in the municipal housing councils. Under a PT government, those CSOs allied with the PT may participate more, leading to questions as to whether the party in power biases the playing field. Lastly, the party in power influences the appointment of housing secretariat officials and their respective ideological predispositions. The commitment of officials to participatory governance and to certain housing policy solutions over others should influence both the nature of deliberative decision making within councils and the policy outcomes they produce.

I argue that the PT's strong influence on the three facets of the policy process in municipal housing councils should significantly alter the policy outcomes council's produce. In other words, where a PT government is in power, I argue that municipal housing councils will be more strongly associated with adoption of social housing programs benefiting the poor. These councils should more directly respond to the demands of CSOs, corresponding to adoption of a variety of programs from new construction to urbanization of existing communities.

Role of the Private Sector

Private sector interests, including real estate and construction associations, often occupy seats on municipal housing councils. Because much of the research on participatory governance institutions in Brazil has focused on participatory budgeting initiatives, which do not generally formally involve private sector actors, identification of the role of the private sector in participatory governance institutions has been limited. In regard to housing policy, however, the role of the private sector cannot be ignored. Housing as a social good cannot be separated from the larger private sector market for real estate and construction. The private sector, defined by profit motive, has a stake in the value of land, the distribution of public sector contracts, and public financing available for potential homebuyers. How these interests influence the policy process of municipal housing councils is key to understanding civil society–state dynamics.

I argue that the private sector influences the policy-making process in municipal councils based on their relative strength on the council to affect the agenda and voting outcomes and their relationship to government officials. Where the private sector plays a strong role on the council, government–private sector alliances may develop, stifling transparency of information provided to CSOs. Whether these alliances develop, however, may be in part based on the ideology of the party in power in the municipal administration and its past relationship to the private sector. Where close alliances do exist, the private sector may have greater access to government officials, thereby limiting the playing field for the policy-making process. In some cases, private sector interests may align with government officials to influence votes and the council's agenda. When this occurs, the nature of deliberative decision making shifts in favor of private sector interests.

Because the role of the private sector in municipal housing councils is strongly tied to the party in power, I argue that across cases the party in power should dictate the influence of the private sector in policy decision making. Of course, it would be naïve to believe that officials from the PT are never influenced by the private sector. But, as a leftist party most closely associated with social movement actors across the board PT mayors should be less likely to build alliances with private sector interests. I expect that the presence of a PT mayor to mitigate the role of the private sector, increasing the influence of other civil society actors. As stated previously, therefore, the presence of a PT mayor where housing councils exist should be more strongly associated with an increase in housing program adoption.

Strategies of Civil Society Organizations

The strategies of civil society may be more important than the density of CSOs in a municipality for determining the policy process in participatory governance institutions.[15] While there might not be a perfect "type" of civil society for ensuring an efficient and effective policy process in the councils, as Wampler suggests, the combination of contestation and cooperation strategies by CSOs may avoid co-optation by government interests as well as contentiousness among actors to increase the relevance of participatory governance institutions.[16]

In all participatory governance institutions, CSOs are largely responsible for pushing the government to ensure they function as representative institutions. To secure transparency in policy making in municipal housing councils, CSOs most likely have to adopt a conscious strategy to demand documents be made available to them. In addition, CSOs need the capacity to analyze budgetary and other bureaucratic documents. CSOs may receive information to which they would otherwise not have access, but they have to adopt careful strategies to ensure the transfer of information occurs. Second, in order to guarantee that participatory governance institutions level the playing field in terms of access, CSOs must adopt a strategy of participation in formal institutions versus a repertoire of more radical tactics. Finally, to ensure effective deliberative decision making, CSOs in municipal housing councils need to act as a cohesive unit, particularly when it comes to voting and negotiating with government officials for common demands.

In terms of policy outcomes resulting from the presence of a municipal housing council, the strategies of CSOs most likely influence the types of housing programs and willingness of government officials to direct resources to housing solutions. The shape of civil society strategies with regards to councils—whether they choose contestation or cooperation—may still be reliant on their traditional relationship with the party in power. Therefore, across cases, I argue that the party in power incorporates some of the effects of the strategies of CSOs. CSOs may be more likely to cooperate under the administration of their allies—traditionally from the PT. Based on a less combative policy-making process, where a PT mayor is in power the councils should be associated with a greater adoption of housing programs.

Table 5.1 is a summary of the hypotheses suggested by this discussion.

OVERVIEW OF THE CASES

The cities of São Paulo, Santo André, and Salvador differ based on a number of factors, including the independent variables of interest discussed previously: the institutional rules of municipal housing councils, traditions of political leadership, private sector power, and CSO strategies. In terms of tradition of political leadership, São Paulo swings back and forth between the left and right, Santo André has a strong PT orientation, and Salvador remains under conservative administration. São Paulo's real estate and construction sectors are the most dominant in housing politics, while in Salvador the private sector also maintains a combative relationship

Table 5.1 Hypotheses

	Institutional Rules	Party in Power	Private Sector Role	CSO Strategies
Transparency	Oversight powers should promote greatest level of transparency.	Where the PT is in power, the administration should be more willing to provide information to CSOs.	Private sector alliances with government officials may limit transparency.	CSOs need to make demands in order to receive information from government officials.
Leveling the Playing Field	Greater segmentation of members leads to competition and stifles the playing field.	Where the PT is in power, allied CSOs will have greater access and voice.	Private sector alliances with government officials will bias the playing field.	CSOs must adopt a strategy of participation in order to ensure a level playing field.
Deliberative Decision Making	Where the rules indicate a greater frequency in meeting times, councils should engender greater deliberative decision making.	Under a PT government, the commitment of government officials should increase deliberative decision making.	Greater private sector influence may shift the agenda of the councils away from CSO demands.	CSO cohesion increases deliberative decision making in the councils.
Distribution of Resources	Oversight powers are associated with adoption of social housing programs.	Where housing councils exist, a PT administration is associated with adoption of more social housing programs.	The influence of the private sector on housing program adoption, where councils exist, is mediated by the party in power.	The party in power mediates the impact of CSO strategies, where housing councils exist.

with civil society. While São Paulo has a strong history of neighborhood associations, vocal social movements, and professional NGOs, Santo André is a smaller city with a less contentious civil society environment. As the largest city in the Northeast of Brazil, Salvador is known for weaker civil society, though demands for addressing the great housing needs in the city have grown increasingly loud in recent years.

SÃO PAULO

São Paulo is the largest city in Brazil and is known for its concentration of wealth and economic power. Located in the Southeast region of the country, the city is representative of megacities around the world in terms of the scale and variation in housing problems. This city of 10.9 million residents includes 1,567 registered favelas; 1,060 irregular settlements; 523 public housing buildings; and 1,698 cortiços (tenement houses).[17] The government estimates that about 350,000 families live in favelas, though housing movement leaders estimate the number to be about twice as high. According to Benedito Barbosa, an attorney representing the CMP (Central dos Movimentos Populares), another 3 million people live in irregular settlements and areas of environmental risk, and nearly 1 million reside in overcrowded and unsafe tenement housing.[18]

Though these numbers only estimate the problem, it is clear that the city is in great need of large-scale interventions to address the quantitative and qualitative housing deficits. The main message in the government's promotional materials is that the scale of interventions must be in line with the size of the city. In fact, São Paulo has a diverse array of programs to provide housing units, improve infrastructure in the favelas, and provide land titles for residents of informal settlements. The city's two largest favelas, Heliopolis with an estimated 70,000 residents and Paraisopolis with 60,000 residents, have received long-term attention from the government, though the problems of inadequate housing, lack of services, and land insecurity clearly persist. Paraisopolis sits next door to an upscale condominium complex and illustrates the classic problem of inequality in this city where rich and poor fight for prime real estate close to the center of the city and employment opportunities.

Municipal Council for Housing

Participatory governance institutions in the city of São Paulo, including the Municipal Council for Housing, have been strongly linked to the intermittent presence of PT administrations. PT Mayor Luiza Erundina (1989–1992) first proposed the law to create the Municipal Council for Housing in São Paulo, but the law did not pass in the city council until 2002, when the PT had the added advantage of dominating the city council under the administration of PT mayor Marta Suplicy. Social movements, especially the UMM-SP (União dos Movimentos da Moradia-São Paulo), expressed a strong desire for the council and were heavily involved in the process of negotiating its terms. Unlike the other two cases discussed here, in São Paulo the Company for Housing (COHAB), a public-private entity, manages the implementation of the municipal housing fund. Though the housing council approves the annual budget for the fund and receives a year-end accounting of how the money was spent, day-to-day operations of the budget are in the hands of COHAB. This sets up a further layer of tension between social movements, which are concerned with providing no- or low-cost housing solutions to the poor, and COHAB, which is concerned with recouping government-backed loans and enabling private sector development.

SANTO ANDRÉ

The city of Santo André is best known for the strength of manufacturing unions and for its long-term administration by the PT.[19] The city is part of the ABC region in metropolitan São Paulo, which also includes the municipalities of São Bernardo do Campo and São Caetano do Sul.[20] Unions in Santo André and these other two cities grew along with the automobile and steel industry up until the 1980s, when many of the manufacturers left the city, leading to an economic decline in the late 1980s and 1990s. The PT was born out of the union movements in the ABC region, of which President Lula was a strong leader and a force for the creation of the new PT in the late 1970s and early 1980s. By 2008, the PT had been in power in the municipality for all but four years since democratization.[21] Though Santo André is a smaller city by Brazilian standards, with approximately 670,000 residents,[22] about 115,000 citizens or 16% of the municipal population live in favelas. According to a survey conducted by the municipal government, the city maintains a housing deficit of about 24,300 units.[23]

Despite Santo André's presence in the shadow of São Paulo, the city has been recognized by international donors and scholars for its innovations in development programs and participatory politics. The city has won several international prizes for best practices, including a prize in 2005 from the United Nations Development Program for taking action on each of the eight Millennium Development Goals. According to the municipal administration, housing policy focuses on both new construction and improving living conditions in favelas.[24] Like the majority of Brazilian cities, most of the growth of favelas has been in the periphery, which the government aims to address by increasing the legal residential housing market and promoting integration of favelas into the formal city through sanitation, mobility, and dignified housing (moradia digna).

Municipal Council for Housing

As in São Paulo, a PT government established the Municipal Council for Housing in Santo André. Mayor Celso Daniel created the Secretariat for Housing and proposed the creation of the housing council during his first administration from 1989 to 1992. The council did not begin to function until 2000, however, under Daniel's second administration. The council consistently holds meetings the last Tuesday of every month in order to provide continuity in decision making, according to council members. In 2006, the municipality was also one of the first to create and pass a Municipal Master Plan for Housing, which includes specific mention of the importance of the housing council for institutionalizing civil society influence on policy making and administration of the housing fund. The municipality also has a general participatory budgeting process, which does fund some housing projects, but the housing council members state that their council is still necessary to provide the consistency needed to solve technical concerns for housing projects and as a space where housing associations can come on a regular basis to solicit funds and technical assistance for their projects.

SALVADOR

Salvador is often referred to as the Afro-Brazilian capital of the country, with a strong legacy of slavery and African cultural heritage. It is the largest city in the Northeast with nearly 3 million residents, but is also the poorest of the cases reviewed here with an income per capita of R$341.[25] Table 5.2 provides a comparison of basic indicators in the three case studies and shows that inequality is also quite high in Salvador with a Gini coefficient of .66. A 2000 housing census in the city approximated the housing deficit, or number of inadequate housing units, at 81,000 out of 651,000

Table 5.2 Comparative Statistics for Case Studies

	São Paulo	Santo André	Salvador
Civil Society Density: Nonprofits and Foundations per Capita	0.0019	0.0014	0.0010
Population	10,900,000	669,592	2,673,560
PT Mayor (2004–2008)	No	Yes	No
Percentage Urban	0.941	1	0.999
Municipal Budget per Capita	R$632	R$504	R$287
Income per Capita	R$610	R$513	R$341
Gini Coefficient	0.62	0.53	0.66

housing units in the city.[26] This number obscures the concentration of the population living in the "informal city": approximately 60% of the city's population lives in the irregular and clandestine settlements. The same study found 89,000 vacant units in the city in need of renovation and access to basic services. Many of these vacant units are located in the historic center of the city, designated a UNESCO World Heritage Site. The right to these properties represents a constant tension between movements that occupy the buildings and officials and developers who want to "clean up" the area for tourism.

Municipal Council for Housing

The Municipal Council for Housing in Salvador began in 2007 under the administration of Mayor João Henrique Carneiros from the PDT (Partido Democrático Trabalhista).[27] During his first election campaign in 2004, Carneiros brought the PT into his coalition, and once in office named a PT-friendly secretary for housing. Under the direction of this secretary, Dr. Angela Gordilho Souza, the Municipal Council for Housing was established by law in 2006. By all accounts, though, by 2008 the council did not yet have a set pattern of meeting or responsibilities. By law the council is supposed to meet every four months, though in practice meetings are more irregular.

THE POLICY PROCESS IN MUNICIPAL HOUSING COUNCILS

In this section I assess the role of institutional rules and civil society–state dynamics in promoting transparency, a level playing field, and deliberative decision making in each case.

Transparency

Transparency involves the reduction of clientelistic behavior and the transmission of greater information to citizens. Scholars argue that public channels for negotiation, which mitigate the use of traditional clientelistic bargaining, create transparency.[28] Municipal housing councils create a public forum for discussion and a link to information between government officials and civil society that never existed before. Rather than relying on bilateral meetings with officials, policy and program decisions should be made in public with negotiation among multiple actors.

As I have already argued, the institutional responsibilities assigned to municipal housing councils should in part determine their transparency. Table 5.3 provides a comparison of the official responsibilities granted to each of the case study housing councils.

Table 5.3 Responsibilities of Municipal Councils for Housing, MUNIC Survey 2008

Responsibilities	São Paulo	Santo André	Salvador
Consultative	No	No	Yes
Deliberative	Yes	Yes	Yes
Normative	No	Yes	No
Oversight	No	Yes	Yes

According to the survey, Santo André and Salvador have oversight powers, which should be significant for transparency. In practice, however, I find that the legal responsibilities afforded to the councils may not be entirely representative of the duties of councils in reality. According to a researcher I spoke with at the Instituto Pólis in São Paulo, laws often do not dictate how the councils function in practice. For instance, the survey indicates that the São Paulo council does not have oversight responsibilities, though in practice I found that the council does have the power to approve or disapprove accounting statements for the municipal housing fund. In Salvador, on the other hand, the council does technically have oversight responsibilities, but the council is not presented with budgetary documents. The case studies, then, do not suggest that the written institutional rules for responsibilities are critical determinants in transparency.

I do find, however, that the party in power plays a large role in generating transparency. For example, in both São Paulo and Salvador, PT-affiliated housing secretaries initiated the position of "liaison" within the housing secretariat. The role of the liaison is to facilitate the transfer of information between the government and social movements and to negotiate conflicts. In São Paulo this position existed only under the Suplicy government (PT). The two liaisons were integral in negotiating the establishment of the council and in setting the early agenda for mutirões (collectively built projects) and subsidized housing projects in the city center. When José Serra (PSDB [Partido da Social Democracia Brasileira]) came in as mayor, his administration actively worked to limit the role of civil society within government and discontinued the incorporation of liaisons. In Salvador, the liaison position began under Dr. Souza from the PT, but has been retained so far under the more-conservative government. The liaison has played a particularly important role in negotiating meetings between CSOs and the housing secretary and delivering the demands of protestors. In order to keep his job, however, this liaison must walk a fine line between offending the current government and appeasing CSOs. Movement leaders describe his role as "delicate," and in the end his role is limited. He does not appear to play a significant role in reducing clientelistic relationships nor is he provided with significant information to transmit to CSOs. The party in power, then, matters for the level of transparency generated by this position.

I also find that the relationship between the private sector and government officials influences transparency in the councils, though as expected the party in power mitigates the dynamic. In all three cities studied, I find a close connection between the party in power and the nature of private sector involvement in the councils. Where a more conservative government is in power, housing secretariat officials tend to come from the private sector. For instance, under the current administration of PSD (Partido Social Democrático) mayor Gilberto Kassab in São Paulo, many housing secretariat officials have close ties with the major real estate association in the city.[29] CSOs criticize the closeness of these ties and the unlimited access the private sector has to housing officials. CSOs argue that this relationship reduces transparency because they are often cut out of negotiations between private sector associations and government officials. In Salvador, as well, the current PDT-affiliated secretary for housing came from the real estate sector and does not appear interested in working with the council. He does not schedule regular meetings, and CSOs report they have not had access to any budgetary information or other internal documents. In contrast, in Santo André the private sector is not involved in the municipal housing council. This appears to contribute to the open and noncombative relationship between civil society and government officials in the council.

Lastly, in my review of the case studies I do find some evidence that the strategies of civil society contribute to the level of transparency achieved in the housing councils. In a contentious environment like São Paulo, civil society must be willing and have the capacity to make demands of the government in order to force it to provide information. For instance, in council meetings I witnessed members from social movements asking numerous clarification questions on budget documents they were given by the housing secretariat—sometimes lasting for hours—until they were satisfied they had the full and correct information. Civil society in Salvador—more radical with less capacity for analyzing complex bureaucratic details—is not as able to hold the government accountable for providing full budgetary information. In Santo André, the neighborhood associations involved in the councils appear more concerned with receiving technical assistance for their individual projects and less concerned with the government's overall spending patterns. Due to the noncombative relationship in Santo André, the government is more willing to share information without significant pressure, but access to full information is not a strategy of council members. The relationship between the PT administration and the council members is one of trust. Though seemingly beneficial, over time this trust may have a negative side if it leads to focusing on individual payoffs rather than demanding transparency.

Based on these three case studies, the party in power seems to contribute the most to ensuring transparency within municipal housing councils. Both the role of the private sector and CSO strategies are based on relationships created by the party in charge of the municipal administration. Written institutional rules dictating responsibilities of the councils do not appear to determine council activities in practice.

Level Playing Field

By definition, participatory governance institutions should increase the involvement of previously excluded segments of society, thereby leveling the playing field in terms of access to policy making. The rules for the composition of the councils should in part dictate who is provided with access through the council process. Across the three cases there is variation in the rules for membership. In São Paulo, there is a distinction in the housing council between social movements and civil society: 16 seats are reserved for members from social movements and 16 seats are reserved for civil society. Civil society includes members from unions, universities, NGOs, and business associations. The remaining 16 seats in the 48-person council are reserved for government officials. This structure sets up a tripartite division between social movements, other CSOs (including business associations), and government officials. Members serve two-year terms, with representatives from civil society and government agencies selected within meetings of their own groups, that is, unions select a representative within themselves. Members from social movements, however, are elected in citywide elections. In the 2007 election, approximately 33,000 votes were cast for social movement representatives.[30]

The council in Santo André has 16 members with half from civil society, including social movements, and half from the government. By decree, the president of the council is from civil society and the president of the Municipal Fund for Housing is from the government. Though larger, the housing council in Salvador has a similar composition with 16 members from civil society and 16 members from government agencies. Like in São Paulo, civil society representation in Salvador is further divided between social movements and "other" groups such as NGOs. In 2007, social movements held one meeting in which they chose members amongst themselves and CSOs, including NGOs, trade associations, and unions, held their own meeting to select representatives.

Does one form of council composition create a more level playing field than the others? All three include at least half representation from civil society. What differs across cases is the differentiation between "civil society" and "social movements" and the requirements for the inclusion of private sector representatives. In São Paulo, the separation of civil society and social movements sets up a division between members, strongly based on class differences. Social movement members often come from housing occupations and can be fairly radical in their demands. "Civil society" members, in contrast, come from NGOs, universities, and the private sector and are generally from middle- to upper-income backgrounds and tend to be somewhat more measured in their deliberations. In Salvador, the contrast exists, but because professionalized NGOs are not as prevalent in Salvador as in São Paulo, the distinctions are not as strong. To some extent, in both cases the voices of social movement members are subordinated to those of NGO leaders who may be considered more educated or polished. By distinguishing membership, the institutional rules do bias the playing field.

In addition, I find that the rules for membership matter for leveling the playing field inasmuch as they shape the participation of private sector associations. In São Paulo business interests occupy five or six seats on the council, forming a considerable voting block. In Santo André the council rules do not mandate the participation of a private sector representative, and no one from the private sector has stepped up to be included. In fact, according to housing secretariat officials, the private sector is not involved in social housing policy making in Santo André. In Salvador, as the city grows and business interests organize in the Northeast of Brazil, the role of the private sector becomes more important. Council regulations in Salvador mandate the participation of two members from private sector entities out of the 32-member council. Though the private sector in Salvador clearly has a voice in decision making, social movements and NGOs also significantly outnumber them.

Given that municipal housing councils decide issues related to housing construction, land use, and infrastructural development, the private sector has a legitimate role to play in the councils' decision making. In the case studies, however, the inclusion of private sector representatives appears to lead to greater contestation among members, which may reduce the voice of previously marginalized voices from neighborhood associations, social movements, and NGOs. For example, in São Paulo there is constant tension between the private sector association representatives and social movements over redevelopment of the city center. Many of the most vocal social movement members call for renovation of old buildings to house those currently occupying these largely abandoned buildings. Representatives of the private sector associations, however, would prefer to see these buildings expropriated and developed by the private market. Finding common ground on policies to address the redevelopment of the city center has proven difficult and has led to arguments and gridlock within the council.

Regarding the effect of the party in power on leveling the playing field, in the case studies I find that the party in power largely determines *which* CSOs are involved in the housing council. This is most strikingly seen in São Paulo, where council membership completely changed between the Suplicy (PT) and Serra (PSDB) governments. While mostly PT-affiliated movements occupied seats in the Suplicy administration, the Serra administration directly supported and "encouraged" the election of newer, weaker opposition groups to the council in 2005. According to one state government official who was a housing council member under Suplicy and Serra, the movements on the council under Serra were co-opted by the government and the council barely operated. In the 2007 elections, then, the "first-term"

PT-affiliated representatives launched a coordinated campaign using a unified ticket to regain their seats in the third term. In Santo André, all of the
neighborhood associations and unions represented on the housing council
appeared to be affiliated with the PT government. In Salvador, when the
housing secretary came from the PT, PT-affiliated social movements say they
felt welcome in the housing secretariat and hoped that the municipal housing council would provide them with real voice. Since Dr. Souza left her
position, the same social movements participate, but they report a feeling
of prejudice against their members and a lack of interest in hearing their
demands on the part of the new housing secretary.

The party in power may encourage some civil society groups to participate while limiting the participation of others. In Santo André, while council
members state they are receptive to all voices, the strength of the PT may
in practice drive away non-PT-affiliated groups from participating. In São
Paulo, the party in power may also prevent certain groups from participating, though with experience the leftist social movements of São Paulo have
learned to ensure their participation by collaborating at council election
time. PT-aligned and more radical CSOs in Salvador also displayed less enthusiasm for the participatory process under a non-PT government.

Finally, how do the strategies of civil society influence the playing field in
municipal housing councils? In the case studies, civil society strategies affect
the interest of groups to participate in formal government institutions and
its willingness to negotiate with government officials rather than engaging
in more radical tactics. On a continuum of contestation versus cooperation,
civil society in Salvador falls on the end of the spectrum toward contestation, while São Paulo falls in the middle and Santo André lies at the other
end toward cooperation.

In Salvador the largest social movement for housing is the Movimento
Sem Teto do Salvador (Roofless Movement of Salvador [MSTS]). The MSTS
was founded in 2003 and its main strategy is the occupation of land and
buildings it believes are not fulfilling their social function as required by the
Brazilian Constitution. By the fall of 2008 the MSTS had 22 occupations,
the majority of which were in abandoned buildings near the center of the
city. Following occupations, members of the movement engage in protests
to the housing secretariat, and leaders then negotiate with the municipal,
state, and federal governments to solicit funding for construction projects
to meet their members' needs. All four of the primary national movements
for housing also have affiliates in Salvador and membership on the housing council.[31] Following the UNMP's (União Nacional dos Movimentos por
Moradia Popular) call to demand the creation of and participation in housing councils, the União da Moradia Popular-Bahia (UMP-BA) was the primary force behind the creation of the housing council in Salvador. However,
the self-build projects for which the UMP-BA secured federal and municipal
contributions began with occupation of land, followed by protest and negotiation in much the same manner that the MSTS secures projects. Though a

few small NGOs assist the movements in their advocacy and participate in the council, the main forces for securing housing programs and policies are these and other housing movements, which rely first and foremost on occupation and protest to ensure benefits for their members. Lack of commitment to the process among some social movements, therefore, does reduce the effectiveness of the housing council in leveling the playing field.

In contrast, civil society in Santo André adopts a largely nonconfrontational strategy. The main participants on the housing council from civil society are the Housing Cooperative of Public Servants (ServiCoop) and neighborhood-based housing associations. As mentioned, housing associations bring their requests for assistance to the housing council. These requests generally involve urbanization rather than new construction. Direct action by civil society in Santo André is extremely rare, while cooperation with the government has become the strategic norm.

Finally, CSO strategies in São Paulo run the gamut, from occupations and large-scale protests to participation in housing councils and election to public office. The most organized movement is the UMM-SP, though the MSTS and several other groups regularly carry out occupations in the center and periphery of the city. The UMM-SP began in 1987 as an umbrella for 42 housing associations, which fight for participation at all levels of government, self-build projects, a mix of credit and subsidies, help for housing tenements, and assistance for people at the lowest income levels. Though their slogan officially calls for direct action through "occupation, resistance and construction," the UMM-SP invests considerable time in the housing council and is the leader in holding the government accountable for its promises of participatory governance. In addition to social movements, São Paulo is the center of the country for NGOs working on urban policy issues. The Instituto Pólis has a regular seat on the housing council and publishes and lectures widely on the importance of participatory governance institutions. CSOs in São Paulo have certainly not abandoned direct action in the form of occupations and protests, but rather rely on a mix of strategies, which includes making their demands within the formal, public forum of the municipal housing council. Their commitment to participate adds to the effectiveness of the council in leveling the playing field for policy making.

In sum, rules defining the make-up of council membership, the ideology of the party in power, alliances with the private sector, and the level of contentiousness in civil society all shape the playing field within municipal housing councils. In the end, however, I find that the party in power again largely controls the other three variables to influence the effectiveness of housing councils.

Deliberative Decision Making

Deliberative decision making as a goal of participatory governance institutions implies that civil society has a significant voice in policy making, particularly in terms of agenda setting and final decisions of the institution. Across municipalities, civil society has varying degrees of influence over the housing council's agenda. In addition, the mechanisms for final decision making—voting, verbal agreements, or no real powers—differ across cases. While the institutional rules should dictate how often housing councils meet, and therefore how relevant they are to policy making, the dynamics between civil society and the state also shape the agenda and means for decision making within housing councils.

In the aggregate data on municipal housing councils from the MUNIC survey in 2008, government representatives only report whether the council met during the year. The data do not specify how often the councils met or the number of meetings per year required by the law or decree establishing the council. The case studies, however, provide evidence to suggest that the frequency of meetings is a function of the pressure civil society places on government officials and the incentives of officials to please their constituencies by engaging in participatory processes.

In the case studies I again find that the party in power strongly influences the council's agenda and the ultimate power of civil society to affect decision making. For instance, in São Paulo the agenda and decision-making power shifted significantly from the Suplicy (PT) administration to the current Kassab (PSD) administration. Officials from the Suplicy administration report that most of the influence on housing policy and programs in São Paulo came directly from the housing movements, stating that "the movements have too much influence" ("os movimentos tem influencia demais"). Government officials were motivated to respond to the demands of social movements and housing associations in order to maintain their electoral bases of support. Under the Suplicy administration the housing council was heavily involved in allocating resources and creating regulations for mutirão projects, communally built housing projects strongly favored by many of the social movements on the council. Movements report that they felt they were making progress in influencing policy decisions. Today, however, both government officials and social movement leaders assert that the council has become more a space for deciding programmatic regulations and bureaucratic details than for defining policy priorities. Issues for discussion in the council include such topics as eligibility criteria for housing programs, FMH (Fundo Municipal de Habitação) budget details, year-end accounting reports, what to do about loan defaults, contracts with construction companies, acquisition of buildings in the city center, maintenance of public housing complexes, and land titling for specific communities.

According to housing secretariat officials in the current Kassab administration, movements "think" they have a great deal of power. However, officials state that their first priority is to deal with those on the formal housing registry waiting list rather than attending to the needs of protestors or movement representatives knocking on their doors. Superintendent for Social Housing Elisabete França argues that the council should decide issues such as how to improve the urbanization of favelas, how to make the mutirão projects more efficient, how to create more integrated programs, or where to find more resources.[32] In other words, the council should decide regulations and search for resources to address the priorities established by government officials within the secretariat. She says this distinction must be very clear because the movements have a tendency to want to make their members and issues the priority. Social movement and NGO leaders fighting for a stronger voice argue that this attitude is precisely the reason behind the failure of the council to further pro-poor policy in the city. While the government pays some lip service to the need for participatory decision making, it withholds "real decisions" from the council's control. According to Evaniza Rodrigues, leader in the UNMP, the government decides what projects fall under the council's jurisdiction, and if it is interested in pursuing specific programs, the government takes them outside of council control.[33]

The housing council in Santo André is remarkable for its congeniality and agreement on the agenda and programmatic issues. In monthly council meetings, housing associations, most of which have members on the council, make requests for money for construction materials and technical assistance to complete projects. The council's role is then to approve the allocation of resources from the municipal housing fund. In addition to funding, the council decides conflicts within favelas over land claims and priorities for regularization of land. The council is not deciding broad policy priorities, but civil society seems satisfied with the status quo policy direction. In interviews, civil society leaders and government officials alike stated that the main challenges to addressing housing needs were the rising price of land and a lack of capacity within the government to implement large-scale projects with money available from the federal level.

I attribute this lack of conflict and ease of deliberative decision making to the long-running administration by the PT in Santo André. One long-term PT-affiliated government official on the council stated, "We don't really have conflicts with each other because everyone is comfortable and we all have the same objective."[34] The municipal housing council is able to effectively engage in deliberative decision making because both civil society and government officials have incentives to cooperate: civil society to voice its requests for assistance and officials to please their constituents.

Finally, in Salvador the party in power also influences the nature of deliberative decision making. In Salvador civil society is still engaged in a cycle of protest and negotiation to ensure the government complies with the council's mandate. From its creation in 2007 until the end of 2008, the council met a total of five times at irregular intervals. During my visit to Salvador in November 2008, social movements took to the streets with a list of demands for the housing secretary, one of which was to schedule the next meeting of the housing council. Though it was not clear that the protest was necessary to ensure the next meeting of the council would occur, the process of public protest followed by negotiation and action is still firmly entrenched in the repertoire of Salvador's housing movements.

When the council did meet, members reported that the discussions centered on the municipal government's role as the link to federal government resources. Housing movements presented proposals for local projects benefiting their members, and the council voted on which proposals to send forward to the federal government for selection. Of the 20 projects forwarded to the federal level, the Ministry of Cities approved only one project for R$1 million. In the end, federal officials rather than the municipal government, civil society, or the council decided on which project should receive priority.

The tradition of conservative party administration in Salvador largely creates the lack of incentives for both civil society and government officials to ensure deliberative decision making. The dynamic between civil society and municipal government officials in Salvador remains mired in traditions of patron-client relationships and disdain for the "other" side. Salvador has a history of conservative politics, administered by a single family for most of the last few decades. Social movements, NGOs, and construction associations view the municipal government as an unwilling partner in providing resources, including land and money, to complement federal government programs. They view the council as a *future* mechanism to hold the government accountable for resource contributions, but know that it will be a long process of maintaining pressure to ensure compliance with the council's participatory mandate. In the meantime movements compete for scarce municipal resource contributions, while looking to the state and federal levels for primary funding of construction and urbanization projects. For their part, current municipal government officials appear completely uninterested in the participatory process of the council. The housing secretary had not attended a single meeting, and housing officials I spoke with either did not know about the council's meetings or were reluctant to discuss details.

While the council aims to reduce clientelism and serve as a space for deliberative policy making, the government does not appear to have the will to carry out the council's mandate. The council increases the ability of diverse voices to reach the government agenda, but it is not clear that the minimal incorporation of CSOs into the council will significantly change the policy-making process in the near term.

How does the private sector, then, influence deliberative decision making in each of these cases? Of the case studies, only in São Paulo does the private sector exert a considerable influence on the agenda and voting outcomes of the housing council. The strongest private sector member is SECOVI, an association of real estate interests, which began in São Paulo but now operates chapters across the country. Representatives from SECOVI say they participate in the council because they have a stake in improving the city overall; however, they are candid in acknowledging their main objective must always be profit. According to one SECOVI representative, they are primarily concerned with (1) the federal government losing money from social housing programs because of borrower defaults, and (2) the impact of public investments on the price of real estate. These concerns translate into agenda setting for the council. For example, a SECOVI representative stated that "the goal of the private sector is to produce new housing and we do not have a direct interest in urbanizing the favelas."[35] They are therefore more likely to push for construction programs over urbanization programs. Whether they get their way in agenda setting depends largely on who is in charge. As stated above, under non-PT governments in São Paulo, housing secretariat officials tend to be appointed from the private sector. SECOVI acknowledges that they have a much better relationship with the current secretary of housing, who used to work with the association, than they ever had with officials under the Suplicy government. This close relationship allows them better access to government officials outside of the council, but also provides them with allies from the government on the council when the agenda is set and votes are held on specific issues. SECOVI also works closely with SINDUSCON, an association of construction companies, to discuss issues before meetings and present a united front in the council.

In the other two cases, where the private sector does not play a strong role on the council itself, business interests do still play a role in what the municipality is able to accomplish in terms of social housing policy. In Santo André, housing council members report that they are severely limited in developing new programs by the rising value of real estate in the city. Both civil society members and government officials on the council seem to accept the rise in prices as a legitimate reason why the government cannot do more to reduce the housing deficit. Though civil society members report they would like to see more zoning for social housing (Zonas Especiais de Interesse Social [ZEIS]), they have not formed a protest movement to demand reform. Given the lack of private sector participation in the council, they do not have a natural enemy with whom to contest zoning rules and they are unlikely to directly challenge the allied-PT government's current policies. The lack of private sector involvement, therefore, limits conflict and encourages cooperation.

In Salvador, social movements strongly distrust the private sector, particularly since the government removed many poor residents in order for business interests to capitalize on the renovation of the historic city center in the 1990s. This distrust carries over to the current secretary of housing who was appointed from the private sector. Even without significant private sector participation in the council, civil society members' animosity toward business interests does affect the ways in which they approach government officials they associate with the private sector. Civil society's expectations for cooperation remain low, which may in turn spur continued direct protest rather than negotiation in the council to make its voice heard.

The relative strength of the private sector determines shifts in power relations, shapes the council's agenda, and influences outcomes. In São Paulo, the participation of a strong private sector causes derisiveness in the council that does not affect the other two councils. Still, in the other two cases the traditional lack of involvement in Santo André and the animosity between sectors in Salvador influences cooperation or conflict even without the private sector's direct participation in the councils.

Finally, how do the strategies of CSOs affect deliberative decision making? In São Paulo, movements have learned to work in coordinated networks to promote their collective interests. Before each meeting of the full council and meetings of the council's executive commission, social movement leaders hold a private meeting to review the coming agenda and supporting documents provided by the housing secretariat. In these meetings, members reach consensus on their response to each agenda item in order to present a united front when the full council or executive commission meets. For instance, before the full council was to address the issue of payment defaults in public housing units, social movements decided they would press the government to understand why people are not paying and urge them to conduct a more detailed study of the problem. Movement leaders say these pre-meetings also offer an opportunity to discuss and debate the complex bureaucratic issues presented to the council, which they would not be able to respond to on the spot. The strategy to voice demands as a united front in council meetings, however, means that their opinions are added to the record, but they do not necessarily change the final outcomes when votes are cast. Private sector interests, government officials, and unallied members may still have the votes to overrule other voting blocks. In Santo André, the lack of conflict between groups leads to faster decision making, though certainly less debate over the nuances of decisions. The tradition in Salvador of bargaining for benefits for members of individual movements following occupations leads to negotiations for these specific groups within the council rather than broader policy discussion and debate.

CONCLUSIONS FROM CASE STUDIES

In the case studies both the institutional rules and civil society–state dynamics strongly influence the activities of the municipal housing councils. None of the three cases exhibits the ideal model of participatory governance, if such a thing exists, but the variables presented here increase our understanding of the institutional rules and factors shaping civil society–state dynamics, resulting in an "imperfect" policy process in municipal housing councils.

My analysis of the case studies closely aligns with my expectations of how the institutional rules and civil society dynamics shape the effectiveness of municipal housing councils. In terms of transparency, however, I do not find that the rules for council responsibilities match the activities of the councils in practice. This leads me to conclude that civil society–state dynamics must be more important for transparency than legal responsibilities. For a level playing field, the party in power largely determines the relationships among actors and the access and voice of civil society. In particular, the inclusion of private sector members aligned with more conservative governments may reduce the access and voice of CSOs, thereby limiting the ability of municipal housing councils to include previously marginalized groups in policy making. Finally, the councils vary significantly in their agendas and mechanisms for deliberative decision making. In the end, however, the party in power strongly influences the agenda and the relative strength of civil society in negotiating their demands.

DISTRIBUTION OF PUBLIC GOODS: OUTCOMES OF MUNICIPAL HOUSING COUNCILS

In the previous section I assessed the variables that influence the policy process in municipal housing councils. In this section, then, I seek to understand the influence of the policy process on outcomes. How and when does the policy process in participatory governance institutions shape the resulting policy and program decisions?

Based on the case studies, I seek to test the influence on outcomes of two primary variables: the party in power and the rules governing housing council responsibilities. The case studies indicate the centrality of the party in power to transparency, a level playing field, and deliberative decision making. All of these factors from the policy process should coalesce to shape the role of the housing council in encouraging adoption of social housing programs, in line with the demands of CSOs. Contrary to my initial expectations, the institutional rules for council responsibilities did not seem to largely impact the policy process, particularly in terms of transparency. Scholars argue, however, that increasing transparency is a primary function of participatory governance institutions and is central to generating accountability of government officials. Here I aim to test whether across cases the rules for council responsibilities are linked to greater accountability of the government as measured by adoption of social housing programs to benefit the poor.

Using the dataset developed in Chapter 3, I run a series of probit regression models. My first hypothesis is that where the PT is in power, municipal councils for housing should be associated with the adoption of a greater number of municipal housing programs. In addition, the housing councils should be more highly correlated with municipally funded housing programs, demonstrating a higher level of commitment to housing from the municipal administration. My second hypothesis is that where councils are given the power for governmental oversight, greater transparency and hence accountability should lead to a greater number of social housing programs. In the end, I aim to provide greater evidence to suggest when participatory governance institutions in the form of municipal housing councils do provide a more equitable distribution of public goods.

STATISTICAL MODELS

Dependent Variables

I test the model against three groups of dependent variables: (1) an index of housing programs, which sums the total number of housing programs by type adopted in the municipality; (2) individual categories of housing programs; and (3) individual categories of municipally funded housing programs. In Chapter 3, I found that the presence of a municipal housing council significantly increased the probability of governments adopting each type of housing program as well as a greater number of housing programs as measured by the index. Here I add a third dependent variable to the analysis, through which I seek to assess the role of municipal housing councils in persuading the municipal government to invest more of its own resources into housing rather than relying on federal or state transfers.

In the case studies, particularly in Salvador, I found that the housing council was used to generate proposals for projects selected by the federal government. Though accessing newly available sums of federal money is critical to addressing the scale of housing challenges in Brazil, I assess whether the presence of a housing council also leads municipal governments to contribute more resources to housing programs themselves. Table 5.4 presents the percentages of housing programs funded either through partnerships between the federal and municipal governments or by the municipal government alone. The table illustrates significant variation in funding patterns depending on the type of program. For instance, in municipalities with programs to construct new units, 68% are funded in partnership with the federal government. Less than a quarter of municipalities with construction programs fund these types of programs independently. On the opposite end of the spectrum, programs to provide materials,

Table 5.4 Source of Funding for Municipal-Level Housing Programs

	In Partnership with the Federal Government	Solely Municipal Government Resources
Construction of New Units	68%	22%
Offer Materials	8%	88%
Offer Plots of Land	9%	89%
Regularization of Land Titles	26%	65%
Acquire Units	65%	25%
Improve Units	37%	56%
Urbanization	58%	47%

plots of land, and land titles tend to be solely municipally funded. The statistical analysis will test whether the presence of a municipal council alters these relationships. In addition, the results will demonstrate whether municipal councils for housing under the leadership of a PT administration or with key oversight responsibilities increase the likelihood of independently funded housing programs.

Key Independent Variables

The key independent variables for this analysis assess the relationships between the PT, institutional rules, municipal councils, and housing programs across contexts. To test the relationship between the party in power, municipal housing councils, and housing programs, I add an interaction term. Theoretically, on its own the party in power may influence the adoption of social housing programs. Previous research suggests that left-leaning governments, including the PT in Brazil, are associated with an increase in social programs.[36] The statistical analysis in Chapter 3, however, did not bear out this hypothesis: the presence of a PT mayor in power was not associated with a greater likelihood of housing program adoption. By adding an interaction term for the party in power and the existence of a municipal housing council, I seek to measure whether the association between housing councils and programs changes when the mayor is from the PT. In other words, does the presence of a PT mayor increase the probability of program adoption where housing councils exist? Across Brazil, in 2005 there were 413 mayors from the PT.

In addition, to test the role of institutional rules, I include dummy variables for whether the councils have consultative, deliberative, normative, and oversight responsibilities. Note that councils may have more than one type of responsibility. As shown in Table 5.5, the great majority of councils have deliberative responsibilities, meaning the councils are established to debate policies and programs, but do not necessarily have the right to request budget or other evaluative information regarding the government's activities. The statistical analysis will indicate whether the type of responsibility afforded to municipal housing councils significantly alters the outcomes. Because these questions apply only to those municipalities with housing councils, the sample size is limited to these municipalities.

Table 5.5   Percentage of Councils with Each Type of Responsibility

Responsibility	Percentage of Councils
Consultative	49%
Deliberative	78%
Normative	33%
Oversight	44%

Additional Factors Influencing Housing Program Adoption

To the model I also add two categories of control variables, informed by the preceding case study analysis regarding the process in participatory governance institutions.

Make-Up of the Legislature

I include a measure of the percentage of seats in the municipal legislature held by members of the PT. Since the number of seats in municipal legislatures (camaras municipais), akin to city councils in the United States, varies by the size of the municipality, I use the percentage of seats occupied by PT members rather than simply the number of PT members. Theoretically, if the majority in the legislature is from the same party, there should be less legislative gridlock, including for policy and resource allocation decisions forwarded by the housing councils. Case studies suggest that legislation to create municipal housing councils may be easier to pass under PT administrations. This leads me to wonder whether the orientation of the legislature also has an effect on the adoption of housing policies and programs. Controlling for the make-up of the municipal legislature should further identify the role the party of the legislature plays in determining housing policy outcomes.[37]

Regional Variation

I include regional dummy variables in this analysis to control for possible effects of political tradition. The Northeast of Brazil is known for more conservative administration and a legacy of clientelism stemming from the sugar plantation economy and slavery.[38] The development of civil society in the Northeast is thought to have been stifled in comparison to the South and Southeast, where politics are traditionally more liberal, though business oriented, in the major cities.[39] After reviewing the case studies, I expect that as compared to the Southeast region, municipalities in the North and Northeast are particularly less likely to adopt social housing programs because of the lack of civil society influence and strength of conservative political traditions. The Southeast region is left out of the statistical models to provide comparison with the other four regions.

RESULTS: PARTY IN POWER

Individual Programs

Here I test whether the presence of a PT mayor changes the relationship between municipal housing councils and adoption of social housing programs. Table 5.6 first shows that where there is no PT mayor, the housing

Table 5.6 The Relationship between the PT, Municipal Housing Councils, and Individual Housing Programs

	Construction of Units	Acquire Units	Improve Units	Offer Materials	Offer Plots of Land	Regularization	Urbanization
Housing Council Exists	0.26***	0.18**	0.27***	0.16**	0.17**	0.25***	0.18**
	(0.07)	(0.07)	(0.06)	(0.06)	(0.07)	(0.07)	(0.08)
Housing Council × PT Mayor	0.26	-0.23	0.20	-0.18	-0.06	-0.09	-0.01
	(0.17)	(0.18)	(0.16)	(0.16)	(0.17)	(0.17)	(0.20)
PT Mayor	-0.08	0.13	0.04	0.23*	-0.08	0.26**	-0.01
	(0.12)	(0.13)	(0.12)	(0.12)	(0.13)	(0.13)	(0.16)
Fund for Housing	0.25***	0.09	0.04	0.09	0.19***	0.14**	0.15**
	(0.06)	(0.07)	(0.06)	(0.06)	(0.07)	(0.07)	(0.08)
Population, 2005 (log)	0.19***	0.12***	0.06*	0.08**	0.10***	0.35***	0.42***
	(0.04)	(0.04)	(0.03)	(0.03)	(0.03)	(0.04)	(0.04)
Percent Urban Population (log)	0.14**	0.04	0.18***	0.20***	0.26***	0.03	0.03
	(0.06)	(0.07)	(0.06)	(0.06)	(0.06)	(0.07)	(0.08)
Municipal Budget per Capita (log)	0.49***	0.18**	0.19**	0.37***	0.27***	0.34***	0.45***
	(0.08)	(0.08)	(0.07)	(0.07)	(0.08)	(0.08)	(0.09)
Gini Coefficient, 2000	1.26***	0.24	1.99***	1.28***	0.01	-0.03	0.99*
	(0.42)	(0.49)	(0.41)	(0.42)	(0.45)	(0.48)	(0.53)
Income per Capita (log)	0.07	0.11	-0.11	-0.17**	0.04	0.17*	0.05
	(0.09)	(0.10)	(0.08)	(0.08)	(0.09)	(0.10)	(0.11)
Civil Society Density (log)	-0.04	-0.02	0.13***	-0.07**	0.03	-0.09**	-0.11**
	(0.04)	(0.04)	(0.04)	(0.04)	(0.04)	(0.04)	(0.05)
Favelas Exist	-0.00	0.06	-0.04	-0.06	-0.00	0.30***	0.38***
	(0.05)	(0.06)	(0.05)	(0.05)	(0.05)	(0.06)	(0.06)

	(1)	(2)	(3)	(4)	(5)	(6)	(7)
Percent of PT Muni Legislators	0.12	0.33	-0.13	-0.22	0.11	0.17	0.50
	(0.25)	(0.28)	(0.24)	(0.24)	(0.26)	(0.28)	(0.32)
Northeast	0.37**	0.19	0.03	0.27	0.56***	-0.05	1.05***
	(0.18)	(0.22)	(0.21)	(0.22)	(0.22)	(0.23)	(0.24)
North	0.67*	0.78**	0.30	0.28	0.74*	1.06***	1.05**
	(0.38)	(0.40)	(0.37)	(0.36)	(0.44)	(0.40)	(0.46)
Center–West	0.19	-0.12	-0.01	0.57***	0.52***	0.60***	0.67***
	(0.17)	(0.20)	(0.17)	(0.18)	(0.18)	(0.17)	(0.19)
South	0.63***	0.26**	0.08	0.57***	0.52***	0.11	0.30**
	(0.12)	(0.13)	(0.10)	(0.12)	(0.13)	(0.13)	(0.14)
Constant	-6.39***	-4.39***	-2.01***	-4.40***	-4.12***	-8.29***	-10.35***
	(0.83)	(0.87)	(0.76)	(0.78)	(0.82)	(0.88)	(0.98)
Observations	4093	4093	4083	4080	4093	4093	4083

Standard errors in parentheses. *** p < 0.01, ** p < 0.05, * p < 0.1.
State dummies also included in model.

council is significantly related to the adoption of all types of programs. Where there is a PT mayor, the relationship is unchanged. The existence of the municipal housing council institution appears to have a greater effect on housing program adoption than the party in power.

The results also indicate that the percentage of the municipal legislators from the PT is not associated with housing program adoption. The relationship between region and housing program adoption appears to be significant, but not steady across programs and regions. The results do, however, appear to contradict my expectations. Compared to the Southeast region, the North and Northeast regions are positively related to the adoption of various housing programs.

Program Index

Again, contrary to my hypothesis from the case studies, across contexts the results do not provide evidence that the presence of a PT mayor in combination with a housing council increases the likelihood of municipalities adopting multiple social housing programs. Table 5.7 displays the results from a negative binomial regression, including an interaction term for the presence of a PT mayor and housing council.[40]

The positive and significant coefficient for the housing council variable indicates that the housing council is positively associated with the adoption of multiple housing programs where there is not a PT mayor in municipalities across Brazil. The interaction term then shows that the effect is not significantly changed by the presence of a PT mayor: housing councils do influence program adoption, but the presence of a PT administration does not enhance the effect.

Municipally Funded Programs

The 2008 MUNIC survey also asks questions about the source of funding for housing programs. Particularly since President Lula assumed office in 2003 and the National System for Housing in the Social Interest was created in 2005, many municipalities have applied for and received federal funding for all types of programs. As the case study in Salvador showed directly, members often use housing councils as mechanisms to access federal funding. In doing so municipalities may choose not to allocate their own resources for housing. However, convincing municipal government officials to allocate municipal funds for housing programs may indicate a further commitment by the municipal government to meet civil society demands. The dependent variables in Table 5.8 are coded 0 or 1 based on whether the municipality has a program supported by the municipal government. The presence of a PT administration, which may be friendlier to CSOs, combined with a municipal council for housing should lead to increasing commitment of municipal resources to housing.

Table 5.7 The Relationship between the PT in Power, Municipal Housing Councils and a Program Index

Variables	Program Index
Housing Council Exists	0.19***
	(0.03)
Housing Council × PT Mayor	−0.02
	(0.08)
PT Mayor	0.06
	(0.06)
Fund for Housing	0.13***
	(0.03)
Population (log)	0.15***
	(0.02)
Percent Urban Population (log)	0.14***
	(0.03)
Municipal Budget per Capita (log)	0.28***
	(0.04)
Gini Coefficient	0.83***
	(0.22)
Income per Capita (log)	−0.02
	(0.04)
Civil Society Density	−0.01
	(0.02)
Favelas Exist	0.06**
	(0.03)
Percentage of Vereadores from the PT	0.06
	(0.13)
Northeast	0.45***
	(0.10)
North	0.49**
	(0.21)
Center–West	0.27***
	(0.09)
South	0.40***
	(0.06)
Constant	−3.31***
	(0.38)
Observations	4093

Standard errors in parentheses. *** $p < 0.01$, ** $p < 0.05$, * $p < 0.1$.
State dummies also included in model.

Table 5.8 The Relationship between Housing Councils, the PT, and Municipally Funded Housing Programs

Variables	Construction of Units by Muni	Acquire Units by Muni	Improve Units by Muni	Offer Materials by Muni	Offer Plots of Land by Muni	Regularization by Muni	Urbanization by Muni
PT Mayor	-0.15	-0.61	0.15	-0.17	-0.39	-0.43*	0.04
	-0.2	-0.42	-0.18	-0.25	-0.33	-0.25	-0.33
Housing Council	0.07	-0.09	0	-0.08	-0.1	0.07	0.16
	-0.09	-0.16	-0.09	-0.13	-0.17	-0.13	-0.16
Council × PT Mayor	0.34	0.44	-0.18	0.11	0.14	0.03	-0.17
	-0.23	-0.5	-0.23	-0.3	-0.39	-0.29	-0.38
Housing Fund	-0.12	-0.02	-0.04	-0.17	-0.01	-0.07	-0.13
	-0.08	-0.16	-0.09	-0.12	-0.16	-0.13	-0.16
Population, 2005 (log)	0.13***	0.18**	-0.06	0.04	-0.01	0.13**	0.01
	-0.04	-0.08	-0.05	-0.07	-0.08	-0.07	-0.07
Percent Urban Population, 2000 (log)	0.07	0.16	0.12	0.06	0.10	0.31**	0.18
	-0.09	-0.18	-0.09	-0.14	-0.18	-0.15	-0.18
Municipal Budget per Capita, 2005 (log)	0.55***	0.43**	0.29***	0.30*	0.11	0.53***	0.42**
	-0.10	-0.20	-0.12	-0.16	-0.20	-0.16	-0.17
Gini Coefficient, 2000	1.72***	0.19	0.35	0.83	2.65**	1.73*	0.27
	-0.59	-1.16	-0.61	-0.92	-1.26	-1.00	-1.10
Income per Capita, 2000 (log)	-0.13	-0.27	0.03	-0.27	-0.32	-0.24	-0.10
	-0.12	-0.26	-0.13	-0.20	-0.26	-0.21	-0.22

	(1)	(2)	(3)	(4)	(5)	(6)	(7)
Civil Society Density (log)	-0.08	0.08	-0.20***	0.11	0.00	-0.02	0.05
	(0.05)	(0.10)	(0.05)	(0.08)	(0.11)	(0.09)	(0.11)
Favelas Exist	0.14**	-0.12	-0.02	-0.10	-0.14	0.06	-0.05
	(0.07)	(0.13)	(0.07)	(0.11)	(0.14)	(0.11)	(0.13)
Percent of PT Muni Legislators	-0.85**	-0.03	-0.17	-1.23**	-0.54	-0.30	-1.11
	(0.35)	(0.69)	(0.35)	(0.50)	(0.67)	(0.55)	(0.70)
Northeast	-1.02**	0.13	-0.71**	0.55	-0.38	-0.21	-1.0**
	(0.48)	(0.51)	(0.33)	(0.41)	(0.46)	(0.47)	(0.50)
North	0.45	2.24***	-0.43	-1.21*	0.18	-0.21	0.25
	(0.75)	(0.64)	(0.69)	(0.72)	(0.54)	(0.81)	(0.69)
Center–West	0.15	0.46	0.12	1.24***	0.24	0.16	0.18
	(0.23)	(0.41)	(0.29)	(0.47)	(0.41)	(0.27)	(0.43)
South	0.23	-0.03	0.60***	0.36	0.91***	0.76***	-0.55*
	(0.14)	(0.30)	(0.18)	(0.25)	(0.34)	(0.24)	(0.29)
Constant	-6.45***	-3.69*	-2.97***	0.28	0.42	-4.41***	-1.90
	(1.04)	(2.02)	(1.15)	(1.72)	(2.18)	(1.55)	(1.74)
Observations	2511	640	1883	1457	867	855	578

Standard errors in parentheses. *** p < 0.01, ** p < 0.05, * p < 0.1.
State dummies also included in model.

Again, contrary to expectations, the results shown in Table 5.8 indicate that the housing council has no effect on municipally funded programs regardless of whether or not a PT mayor is in charge. Interestingly, the results do indicate a negative correlation between several municipally funded programs and the Northeast versus the Southeast. In the previous models, the Northeast regional dummy variable was positively related to many different types of housing programs compared to the Southeast region. This appears to indicate that municipal governments in the Northeast tend to rely much more heavily on federal and state transfers rather than dedicating their own resources. Even controlling for the size of the municipal budget, region still appears to play a role in the commitment of the municipality to social housing policy.

RESULTS: COUNCIL RESPONSIBILITIES

Though the case studies did not illustrate the importance of responsibilities afforded by law, theoretically they should in part influence the policy process and the resulting policy outcomes. The ability to approve accounting documents in oversight councils should increase the likelihood that civil society will influence the process and create pressure to prioritize social housing. In order to test these claims I added dummy variables for each of the four responsibilities: consultative, deliberative, normative, and oversight. Including the responsibilities in the same models as Tables 5.6, 5.7, and 5.8 necessarily reduces the sample to only municipalities where housing councils exist (i.e., an official first answers affirmatively on the survey that the municipality has a housing council before answering questions about the responsibilities of the council).

The results in Table 5.9 indicate that across contexts, councils with oversight responsibilities are positively related to the program index and four of the seven types of programs. None of the other responsibilities demonstrate a positive relationship with the program index, nor is there any clear relationship to individual programs. In addition, as shown in Table 5.10, there is no clear pattern for the effect of any of the responsibilities on municipally funded programs. Leaving aside the mode for funding, councils reporting oversight responsibilities do appear to have the greatest impact on program outcomes compared to councils without the power to oversee accounting decisions.

Unlike in the previous model regarding municipally funded programs, in this model the regional differences are largely insignificant. The difference is that this model is restricted to municipalities with existing housing councils. This is to say that in municipalities with housing councils rather than all municipalities, there is not a negative correlation between the Northeast region and municipally funded programs, as compared to the Southeast region. This may signify that the existence of a municipal housing council

Table 5.9 The Relationship between Council Responsibilities and Housing Program Adoption

Variables	Program Index	Construction of Units	Acquire Units	Improve Units	Offer Material	Plot of Land	Regularization	Urbanization
PT Mayor	0.05	0.21	-0.18	0.21	0.06	-0.12	0.27*	-0.05
	(0.06)	(0.15)	(0.15)	(0.13)	(0.13)	(0.14)	(0.14)	(0.16)
Consultative	0.00	-0.11	-0.03	-0.10	-0.04	0.03	0.24***	0.03
	(0.04)	(0.09)	(0.09)	(0.08)	(0.08)	(0.09)	(0.09)	(0.10)
Deliberative	-0.02	0.00	-0.05	-0.12	0.01	-0.00	0.08	-0.05
	(0.04)	(0.10)	(0.11)	(0.09)	(0.09)	(0.10)	(0.11)	(0.11)
Normative	-0.07	0.04	-0.22**	0.01	-0.02	-0.13	-0.21**	-0.16
	(0.04)	(0.10)	(0.11)	(0.09)	(0.09)	(0.10)	(0.10)	(0.11)
Oversight	0.13***	0.16*	0.26***	0.13	0.11	0.21**	0.17*	0.15
	(0.04)	(0.09)	(0.09)	(0.08)	(0.08)	(0.09)	(0.09)	(0.10)
Housing Fund	-0.01	0.05	-0.04	-0.08	-0.10	0.07	-0.05	0.12
	(0.04)	(0.10)	(0.10)	(0.09)	(0.09)	(0.10)	(0.10)	(0.12)
Population, 2005 (log)	0.12***	0.17***	0.12**	0.04	0.07	0.07	0.36***	0.38***
	(0.02)	(0.06)	(0.06)	(0.05)	(0.05)	(0.05)	(0.06)	(0.06)
Percent Urban Population, 2000 (log)	0.13**	0.07	-0.10	0.24**	0.24**	0.30**	0.08	0.05
	(0.05)	(0.11)	(0.12)	(0.11)	(0.11)	(0.12)	(0.13)	(0.14)
Municipal Budget per Capita, 2005 (log)	0.22***	0.60***	0.16	0.28**	0.25**	0.14	0.30**	0.47***
	(0.05)	(0.14)	(0.14)	(0.12)	(0.12)	(0.13)	(0.14)	(0.15)
Gini Coefficient, 2000	0.54	2.01**	0.64	1.45**	0.52	0.04	0.12	0.78
	(0.33)	(0.79)	(0.80)	(0.71)	(0.71)	(0.75)	(0.80)	(0.86)
Income per Capita, 2000 (log)	0.03	0.38**	0.14	-0.13	-0.23	0.04	0.14	0.14
	(0.07)	(0.16)	(0.16)	(0.14)	(0.14)	(0.15)	(0.16)	(0.18)

(Continued)

Table 5.9 (Continued)

Variables	Program Index	Construction of Units	Acquire Units	Improve Units	Offer Material	Plot of Land	Regularization	Urbanization
Civil Society Density (log)	-0.03	-0.11	-0.15**	0.16***	-0.11*	0.06	-0.10	-0.14*
	(0.03)	(0.07)	(0.07)	(0.06)	(0.06)	(0.07)	(0.07)	(0.08)
Favelas Exist	0.07*	-0.02	-0.03	-0.04	-0.10	0.07	0.46***	0.43***
	(0.04)	(0.09)	(0.10)	(0.08)	(0.08)	(0.09)	(0.09)	(0.10)
Percent of PT Legislators	0.04	-0.12	1.02**	0.06	-0.41	-0.19	-0.26	0.81*
	(0.19)	(0.43)	(0.45)	(0.40)	(0.39)	(0.43)	(0.44)	(0.48)
Northeast	-0.10	1.12*	0.50	-0.03	-0.69	0.82*	-0.48	0.18
	(0.23)	(0.63)	(0.50)	(0.47)	(0.59)	(0.49)	(0.60)	(0.57)
North	0.36	-0.70	0.60	-0.93	0.34	0.97	0.43	0.35
	(0.45)	(0.59)	(0.95)	(0.64)	(0.56)	(0.90)	(0.59)	(0.58)
Center–West	0.34***	0.45	0.03	0.36	0.68**	1.04***	0.37	0.32
	(0.12)	(0.31)	(0.29)	(0.27)	(0.27)	(0.28)	(0.30)	(0.33)
South	0.15*	0.56**	0.29	-0.17	0.32	0.55***	0.09	0.24
	(0.09)	(0.23)	(0.20)	(0.19)	(0.20)	(0.21)	(0.20)	(0.22)
Constant	-2.38***	-8.964***	-5.09***	-1.03	-2.43**	-2.56**	-7.91***	-10.27***
	(0.54)	(1.50)	(1.35)	(1.23)	(1.24)	(1.30)	(1.40)	(1.50)
Observations	1352	1349	1335	1349	1349	1351	1345	1349

Standard errors in parentheses. *** $p < 0.01$, ** $p < 0.05$, * $p < 0.1$.
State dummies also included in model.

Table 5.10 The Relationship between Municipal Housing Council Responsibilities and Municipally Funded Housing Programs

Variables	Construction of Units by Muni	Acquire Units by Muni	Improve Units by Muni	Offer Materials by Muni	Offer Plots of Land by Muni	Regularization by Muni	Urbanization by Muni
PT Mayor	0.32* (0.16)	-0.13 (0.35)	0.11 (0.17)	-0.11 (0.23)	-0.52 (0.34)	-0.34 (0.21)	0.00 (0.28)
Consultative	-0.03 (0.11)	-0.23 (0.22)	-0.02 (0.11)	0.14 (0.16)	-0.20 (0.22)	-0.01 (0.16)	-0.31 (0.19)
Deliberative	0.33** (0.13)	-0.10 (0.27)	0.18 (0.13)	0.22 (0.19)	0.29 (0.23)	0.14 (0.18)	-0.09 (0.23)
Normative	-0.03 (0.12)	0.03 (0.26)	-0.19 (0.12)	-0.08 (0.19)	0.32 (0.23)	-0.07 (0.18)	0.38* (0.21)
Oversight	0.05 (0.11)	0.19 (0.21)	0.30*** (0.12)	-0.13 (0.16)	-0.14 (0.20)	-0.01 (0.16)	-0.32* (0.19)
Housing Fund	-0.05 (0.12)	0.07 (0.26)	-0.11 (0.12)	-0.08 (0.18)	-0.04 (0.25)	-0.20 (0.20)	-0.11 (0.26)
Population, 2005 (log)	0.14** (0.06)	0.19* (0.11)	-0.09 (0.07)	-0.01 (0.10)	-0.05 (0.13)	0.10 (0.09)	-0.17 (0.10)
Percent Urban Population, 2000 (log)	0.31** (0.14)	0.54* (0.31)	0.31** (0.14)	0.34 (0.22)	0.62* (0.34)	0.45* (0.26)	0.29 (0.32)
Municipal Budget per Capita, 2005 (log)	0.76*** (0.15)	0.61** (0.30)	0.38** (0.17)	0.37 (0.25)	0.26 (0.32)	0.46** (0.22)	0.19 (0.26)
Gini Coefficient, 2000	1.69* (0.92)	1.13 (1.90)	0.08 (0.95)	0.30 (1.44)	3.79* (1.94)	3.54** (1.50)	1.99 (1.72)
Income per Capita, 2000 (log)	-0.30 (0.20)	-0.67 (0.42)	0.06 (0.21)	-0.51 (0.32)	-0.53 (0.44)	-0.30 (0.32)	0.21 (0.35)

(Continued)

Table 5.10 (Continued)

Variables	Construction of Units by Muni	Acquire Units by Muni	Improve Units by Muni	Offer Materials by Muni	Offer Plots of Land by Muni	Regularization by Muni	Urbanization by Muni
Civil Society Density (log)	-0.08	-0.07	-0.21**	0.17	0.08	-0.12	0.05
	(0.08)	(0.17)	(0.09)	(0.13)	(0.18)	(0.14)	(0.17)
Favelas Exist	0.18*	-0.01	0.07	-0.08	-0.28	0.02	0.30
	(0.11)	(0.21)	(0.11)	(0.17)	(0.21)	(0.17)	(0.22)
Percent of PT Muni Legislators	-1.24**	0.14	-0.88*	-1.32*	0.36	-0.83	-1.36
	(0.52)	(1.00)	(0.52)	(0.75)	(1.14)	(0.79)	(1.03)
Northeast	0.043	0.89	0.22	-1.28	-0.29	-0.20	1.08
	(0.49)	(1.04)	(0.95)	(1.01)	(0.93)	(0.93)	(0.88)
North	0.13		-0.73**			-1.43*	0.12
	(0.65)		(0.36)			(0.84)	(0.62)
Center–West	0.25	0.42	-0.16	0.57	0.38	0.54	-0.11
	(0.32)	(0.63)	(0.38)	(0.57)	(0.66)	(0.44)	(0.59)
South	0.36	0.30	0.33	-0.13	0.40	0.89***	0.38
	(0.25)	(0.48)	(0.28)	(0.36)	(0.47)	(0.34)	(0.41)
Constant	-7.37***	-4.47	-3.22*	2.30	1.00	-4.66**	-0.93
	(1.54)	(2.90)	(1.71)	(2.53)	(3.45)	(2.22)	(2.59)
Observations	974	255	769	561	350	428	280

Standard errors in parentheses. *** $p < 0.01$, ** $p < 0.05$, * $p < 0.1$.
State dummies also included in model.

reduces the negative effects of regionally based clientelism and traditional neglect of housing issues.

PROCESS VERSUS OUTCOMES: FINDINGS ACROSS CASE STUDIES AND STATISTICAL ANALYSIS

Though the case studies provide strong evidence to suggest that the party in power influences the civil society–state dynamics in the policy process within municipal housing councils, quantitative results do not confirm the importance of the PT in power for program outcomes in the larger universe of cases. The institution of municipal housing councils, providing some level of transparency, inclusion of civil society, and deliberative decision making, appears to function across contexts to produce pro-poor outcomes, regardless of the party in power. Looking further into whether institutional rules are associated with redistribution of public goods, the ability to oversee government finances seems to make the largest difference in program implementation. In the aggregate, institutional rules do make a considerable difference for program outcomes. Still, questions remain regarding the influence on municipal budget allocation for social housing programs and the effect municipal housing councils may have in shifting prioritization of municipal funding.

The PT's insignificant association with housing outcomes across contexts leads me to return to the case studies for answers. Though speculative, first I question whether the ideology and the commitment of the PT to participatory governance may in fact vary across the country. Though the PT is considered to be one of the most ideologically coherent parties in Brazil, in general party platforms in Brazil are weak and party switching among politicians is common. Across the country, from urban to rural areas the PT may not operate in the same manner. Even in São Paulo where the Suplicy (PT) government relied on the support of housing and urban reform movements, the relationship with civil society within the housing council was far more contentious than in the smaller city of Santo André, where the PT had been in charge for many years. In addition, looking to PT-administered housing councils in São Paulo and Santo André in comparison to the council under a PT housing secretary in Salvador, I recognize the constraints in Salvador that may limit the effect of the party in power. Most significantly, Salvador suffers from severe resource constraints.

This leads me to consider the role that resource constraints play across municipalities. Municipal resource constraints may limit government responsiveness regardless of party affiliation and deserves explicit mention. Across statistical models, the municipal budget per capita is consistently positively associated with the adoption of housing programs. This suggests that the decisions of municipal administrators and housing councils are strongly conditioned by municipal budgets, regardless of which party is in power. As a result, municipal officials may choose to implement less costly programs or use housing councils more to access federal funds than to re-prioritize municipal allocation of resources. Where there are strong alliances between a PT administration and civil society, the housing council may still have some effect in reprioritizing social housing needs. However, to save money housing secretaries may enact programs that do not require large financial investments, such as regularization or providing plots of land, or they may view the role of the council as a link to the federal system rather than as administrator of municipal funds. Either way, the ideology of the party in power is unlikely to change the reality of local revenue scarcity, at least in the short term.

In Salvador, where the municipal budget per capita remains well below the other two cities, the only program the municipal government supports is regularization of land titles for people living on city-owned land. The previous secretary for housing explained to me that the municipal government invests in regularization of land titles because it is cheap. The cost for regularization is about R$200 per family, while building a new house costs R$25,000 and urbanization costs between R$5,000–R$17,000 per household. According to an official in the municipal secretariat for housing, the only real projects underway in Salvador in 2008 were two self-build projects directed by housing associations, financed by the federal government. The municipality contributed only the land and construction of a community meeting area for one of the projects. Officials stated that any new projects would also have to be approved and financed by the federal government due to lack of municipal resources. Members of the housing council have not succeeded in pressing the municipal government to increase its contributions to housing programs through the municipal housing fund. According to the former secretary for housing, there are no municipal funds in the fund: "They have a Fund without funds."[41] In practice this means that the Municipal Council for Housing in Salvador is completely unable to make any budget allocation decisions. Instead, the housing council is used as a pass-through for federal funding proposals.

In addition, the statistical models may suffer from omitted variable bias. Several of the contextual variables, which I find to matter in the qualitative analysis, cannot be measured directly in the statistical analysis. For instance, the capacity of civil society may matter across cases for generating accountability and responsiveness. Though I hypothesized that transparency, and hence accountability, resulting from municipal housing councils would be stronger under PT administrations where CSOs maintain strong alliances with government officials, the capacity of civil society may in fact be a stronger factor than alliances in ensuring transparency. A coordinated network of CSOs serving on a council may make requests for information, process complex accounting documents, and formulate coordinated responses within the confines of the councils and to their membership bases, which is not possible for civil society in other municipalities. The contrast in civil society capacity and outcomes in São Paulo versus Salvador does in fact provide evidence for this claim. Civil society in Salvador currently uses the council to formulate proposals to the federal level rather than demand review of municipal government finances and reprioritization of funds. In São Paulo the transparency afforded by the council as a result of the continued demand for information by CSOs may contribute to the government's responsiveness to housing needs as a major priority in the city, regardless of the party in power. While the statistical model contains a measure for the depth of civil society, it may not capture the capacity of CSOs across municipalities.

Finally, the importance of oversight responsibilities for program adoption may indicate the primacy of transparency for the effectiveness of participatory governance institutions in shifting the distribution of public goods. Though in the case studies I did not find a strong connection between legal responsibilities afforded to the councils and duties in practice, across contexts the rules do appear to matter. Based on the case studies I questioned the reliability of the survey data, given that the responsibilities I witnessed on the ground did not match with the survey responses. Across cases, however, the results do illustrate the expected result that oversight responsibilities matter for transparency and therefore outcomes.

Not all councils are created the same, nor do they produce the same outcomes. As municipalities increasingly adopt into law housing councils in order to comply with the new federal requirement to access funds, administrators and CSOs monitoring the process should be aware that the responsibilities afforded by law matter. Though in the case studies the responsibilities written in law did not correspond directly to activities in practice, in the aggregate the types of responsibilities granted to councils matter.

CONCLUSIONS

This chapter yielded several conclusions regarding policy making and outcomes of participatory governance institutions. First, I find evidence across the case studies that to some extent expectations regarding institutional rules and civil society–state dynamics do play out in practice for the policy-making process. Transparency, a level playing field, and deliberative decision making in municipal housing councils are dependent on the rules that shape council responsibilities, membership, and meeting frequency. To a greater extent, however, I find that the policy process is shaped by civil society–state dynamics: though rules may exist on paper, civil society, government, and private sector actors determine the implementation of those rules. In the case studies, it is the party in power that appears to largely dictate the relationships among actors, and in turn creates transparency, participation, and the ultimate extent of deliberation within municipal housing councils.

Using statistical analysis, I then sought to assess the variables that determine when participatory governance institutions lead to greater distribution of public goods. I find that the party in power is not significantly associated with greater housing program adoption where municipal housing councils exist. This is a surprising result, but in looking back to the case studies I argue that the PT may vary in commitment to participatory governance across the country and municipal budgets may constrain the efforts of PT mayors and housing secretariats across the country. Therefore, though the party in power may matter in some cases, in the aggregate the party is a weak predictor of the effect of participatory governance institutions on program outcomes.

Instead, I find that transparency created by institutional rules matters across contexts. Councils with specific oversight powers appear to have the greatest effect on the adoption of social housing programs across municipalities. These results suggest that institutional rules governing municipal housing councils may be more important than the political party in charge for determining outcomes. Access to budgetary numbers is critical for ensuring accountability. As more and more municipal housing councils are created in response to the federal mandate, it is critical, then, to assess whether these new institutions are created with enough responsibility to alter policy outcomes.

The results of this analysis also bring to light questions regarding mixed-method research. Using multiple methods should serve to strengthen the reliability of findings. When case studies tell one story and statistics another, however, researchers have to use both sets of data to tease out the causal mechanisms at work and the plausible explanations for conflicting findings. The real world of politics and policy making is messy, and neither the interpretation of cases nor statistical analysis can truly identify all variables at work. I believe, though, that relying on multiple methods in this study reduces the probability of asserting false conclusions, even if it takes some work to wade through the evidence regarding the process and outcomes of these new institutions.

Participatory governance institutions are not the magic bullet for incorporating diverse voices, promoting transparency, ensuring policy deliberation, and shifting resource distribution toward the poor, but neither are they ineffective institutions for creating social policy change, as skeptics would argue. The dynamic between civil society and the state does change when the two sides agree to meet at one table. While the policy process may never be ideal, across political contexts taking one's seat at the table may be one small step toward policy change.

6   The Creation Effect
Evaluating Commitment in Participatory Governance Institutions

> The council was created because it is necessary to define public policy. It doesn't work for us to determine policies without the principal people involved. Public officials cannot think that they know everything about the necessities of the city. No, a government needs partners. A democratic government facilitates participation and transparency in its administration.
>
> —Former housing secretariat official from the Suplicy (PT) administration in São Paulo[1]

This chapter continues the search to determine *when* and *how* participatory governance institutions make a difference in pro-poor policy adoption. Previous analysis suggests that municipal housing councils are strongly related to the adoption of housing programs, though neither the density of civil society nor the presence of a PT (Worker's Party) government enhances the effect of the councils across contexts. Through case study analysis and a look into the survey data, however, it is clear that not all councils function the same. In the previous chapter the case studies revealed important variation in council formation, responsibilities assigned to councils, and their interaction with civil society, private sector actors, and the state. Statistical analysis then confirmed that the responsibilities allocated to councils are significantly related to housing program adoption.

This chapter examines another important dimension of variation: how the participatory councils were created. Whether the impetus for creation comes from civil society and/or local government officials (bottom-up) or in response to the federal mandate (top-down) could hold important implications for how municipal housing councils function and, ultimately, in the resulting policy outcomes. Who initiates the creation of participatory governance institutions should matter for how seriously they are taken by government and civil society as mechanisms for deliberation. Consequently, the top-down/bottom-up distinction should also hold implications for policy outcomes.

The question for this chapter is motivated by previous research, which finds that the commitment of mayors is critical for ensuring the effectiveness of decentralization reforms, including participatory governance institutions.[2] Not only mayors, but also other relevant government officials must be willing to share control over decision making regarding policy direction and resource distribution in order for participatory institutions to matter. Without a commitment to the participatory process, institutions may exist on paper, but have little say over policy making. In addition, I argue that civil society must also be committed to the process in order for the mechanisms of accountability and responsiveness to work. In many contexts CSOs (civil society organizations) lobby for the creation of participatory institutions, and their involvement is viewed as a foregone conclusion. However, where local participatory institutions are mandated from the federal level, local CSOs may not exhibit the same enthusiasm for the process. Instead they may continue to seek benefits for their members directly from government officials. Without the commitment of CSOs to engage in an open forum for debate, government officials lack incentives to prioritize civil society demands and to invest further in the participatory process. This chapter seeks to provide evidence as to how the commitment of local government officials and civil society actors varies depending on the creation of participatory governance institutions. In turn, I present evidence to suggest that variation in commitment alters the resulting impact of municipal housing councils.

The Brazilian housing system offers an opportunity to assess how the motivation for creation of participatory governance institutions changes both the policy process and resulting outcomes. As stated previously, the Brazilian National System for Housing in the Social Interest (SNHIS), created in 2005, mandated that all municipalities must have a municipal council for housing by the end of 2009 in order to receive federal funds. To comply with the law in time, many municipalities began creating municipal housing councils in 2005, accounting for much of the increase in councils across Brazil between 2005 and 2008. Before 2005, however, hundreds of housing councils already existed across Brazil: generally at the demand of CSOs or by ideologically motivated government officials. This provides a comparison by which to measure whether councils created before 2005 (bottom-up) function differently than those created after 2005 (top-down). Though the distinction may not hold across all cases created after 2005, even where ideologically motivated officials were apt to create participatory institutions, the federal system imposed a new order to the process that did not exist previously. Case studies in Curitiba and Recife will help to clarify how the process of establishing councils after 2005 differed from the process of creation in São Paulo, Salvador, and Santo André.

With the new system coming into place, answers to questions regarding the impact of creation are timely for ensuring useful participatory governance institutions in Brazil. Moreover, whether effective participatory governance institutions can be mandated from the federal level is particularly relevant to numerous other developing countries adopting similar systems to Brazil's. In the end, whether participatory governance institutions legislated from above lead to the promotion of pro-poor outcomes has implications for Brazil and other developing countries. More broadly, this chapter provides evidence as to whether effective local participation can be legislated from above.

This chapter asks three specific questions: (1) Do municipal governments demonstrate a greater commitment to the participatory process in terms of delegating power and resources where councils are created from the bottom-up? (2) Do CSOs in these municipalities display a commitment to the participatory process and a willingness to demand accountability of the government through the councils? (3) Are pro-poor policy outcomes more likely where councils are created in response to bottom-up versus top-down pressures? For municipal officials, the concept of "commitment" can be defined by the official's willingness to cede control over programs and resources to civil society. Commitment of local officials is then measured by perception of the council's role as well as by whether the council is given deliberative powers and resources to allocate. For civil society, commitment is defined by the enthusiasm of leaders to participate in the housing council process rather than continuing with status quo tactics. In addition, CSO commitment involves the drive to ensure that the local government implements the participatory process and housing programs as promised.

I expect that municipal housing councils created between 2005 and 2008 are more likely a response to the federal mandate rather than local initiative and, therefore, will not generate the type of participatory environment as councils created previously. To provide evidence for this claim, I compare the cities of São Paulo and Santo André, where councils were created by PT governments at the demand of CSOs, to the cases of Curitiba and Recife, where councils have only recently been created in response to the federal mandate. I also include the case of Salvador, where a PT-affiliated municipal housing secretary created a municipal council for housing in part because of ideology and in part as a reaction to the forthcoming requirement to access federal funding. I suspect that municipalities with councils created from the top-down will be less likely than municipalities with councils created from the bottom-up to adopt each type of housing program. In Salvador, Curitiba, and Recife, I expect less commitment from both civil society and government officials to participatory governance, resulting in fewer housing programs. For each case I assess differences in the commitment of local officials and civil society leaders before turning to statistical analysis of municipalities across Brazil. In the end I conclude that the commitment of actors varies along with the impetus for creation of municipal housing councils. In turn, commitment alters the probability that municipal housing councils make a difference in policy outcomes.

WHY SHOULD TOP-DOWN VERSUS BOTTOM-UP INITIATION OF PARTICIPATORY GOVERNANCE INSTITUTIONS MATTER?

Literature regarding the effect of creation on participatory governance institutions is largely based on previous findings related to decentralization. For example, Alfred Montero and David Samuels argue that the outcomes of decentralization fundamentally depend on the political origins of the reforms.[3] Participatory governance institutions are similar to other decentralization reforms in that the federal government transfers resources and responsibilities to the local level. However, participatory governance institutions require a second process of devolving local control to civil society.

Researchers on participatory governance institutions increasingly use the "top-down" versus "bottom-up" distinction to identify the impetus behind creation of the institution. The participatory budgeting process in Porto Alegre, Brazil, created by the PT in 1989, is identified as a "bottom-up" institution because the demand for its creation came from within the city administration.[4] In Porto Alegre and elsewhere, the motivation to create participatory governance institutions on the part of the administration is difficult to disentangle from the demand for participatory governance institutions from CSOs that support the party in power. Many participatory governance institutions also present a clear case for "top-down" imposition. For instance, in 2002, the central government of Peru enacted reforms to establish decentralized, participatory institutions across regions and municipalities.[5] In this case the central government instructed municipalities to create institutions they hoped would promote efficiency and transparency in policy making. In other cases, the distinction in the impetus for creation is less clear.

In every case, though, actors create rules to their benefit and respond to incentives for cooperation and commitment. For example, where the mayor is less favorable to the idea of participation in policy making, he or she may reserve greater control over the process for the administration. Where civil society is clearly demanding the participatory process, the mayor may concede more control to CSOs in an effort to win favor and votes. Further, where the rules of operation are strictly imposed by the central government without concern for local political will, municipal legislatures or mayors may create institutions that conform to federal regulations on paper, but have little say in reality.

In the case of Brazil's municipal housing councils, the operating rules were left to the municipality to decide. Either municipal legislation or executive orders establish the existence of municipal housing councils. Though the federal government mandated that in order to receive federal funds every municipality create a participatory council to manage the municipal housing fund, the federal level did not mandate rules regarding frequency of meetings, composition of membership, responsibilities, or obligations. Even with the top-down imposition of municipal housing councils, therefore, the municipal administration still has significant control in shaping these institutions. Still, based on the locus of demand, I categorize those municipal housing councils created in response to the federal mandate as "top-down" institutions and those created before the mandate as "bottom-up" institutions.

In his study of several types of participatory governance institutions across Brazil, Leonardo Avritzer finds that both political will and civil society willingness to join participatory institutions are key for their effectiveness. He argues that "successful participatory institutions . . . need to be the result of a specific interaction between the political will to initiate a participatory process and civil society actors who can join these institutions."[6] Avritzer reviews the cases of participatory budgeting systems, health councils, and city master planning processes in several Brazilian cities and concludes that the institutional design must match the context. What then happens when municipal councils are imposed by federal mandate across contexts? Though the rules of institutional responsibilities vary across municipal housing councils, the basic structure of the institution is the same. Avritzer's work implies that variation in effectiveness should be expected. Here I seek to understand more completely how the mechanism of commitment of local officials and civil society actors varies where councils are imposed top-down versus created from the bottom-up, changing the outcomes of these participatory governance institutions.

From the beginning, other scholars find that the incentives of local leaders to participate in municipal councils are important for generating real responsibilities and decision-making powers for the councils.[7] Participatory governance institutions need buy-in from mayors to facilitate information sharing between the government and CSOs.[8] The incentives of political society cannot be separated from the reason behind creation of participatory institutions. Without strong demand from civil society for the creation of participatory governance institutions with significant responsibilities, mayors may not have a compelling reason to give up power in the first place.[9] When municipal councils for housing are legislated by the federal government as a prerequisite for receiving federal funds, the incentive for the mayor to comply is to receive funding to deal with pressing social problems. The mayor's incentive is to save municipal resources by creating the institution required to receive federal resources, not to generate dialogue, transparency, and responsiveness to the demands of civil society. Without mayoral buy-in to the merits of participatory democracy, but rather incentives to create an institution on paper without real responsibilities, I argue that municipal councils created in response to a federal mandate will not significantly alter the process or outcomes of policy making. Though municipalities with councils may have more programs funded by federal resources, programs will not represent the diverse demands of civil society, the municipal budget for housing will not increase, and much of the resources for housing will actually remain outside of council control.

Civil society commitment to participatory democracy is also critical for the effectiveness of participatory governance institutions. Though in Chapter 4 I found that the density of civil society was not associated with an increase in the probability of program adoption where municipal housing councils were present, in order for participatory institutions to function, by definition existing civil society must be committed to the process for it to be "participatory." According to the literature, previous existing civil society–state relationships may, in part, determine policy making in participatory governance institutions. Traditionally, CSOs related to housing work bilaterally with local government officials to secure benefits for their members, often in the form of new construction or land rights. Municipal councils may bring CSOs together to negotiate for broader benefits, but cooperation is not guaranteed. In their study of participatory budgeting councils in 10 different Brazilian municipalities, Gianpaolo Baiocchi, Patrick Heller, and Marcelo Kunrath Silva find that the democratizing of civil society through the participatory budgeting process is predicated on preexisting state–civil society relationships.[10] They find that adding a participatory governance institution to the municipality does not automatically generate cohesion among CSOs willing to deliberate with the state on broader housing policy. Andrea Cornwall also finds that the political culture, including a tradition of clientelism, prevented democratic governance from functioning in the cases of health councils she studied.[11] As such, municipal councils may replicate the bilateral CSO-government relationships that previously existed. Though I argue in previous chapters that these bilateral relationships will be mitigated if CSOs see the benefits of collaboration within housing councils, if CSOs are not in favor of the councils from the start, they may not see the value in changing existing relationships. Without CSO buy-in to the process, civil society will not press the municipal government to actually hold meetings, present budgetary numbers for accountability, or bring contentious issues up for a vote. If CSOs do not see the value in committing their time to the process or if they do not have the capacity to engage in meaningful debate, the institutions become little more than rubber stamps for the government's agenda.

While existing literature offers evidence to suggest that political and civil society at the time of creation matter for the effectiveness of participatory governance institutions, few are specific about the mechanisms by which creation influences the way in which the councils function and their eventual outcomes. Using municipal housing councils, I attempt to define the variation in government and civil society commitment, which in turn leads to differences in the outcomes of top-down versus bottom-up generated participatory governance institutions.

MUNICIPAL HOUSING COUNCILS BY REASON FOR CREATION

According to data from the MUNIC survey (Pesquisa de Informações Básicas Municipais), 747 Brazilian municipalities had existing housing councils in 2005. Generally, mayors favoring participatory governance or those who depended on alliances with CSOs demanding the creation of participatory governance institutions established these councils. Between 2005 and 2008, local governments created an additional 962 municipal housing councils. One difference I might expect to see across those councils established before 2005 and those established after the mandate is the presence of a PT mayor. The data in Table 6.1, however, do not show a significant difference in the presence of a PT mayor across municipalities that adopted municipal housing councils before and after 2005. This appears to contradict the common perception that mayors from the PT create participatory governance institutions, which have been a trademark of the party. It is important to note, though, that the data below may not account for the party of the mayor when the municipal housing council was created prior to 2005, since mayoral elections were held in 2004. The data do not report in what year the councils were created or the party of the mayor in that year. Therefore, though the data do not indicate a significant difference in the percentage of municipalities with a housing council under PT administration for 2005 and 2008, it may be that there was a PT mayor in power when the majority of housing councils were created prior to 2005. Regardless of the party in power, before 2005 the mayor likely demonstrated commitment to participatory governance institutions in order to have signed an executive order or approved legislation from the city council.

Other variables do illustrate the differences in municipalities adopting housing councils before and after 2005. Compared to municipalities with housing councils before 2005, municipalities adopting housing councils after 2005 were smaller in population size, had fewer revenues to spend on a per capita basis, were poorer, and had slightly fewer nonprofits and foundations per capita. As Table 6.1 demonstrates, the context in which these municipal housing councils function was somewhat different from the start.

Table 6.2 demonstrates the variation along these variables in the case studies presented in this chapter. Though all five of the cases are large cities,

Table 6.1 Average Characteristics of Municipalities with Housing Councils

	Councils Created before 2005	Councils Created after 2005
Number of Observations	747	962
Housing Fund Exists	79%	78%
Population, 2005	88,509	46,528
Percent Urban Population	64%	65%
Municipal Budget per Capita	743.48	716.61
PT Mayor	11.80%	10.30%
Gini Coefficient	0.55	0.56
Income per Capita	R$231.88	R$191.36
Civil Society Density	0.0035	0.0027
Favelas Exist	42%	43%

Table 6.2 Characteristics of Case Study Municipalities

	São Paulo	Santo André	Salvador	Curitiba	Recife
Population, 2005	10,927,985	669,592	2,673,560	1,757,904	1,501,008
Municipal Budget per Capita	R$632	R$504	R$287	R$549	R$533
Income per Capita	R$610	R$513	R$341	R$620	R$392
Civil Society Density	0.0019	0.0014	0.0010	0.0024	0.0015

there is significant variation in the municipal budget per capita, income per capita, and civil society density (nonprofits and foundations per capita).

In both São Paulo and Santo André, PT governments linked to housing CSOs initiated the creation of the housing councils in the early 2000s. In Salvador, a PT-affiliated secretary of housing pushed to establish the housing council in 2007. Civil society in Salvador supported the creation of the council and has worked collaboratively to ensure its implementation. Curitiba and Recife both established municipal housing councils in direct response to the federal mandate, though the councils were not yet functioning when I visited in fall 2008. These two cities present interesting cases for study because they differ in their approach to participatory politics, by income level, and by the make-up of civil society. Though I introduced the cases of São Paulo, Santo André, and Salvador in the previous chapter, here I present background information to provide context for participatory politics in Curitiba and Recife.

CURITIBA

Curitiba is known worldwide for its early and innovative approaches to urban planning, though within Brazil it is also well-known for its conservative politics. In the 1960s, the government research agency led by Jaime Lerner created Curitiba's first Master Plan, which called for a large-scale bus system and plans for environmental sustainability. Jaime Lerner became mayor in the 1970s under the dictatorship and then won election for two terms in the 1980s-1990s. He was also governor of the state of Parana. The current mayor of Curitiba, Beto Richa from the same center-right PSDB (Partido da Social Democracia Brasileira) party of Jaime Lerner, handily won reelection in October 2008 with 77% of the votes. Curitiba has never had a mayor from the PT, and the city council has only ever had between 10% and 15% representation from the PT. These two factors—a long-standing technocratic orientation to urban planning and the continuous administration by conservative governments—created the situation today in which the municipal government reluctantly implements participatory institutions mandated by the federal government, but maintains firm control over policy decision making.

Curitiba has a strong community of NGOs (nongovernmental organizations), but relatively weak social movements for housing. The development of NGOs rather than social movements is most likely a result of the long tradition of urban studies in the city combined with a highly educated population. The city has a Company for Housing (COHAB), which is a mixed private-public company tasked with implementing housing projects, but the city does not have a secretariat for housing. COHAB manages the municipal housing fund, though there was not a council for housing to accompany that fund until it was created in 2008. As of October 2008, no elections had been held or planned to elect members to the housing council.

NGOs and movements were not lobbying for the implementation of the housing council, though if created they hoped it would be a space for real consultation, deliberation, and transparency. Left-leaning social movements in the city remained suspicious that relationships with municipal officials would change. According to Luiz Herlain, long-term organizer for the Central dos Movimentos Populares (CMP), "The administration will not accept the control of the Council. We need a revolution in customs and leadership. Their concept of democracy is very dangerous as is the relationship between the government and the private sector. There is no transparency and they do not support transparency."[12] This statement reflects the deep-seated skepticism of CSOs regarding the government's perception of civil society as equal partners worthy of decision-making authority. Without the commitment of the municipal government to reform, Herlain and others doubted that participatory institutions could be an effective strategy for policy change in Curitiba.

Nonetheless, as a result of the federal mandate for participatory councils, in the fall of 2008, CSOs in Curitiba were concentrating their efforts on the Council for the City, which met for the first time in June 2008. The focus on the Council for the City matches the city's focus on urban issues as a whole rather than housing as a separate issue, but NGOs and movements also complained that they were afraid housing issues would be overlooked in the council, with transportation and the environment receiving the majority of attention.

RECIFE

Recife is known as the city in the Northeast most oriented toward the left. A PT government has administered the city for much of the past two decades. The mayor from 2001 to 2008, João Paulo Lime e Silva, was a president of the Central Worker's Union (CUT) who participated in housing associations and social movement activities. According to a social movement leader in Recife, João Paulo had a definite sense of commitment to participatory governance. The mayor elected in 2008, João da Costa, participated in student movements before leading the participatory budgeting agency under João

Paulo. The participatory budgeting process attracted about 80,000 participants in 2008 and addressed housing issues based on demand, according to officials from the secretariat for housing. Recife is also well-known as the first city in Brazil to create Special Zones for Social Interest (Zonas Especiais de Interesse Social [ZEIS]). In 1983, the city created these zones to provide land titles and infrastructure to favelas within the city. There is a participatory council to allocate funds for the ZEIS for projects such as those to improve sidewalks, sanitation, sea barriers, and housing units.

Despite this tradition of participation, the creation of the municipal council for housing has not been a smooth process. The law to create the housing council passed in 2007, but as of November 2008, neither elections for members nor a first meeting was set. Members of civil society say they are concerned with how the housing council will be integrated into the Municipal Council for the City, also part of the national system for urban planning under which housing is a component. This is an issue that civil society throughout the country is concerned with: how to integrate housing into the broader institutional structure and urban planning process. Leaders from social movements in Recife understand that the municipality has to have the housing council in order to receive funds from the federal level and that the council has to manage those funds, but they want to make sure the council is also a real space for policy deliberation. According to the Rev. Marcos Cosmo, leader of the Movimento dos Trabalhadores sem Teto (Roofless Worker's Movement [MTST]) in Recife, "Our challenge now is not to get the government to implement the councils, but for the councils to actually achieve results and make things happen. We have to be careful about straying from the strategy of mobilizing our bases and the struggle of the people. If we do this we will see few results."[13] The challenge for Rev. Cosmo and other social movements is to make sure their efforts working with the government actually lead to real change rather than leading to cooptation and stagnation in generating solutions to housing problems.

The four major national movements are a significant presence in Recife, with numerous associations representing local issues, including the needs of residents living in palafitas—dwellings built on stilts above waterways. According to Leonardo Avritzer, one of the reasons Recife may not have had a housing council before the mandate is that they had the ZEIS council, which acts in very much the same way.[14] Avritzer argues that Recife is actually an exceptionally participatory city, but at a very localized level. With the growth of more professional NGOs in the city, however, this may change. For example, FASE (Federação de Órgãos para Assistência Social e Educacional), a policy-oriented NGO, which coordinates the National Forum for Urban Reform, operates in Recife and works alongside the social movements to provide capacity building and advice in negotiating with government officials.

Curitiba and Recife present contrasting cases for study: Curitiba operates under a very technocratic orientation while Recife has already demonstrated commitment to other participatory institutions. Assessing these two case studies as examples of municipalities creating housing councils in response to the federal mandate should provide some control for variation in the administrations' ideological leanings across contexts. At the same time, by comparing these two cities to the other cases of São Paulo, Santo André, and Salvador, I seek to understand the relationships between civil society, government officials, and participatory governance institutions across diverse contexts.

MUNICIPAL GOVERNMENT COMMITMENT TO PARTICIPATORY GOVERNANCE INSTITUTIONS

Do municipal governments where councils are created from the bottom-up demonstrate a greater commitment to the participatory process in terms of delegating power and resources?

While difficult to measure, I argue that commitment of municipal officials can be gauged by perception of the council's role, decision-making powers given to the council, and resources provided for council allocation. When participatory governance institutions are imposed by national legislation, local governments may respond by creating institutions that fulfill the requirement, but do little to incorporate civil society into decision making. In addition, municipal governments may see the creation of participatory councils as a means toward attaining federal resources to address housing needs, thereby alleviating the need for municipalities to direct their own funds toward the problems. Reviewing the case studies and survey data, I argue that where municipalities created housing councils in response to bottom-up pressures, government officials do display a higher level of commitment to the participatory process than where they were created in response to the federal mandate. This commitment is clear in their willingness to engage civil society through the councils and several indicators related to the power of the council.

In each of the five case study cities, I interviewed officials from the main housing agency and asked them to describe the role of the housing council.[15] Their responses demonstrate varying levels of commitment to the participatory process:

São Paulo: Housing secretariat officials stated that the council is a space for social movements and associations to bring their concerns for debate and decide whether programs should continue. Though as evidenced in the quote at the beginning of this chapter, the PT government from 2001 to 2004 directly supported the creation of the housing council, the current PSD (Partido Social Democrático) government has maintained the participatory process. The more conservative PSD government appears wary of allowing civil society to dictate a substantial portion of the agency's resources, but they respect the participatory process and hold regular meetings with social movement and civil society members in which votes on issues are taken and respected. According to Elisabete França, who as the superintendent for social housing is also the executive secretary for the housing council, "the council has an important function as a place to exchange ideas, and my job is to make sure things function within the council."[16] She views the council as an obligation of the government, and though the process of deliberation and decision making is upheld, França clearly views the council more as a space for debate than broad policy change.

Santo André: Government officials reported that the role of the council is to make sure the government follows up on promises made during annual conferences. In this way they view the council as a mechanism for accountability. At a meeting of the housing council in Santo André, members also told me that the role of the council is to discuss housing policies and how to spend money in the Municipal Housing Fund. Through monthly meetings the council provides continuity for policy making and forging connections between the government and civil society.

Salvador: Former secretary for housing Angela Gordilho Souza stated that civil society is responsible for "keeping the councils and the system going across administrations."[17] Without pressure from civil society the administration would not continue to operate the council. According to the current administration in Salvador, the council can provide a space for civil society to communicate needs, but the government was not sure if any municipal money would be available for council control. The current government does not appear to take the participatory process seriously as a means for policy change. In response to my question about whether decisions made by the council were final, a current government official told me that resolutions from the council go to the president of the council, who is the secretary for housing. The secretary then decides if the resolutions are within the law. If the actions recommended are not within the law, then the resolutions are sent back to the council. In this way the power to implement decision still remains with the secretary. Though this process exists in other participatory councils across the country, the government in Salvador seemed particularly reticent about handing final decision-making power over to civil society.

Curitiba: The housing council is viewed as a government-directed process for which civil society needs to be trained to participate. In an interview, the manager of the nascent housing council from COHAB told me that they created the council "to manage the housing fund in order to comply with the law."[18] To them the council's role is not to formulate policy or regulate programs, but simply to provide input into the distribution of the municipal housing fund to meet the minimal federal requirement.

Recife: The secretary for housing speculated that the make-up of programs and policies probably would not change as a result of the council, but that the interaction of council members and their involvement in projects would be beneficial to the implementation of existing programs. The municipal government agreed to carry out the process, but did not expect many changes as a result. In Recife, the PT government in power recognized the importance of participatory governance institutions as part of the party's ideological platform, but given the reality of a fragmented and sometimes radical civil society for housing in the city, government officials were not sure how the process would work there.

Dividing the cases by impetus for council creation, from these interviews I find that government officials in São Paulo, Santo André, and Salvador do foresee a stronger role for civil society in holding the government accountable for meeting resident's needs than in Curitiba and Recife. In Curitiba, in particular, the municipal government did not appear to welcome the direction of policy making by civil society. In Recife, as well, though the government respected the input of civil society, officials did not foresee any shifts in policy making as a result of their participation.

Though the words of government officials are important, government commitment to the participatory process may also come out in the institutional rules of the councils and resource contributions for council control. To establish whether there are any clear patterns in the institutional rules of the councils and prioritization of spending depending on creation, I assess municipal-level data from the MUNIC survey, separating municipalities with councils established prior to 2005 from those with councils created after 2005. The main variables of interest for this analysis are council responsibilities, whether the councils met during the year, and the source of funding for housing programs.

COUNCIL RESPONSIBILITIES

As reported in Chapter 5, in 2008 the MUNIC survey asked questions about whether the municipal housing council was consultative, deliberative, or normative, or provided oversight, indicating the extent to which the council actually has power over housing planning decisions. Compared to councils created before 2005, I expect that councils created in response to the federal mandate would be more likely to have consultative powers, but less likely to have the other three types of decision-making responsibilities. In fact, this turns out not to be the case. Table 6.3 shows that though councils created after 2005 are more likely to have consultative responsibilities, they are just as likely or more likely to also have deliberative, normative, and oversight responsibilities. The commitment of government officials, or lack thereof, is not reflected in the responsibilities assigned to councils as I expected.

Table 6.3   Responsibilities of Councils as Stated in Law or Decree

	Where Councils Existed before 2005 (prior to mandate)	Where Councils Began after 2005 (post-mandate)
Consultative	47%	51%
Deliberative	78%	78%
Normative	29%	35%
Oversight	42%	46%

MEETINGS

Whether or not municipal councils meet during the year provides another clue as to whether governments are making the councils a priority. Here there is a big difference between councils created before and after 2005. Only 50% of councils created after 2005 met in the year 2007–2008, while 71% of councils created prior to 2005 met during the same time period. This indicates that there is a significant number of councils created in response to the federal mandate that may simply exist on paper without ever holding a meeting. The reason behind creation does appear to matter for whether councils meet.

FUNDING SOURCES

The source of funding for housing programs is critical for understanding two variables: (1) the control the council has over resources and (2) whether municipalities with councils are actually more likely to contribute to housing programs using their own funds rather than relying on the federal government. Both of these variables reflect the government's commitment to the housing councils as institutions for decision making in allocating resources. For instance, in many municipalities the official fund for housing may be empty, leaving the housing council without any resources to control. The MUNIC survey asked whether the municipal housing fund actually funded programs.

Though councils established across time are almost equally likely to have a municipal housing fund, there is a significant difference in whether the fund actually funded projects. Table 6.4 shows that in municipalities with councils created after 2005, the municipal fund for housing only financed projects in 35% of cases. For councils created before 2005, the fund financed projects in 45% of municipalities. Though the number is perhaps surprisingly low across cases and reflects a lack of commitment to the process among a large portion of municipalities, the fact that councils created in response to the mandate are even less likely to allocate funds to the housing fund suggests that the motivation for creation does have a depressing effect on municipal government commitment.

Table 6.4 Project Funding

	Where Councils Were Created before 2005	Where Councils Were Created after 2005
Housing Fund Exists	0.79	0.78
Housing Fund Funded Projects	0.45	0.35
All Funds in the Fund	0.50	0.55

Unfortunately the survey does not provide data on what portion of the municipal fund for housing comes from municipal resources versus federal transfers. However, the survey does ask about the source of funding for programs within the municipality, regardless of whether the council controls them. If councils do encourage municipalities to take greater responsibility for housing needs, I would expect that municipalities with councils created before 2005 would be more likely to allocate municipal resources to housing needs than municipalities with councils created after 2005. Table 6.5 provides the percentage of programs funded either in partnership with the federal government or solely by the municipal government, split by council cohort. The data show that municipalities with councils created after 2005 are less likely to use municipal resources for programs to construct new units, provide regularization of land titles, improve units, and urbanize favelas.

In sum, municipal government commitment to the housing councils does appear to vary according to the reason for creation, though not uniformly across variables. Table 6.6 provides a summary of the findings related to government commitment.

In interviews, government officials in São Paulo, Santo André, and Salvador did indicate they expected civil society to use the councils to hold the government accountable for addressing housing needs. These perceptions by government officials coincide with several of the variables used here to measure commitment. Though the time of creation is not associated with the responsibilities afforded to the council, creation does matter for whether the council met and whether the fund for housing actually funded programs. In addition, councils created from the bottom-up appear to elicit resources more often from municipal governments than councils created from the top-down. This may indicate that these governments are more likely to use the housing councils to hear civil society demands and respond by increasing municipal resources. By these measures, then, municipal councils mandated by the federal level appear not to have the same level of support, particularly in terms of resources, as those councils created at the demand of civil society or by ideologically driven mayors. This evidence suggests that the reason behind creation matters for whether housing councils have control over decision making and for whether municipal governments increase their support for housing programs.

Table 6.5 Source of Funding for Municipal-Level Housing Programs

	Where Councils Existed before 2005 (prior to mandate)			Where Councils Began after 2005 (post-mandate)		
Type of Program	Number of Observations	In Partnership with the Federal Government	Solely Muni Government Resources	Number of Observations	In Partnership with the Federal Government	Solely Muni Government Resources
Construction	563	75%	31%	689	71%	22%
Offer Materials	339	12%	85%	410	12%	85%
Offer Land	229	9%	90%	278	12%	86%
Regularization	247	30%	73%	298	29%	62%
Acquire Units	146	73%	27%	204	68%	28%
Improve Units	467	35%	63%	518	39%	56%
Urbanization	172	63%	51%	195	63%	48%

Table 6.6 Summary of Variation in Municipal Government Commitment

Government officials' perceptions of the role of the housing council	Where councils were created from the bottom up, officials report a stronger role for civil society and a greater expectation that the council should hold the government accountable.
Responsibilities	Do not vary according to council creation.
Meetings	Bottom-up councils were more likely to actually hold meetings.
Council-controlled fund that funded projects	Bottom-up councils more likely to control a fund that funded projects.
Municipally funded programs	Bottom-up councils more likely to have several types of municipally funded programs.

CIVIL SOCIETY COMMITMENT TO PARTICIPATORY GOVERNANCE INSTITUTIONS

Where housing councils were created from the bottom-up, do CSOs display a greater commitment to the participatory process and determination in demanding accountability of the government through the councils?

In each of the case studies the majority of CSOs were pleased that municipal housing councils had been created in their cities and pledged varying levels of participation. However, while the level of commitment of CSOs is difficult to measure, I do find a difference in how CSOs say they will use the housing councils to negotiate for housing interventions and in their drive to ensure government officials uphold the participatory process. In São Paulo and Santo André, CSOs reported that they brought concerns and requests for assistance to the housing councils. In Salvador, CSOs recognized the importance of using the council to access federal funding, though they did not expect it to automatically generate municipal resource commitment. In Curitiba and Recife, CSOs appeared more hesitant toward their role in ensuring that the councils would be used as mechanisms for responsiveness and accountability. Since the creation of the institutions was a foregone conclusion, CSOs hoped for their effectiveness. But not having fought for their creation, CSOs did not appear to have real strategies in mind for how they would advance their agendas within the councils.

São Paulo—Strong civil society commitment to ensuring responsiveness and accountability through the housing council

Social movements in São Paulo view the creation of the housing council as a significant achievement. While they still have criticisms about the process and the amount of resources they have control over, they participate in the council with intense energy. In interviews, several movement leaders commented that one important victory had been to bring more attention to the needs of residents in the city center. Housing policy in the city traditionally focused on the periphery as the location for large public housing units, but advocates have fought hard to legitimize the idea of low-income housing in the city's economically vibrant center. Though social movements worry that they should not abandon all direct action in favor of participation in the council, they recognize the benefits of collaboration, including participating as a voting block in the council. Professional NGOs in São Paulo have also been instrumental in providing capacity building to movement leaders, increasing their confidence in challenging government and business interests in the council. CSOs use the housing council to negotiate changes in existing programs, the location of future programs, and the allocation of municipal resources.

Santo André—Strong civil society commitment to using the housing council for project assistance

The housing council in Santo André was created mainly at the direction of PT mayor Celso Daniel. Housing associations and local union leaders participate in the council and report that although the participatory process could always be improved, they view the council as a crucial mechanism to access financial, technical, and legal assistance. Close ties between civil society and administration officials in Santo André facilitated the smooth functioning of the housing council. CSOs appeared relatively content with the process and were not inclined to participate in direct action as a means to reaching municipal officials.

Salvador—Pragmatic civil society commitment where government does not provide dedicated resources for housing council control

Civil society in Salvador appears pragmatic in its commitment to the participatory process. As I reported in the previous chapter, though she resigned shortly thereafter, a PT-affiliated housing secretary created the housing council in Salvador as a response to the federal mandate and based on her own ideological convictions. The former secretary was committed to the process and to involving civil society in setting up the institution, but CSO leaders knew that the mayoral administration and the subsequent secretary for housing were not genuinely interested in participatory governance. With the institution in place, however, CSOs recognize the practical opportunity to use the council to coordinate project proposals to send to the federal level. Leaders commented that the council could be a space for demanding transparency and accountability from the municipal government if civil society maintained constant pressure, but under the current government in the short term, CSOs were focused on using the council to access federal-level resources. Protests, land occupations, and bilateral meetings were still a large component of CSO strategies for negotiating with municipal officials.

For example, during my visit the MTST led a protest to the housing secretariat in the city center to demand that the municipal government contribute funds to build new public housing units. The mixed motivations behind creation of the housing council in Salvador seems to have opened the door for participation of civil society in a formal, public space, but without the continued commitment of the municipal administration, the council is more a conduit for federal funding than a mechanism to elicit municipal responsiveness and accountability. Civil society is committed to participating in the council but continues to use other means to access municipal officials.

Curitiba—Divided civil society exhibiting mixed commitment to challenging the government's technocratic approach to governance

Many CSOs in Curitiba appeared largely ambivalent regarding the creation of the new municipal council for housing. In Curitiba there is a strong divide between those CSOs allied with the conservative-leaning administration and those opposed to the administration. Among those CSOs opposed to the administration, leaders told me they welcomed the introduction of all participatory governance institutions, but that the real power remained with the government and private sector in the city. As such, they hoped to use the council as a space to change policies, but in reality they felt the need to retain other strategies, including occupations. The problem with the housing council and other participatory institutions in Curitiba, according to a leader from local NGO Terra dos Direitos, is that the government allows for consultation with civil society without providing any institutional mechanisms for accountability. Though the housing council had not begun functioning, the existing Council for the City was not deliberative and did not allow for voting on issues by members. On the other side, leaders of housing associations allied with the administration expressed their commitment to the council process and stated they would participate alongside government officials. Given their close collaboration with the government, these CSOs are unlikely to challenge current municipal policy.

The inability of opposing CSOs to work together in Curitiba will most likely reduce the likelihood that they present a united front in the council. In addition, even if the housing council encourages both sides of civil society to debate, without institutional mechanisms for accountability, the council may not change the distribution of resources or reorient the government's current technocratic model of governance. In creating the council as a response to the federal mandate, the municipal government was not required to provide voting power to members. CSOs across sides want a space for discussion, but without real power to allocate resources or present policy reforms, unaligned CSOs, in particular, may reduce their commitment to the institution and rely on current occupation strategies instead. Never having formed a united front to demand the housing council, CSOs related to housing are unlikely to come together in the council to make demands for responsiveness and accountability. The council, then, may become a rubber stamp for government proposals.

Recife—Skeptical civil society with some commitment to participate

Civil society in Recife appeared to maintain a fairly pessimistic view of the newly created housing council, which may limit their commitment to the council and their enthusiasm for holding the government accountable for implementing the participatory process. In interviews, CSOs expressed their skepticism regarding both the position of the housing council outside of the Council for the City and the likelihood that the housing council would have any real effect on the housing situation. According to a leader from the MTST in Recife, participatory councils in general "have the capacity to make decisions, but mostly evaluate and propose policies without anything ever reaching the ground."[19] The MTST also disagreed with the setup of the housing council outside of the Council for the City because they were concerned about de-linking housing from other urban issues. Despite this skepticism, the MTST pledged to participate in the housing council, much to the relief of government officials who acknowledged that for the process to work they needed the support of the MTST as the most influential movement in Recife. Many of the other movements stated that they were pleased with their relationship with the secretary of housing and were able to secure meetings with her as needed. The housing council would perhaps save them time in arranging bilateral meetings and would be an open forum to debate policy issues. An advocate from the NGO FASE argued, "Through the council civil society can reach the administration to define goals, allocate resources, and define priorities."[20] In sum, the majority of CSO leaders were interested in the transparency the council would provide and pledged to participate, though several leaders remained dubious that the housing council would improve outcomes for residents in the city. Rather than actively demanding the implementation of the council, many CSO leaders appeared to take a "wait and see" approach.

Across cities, the commitment of civil society does appear to vary based on the motivation behind the creation of municipal housing councils. Civil society in the three case study cities where councils were created in response to CSO demands and ideologically motivated officials seem to be more united in their commitment to holding the government accountable for the implementation of the participatory process and to resident's housing needs. In Curitiba and Recife, divided civil society and skepticism about the ability of the housing council to change policy may limit the effectiveness of the councils in the future.

PROBABILITY OF PROGRAM ADOPTION

Are pro-poor policy outcomes more likely where councils are created in response to bottom-up versus top-down pressures?

Based on the case studies, I find that in municipalities where the housing councils were created in response to top-down pressures, both government officials and civil society leaders appear less committed to making the participatory process work. This leads me to look across contexts to assess whether issues of commitment to participatory governance based on the motivation for council creation affect housing program adoption. Does low government and civil society commitment to municipal councils translate into fewer housing programs within municipalities?

Using the statistical model developed in Chapter 3, I evaluate whether the motivation behind the creation of participatory governance institutions influences policy outcomes.[21] The dependent variables include all types of housing programs: construction of new units, provision of construction material, provision of land, regularization of tenure status, acquisition of housing units, improvement of units, and urbanization programs. In the statistical analysis in Chapter 3, the key independent variable of interest reported the existence of a municipal council for housing in each of Brazil's 5,564 municipalities. Control variables account for the effects of population size, population density, the municipal budget, the party of the mayor, inequality, income, civil society density, and the presence of favelas. Through this analysis I found that the existence of a municipal housing council matters for the adoption of housing programs. Subsequent analyses then found that neither the density of civil society nor the presence of a PT mayor changed the probability of municipalities with housing councils adopting programs, though the responsibility to oversee budgetary matters did make a difference.

Through this analysis I now seek to evaluate whether the reason behind creation alters the likelihood of program adoption. To compare the effects of creation on housing program adoption in 2008, I create two new variables: "council both years" and "2008 council only." For "council both years," 0 = never had a council and 1 = reported having a council in both 2005 and 2008. For "2008 council only," 0 = never had a council and 1 = reported having a council in 2008 only. I hypothesize that regardless of time of creation, municipalities with housing councils are more likely than municipalities without housing councils to adopt all types of programs. Therefore, both variables should be significantly related to each type of housing program. In municipalities with housing councils created prior to 2005, however, housing councils should have the greatest effect on program adoption due to stronger municipal government and civil society commitment. Both government officials and civil society are likely to be more committed to the participatory process in these municipalities, leading to greater responsiveness and accountability of the government to address housing needs.

FINDINGS

Based on probit analysis, Table 6.7 demonstrates that regardless of when they were created, municipal housing councils are significantly associated with the adoption of all types of housing programs.[22] The exceptions to this are programs to offer plots of land and urbanization programs in municipalities with councils created after 2005. Based on this it appears that councils created in response to the mandate may have a smaller impact than those created before 2005, but the difference in impact cannot be directly interpreted from these results.

To gauge the substantive effect, I use the CLARIFY program to simulate the probability of program adoption. Using the same probit models as in Table 6.7, CLARIFY calculates the predicted values for program adoption. Setting all other independent variables to their means, I test the probability of program adoption where housing councils never existed, where they were created between 2005 and 2008, and where they existed prior to 2005. Table 6.8 illustrates the predicted probabilities of program adoption across program type and existence of housing council. With notable exceptions, the numbers demonstrate the increasing likelihood of program adoption, moving from the probability of program adoption where no council existed, to the probability where councils were created after 2005, and then to the probability where councils were created prior to 2005. The exceptions to this finding are programs for regularization and to acquire units, where the associations are not significantly different. In Table 6.9, I then use the predicted probabilities to calculate the differences according to council creation. The center column demonstrates the substantive differences in likelihood of program adoption between municipalities where councils were created before and after 2005. Except for regularization programs and programs to acquire units, the time of creation appears to alter the extent to which housing councils influence program adoption.

DISCUSSION

The statistical results provide support for the hypothesis that participatory governance institutions created in response to bottom-up pressures produce stronger pro-poor outcomes than those created in response to top-down mandates. Compared to municipalities without housing councils, the probability for adoption of almost all the different types of housing programs is twice as high where a council existed since at least 2005. These findings do come with an important caveat: the length of housing council operation may also account for the increased likelihood of program adoption. Unfortunately, the survey does not specify in which year the councils were created. Therefore, I can only use the survey responses in two years, 2005 and 2008, as cutoff points. Councils reported by officials to exist in 2005 could have been created in 2005 or several years prior. The same is true for councils reported by officials to exist in 2008. I cannot distinguish whether the council was created in 2008 or in the years between 2005 and 2008. The length of time in operation would logically seem to influence whether the housing councils had a chance to begin functioning and subsequently influence policy outcomes. Given data limitations, however, I

Table 6.7 The Effect of Housing Councils Created before and after 2005 on Housing Programs

	Construction of Units	Offer Materials	Offer Land	Regularization	Acquire Units	Improve Units	Urbanization
Council Both Years	0.43***	0.18**	0.27***	0.21**	0.15*	0.39***	0.30***
	(0.09)	(0.08)	(0.09)	(0.09)	(0.09)	(0.08)	(0.1)
Council in 2008 Only	0.21***	0.12*	0.1	0.25***	0.16**	0.23***	0.12
	(0.07)	(0.07)	(0.07)	(0.08)	(0.08)	(0.07)	(0.09)
Municipal Housing Fund	0.25***	0.09	0.19***	0.14**	0.09	0.04	0.16**
	(0.06)	(0.06)	(0.07)	(0.07)	(0.07)	(0.06)	(0.08)
Population, 2005 (log)	0.19***	0.07**	0.09***	0.36***	0.13***	0.06*	0.42***
	(0.04)	(0.03)	(0.03)	(0.04)	(0.04)	(0.03)	(0.04)
Percent Urban Population (log)	0.14**	0.19***	0.26***	0.03	0.03	0.18***	0.02
	(0.06)	(0.06)	(0.06)	(0.07)	(0.07)	(0.06)	(0.08)
Muni Budget per Capita (log)	0.49***	0.37***	0.27***	0.34***	0.18**	0.18**	0.45***
	(0.08)	(0.07)	(0.08)	(0.08)	(0.08)	(0.07)	(0.09)
PT Mayor	0.05	0.1	-0.1	0.25***	0.07	0.11	0.05
	(0.08)	(0.08)	(0.09)	(0.09)	(0.09)	(0.08)	(0.10)
Gini Coefficient	1.22***	1.27***	0.00	-0.03	0.24	1.97***	0.99*
	(0.42)	(0.42)	(0.45)	(0.48)	(0.49)	(0.41)	(0.53)
Income per Capita (log)	0.08	-0.16**	0.04	0.17*	0.1	-0.11	0.04
	(0.09)	(0.08)	(0.09)	(0.10)	(0.10)	(0.08)	(0.11)
Civil Society Density (log)	-0.04	-0.07*	0.03	-0.09**	-0.01	0.13***	-0.11**
	(0.04)	(0.04)	(0.04)	(0.04)	(0.04)	(0.04)	(0.05)
Favelas	0.00	-0.06	0.00	0.30***	0.06	-0.04	0.38***
	(0.05)	(0.05)	(0.05)	(0.06)	(0.06)	(0.05)	(0.06)
Constant	-6.40***	-4.34***	-4.01***	-8.29***	-4.33***	-1.99***	-10.25***
	(0.83)	(0.78)	(0.82)	(0.88)	(0.87)	(0.76)	(0.98)
Observations	4,093	4,080	4,093	4,093	4,093	4,083	4,083

Standard errors in parentheses. *** $p < 0.01$, ** $p < 0.05$, * $p < 0.1$.
Model includes state dummies.

Table 6.8   Probability of Program Adoption Based on Time of Council Creation

	No Council	Council Created after 2005	Council Created before 2005
Construction	0.61	0.69	0.76
Offer Materials	0.35	0.39	0.41
Offer Plots of Land	0.21	0.25	0.30
Regularization	0.17	0.24	0.24
Acquire Units	0.14	0.18	0.18
Improve Units	0.44	0.53	0.59
Urbanization	0.09	0.12	0.16

Table 6.9   Difference in Probability of Program Adoption Based on Time of Council Creation

	From No Council to Council Created after 2005	From Council Created after 2005 to Council Created before 2005	From No Council to Council Created before 2005
Construction Materials	0.06	0.07	0.15
Offer Materials	0.04	0.02	0.06
Offer Plots of Land	0.04	0.05	0.09
Regularization	0.07	0	0.07
Acquire Units	0.04	0	0.04
Improve Units	0.09	0.06	0.15
Urbanization	0.03	0.04	0.07

am not able to control for the length of operation, which may in fact bias my findings.

Keeping this caveat in mind, I still draw several conclusions based on the available data and results. First, where councils were created prior to 2005 and the announcement of the federal mandate, it appears that government officials and civil society do maintain commitment to the participatory process over time. The housing councils still have an effect on policy outcomes at least three years after they were created. This provides evidence to confirm that these councils do not just exist on paper, but are having some effect on adoption of programs to benefit the poor. The case studies also confirm this finding that councils continue to have an effect over time. For instance, though leadership changed in São Paulo, the housing council continued to meet regularly and engage in intense debates. Though policies and programs changed over time, as discussed in Chapter 7, the council remained an important space for deliberation and program implementation.

Second, councils created after the announcement of the mandate also have an effect on policy outcomes. Though the effect is not as large as in municipalities where councils existed prior to the mandate, the results provide evidence that there is a positive relationship between housing councils created after 2005 and the likelihood of program adoption. Councils created in response to top-down pressures are not merely institutions on paper set up to receive federal funds. The effect, however, is clearly smaller than where housing councils existed prior to the federal mandate. The case studies provide evidence that the municipal housing councils formed in response to the federal mandate may not garner the same level of commitment from government officials or CSOs. This commitment gap may explain some of the variance in the effect of councils created before and after the mandate. Whether the gap increases or decreases over time may depend on whether the councils generate acceptable results for both government and civil society.

Third, though the effect of the councils is not uniform across program type, the probability of program adoption where councils were created prior to the mandate is generally higher than the probability where councils were created after the mandate. Stronger commitment to the participatory process by government officials and civil society, who were likely involved in the creation of the housing councils, does appear to significantly alter the relationship between the councils and adoption of social housing programs. Given that the results indicate that commitment is a critical variable in participatory governance institutions, imposition of rules from central governments should be viewed cautiously.

CONCLUSIONS

This analysis provided evidence to confirm the claim that the manner in which participatory governance institutions are created makes a difference for how they function and the outcomes they produce. Case study interviews first demonstrated differences in how government officials view the role of the housing councils and civil society's role in policy making. In São Paulo and Santo André where PT governments clearly created municipal housing councils in response to civil society demands and in line with the administration's ideology, the institutions are viewed as spaces for negotiation and deliberation by civil society on programmatic decisions. In contrast, government officials in Curitiba and Recife did not appear to take the councils as seriously as a means for civil society to directly influence policy. Survey data across cases also reveals a lack of commitment by municipal governments to holding meetings and dedicating resources. The reason behind creation of municipal housing councils does matter for how governments both perceive the council's role and respond with time and money.

Though civil society in all the case study cities demonstrated an interest in participating in the housing councils, subtle differences in the attitude of CSOs toward the councils exist. In São Paulo and Santo André, CSOs work collaboratively to solicit benefits through the housing councils, though of course they still argue the process could be improved. In Salvador, CSOs work together to make proposals and to demand that the government take the council seriously. In Curitiba and Recife, however, a lack of cohesion among CSOs may limit the effectiveness of the housing councils. Without significant investment in the process from the beginning, CSOs may not come together to use the councils for making collective demands. The mode of creation does appear to affect the manner in which civil society engages with the participatory process.

Statistical analysis then provides evidence that the variation in commitment of government and civil society actors matters for the influence of municipal housing councils. Councils created prior to the mandate are more strongly related to program adoption than councils created after the announcement of the mandate. Bottom-up councils are more likely to generate pro-poor policy outcomes than top-down councils, though top-down councils also have some effect.

In the end, the findings in this chapter have implications for governments seeking to address social problems through increasing participation in policy making. While participatory governance institutions legislated by the federal government may have some effect on increasing pro-poor policy adoption, the commitment of local government officials and civil society members cannot be ignored. Both officials and CSOs must have incentives to cooperate. Government officials need to take the deliberative role of civil society seriously and respond by providing institutional support and resources. Civil society also needs to view the councils as a worthwhile use of their time where their demands will be heard. Local participation can be legislated from above, but the results may not be the same across contexts.

7 Longevity in Participatory Governance Institutions São Paulo's Municipal Housing Council at 10

> The councils are worth having because they force both sides to dialogue. The state has to consult civil society about the course of policies, though they are insufficient as spaces to decide all questions.
>
> —Government official in São Paulo, Brazil[1]

In the previous chapter I find that the commitment of civil society and government officials is important for determining how participatory governance institutions function and the outcomes they produce. Not only does commitment shape the policy process, but it also has an effect on the distribution of resources and the direction of social housing programs. This finding leads me to question how commitment shapes participatory governance institutions in the long term. Does commitment change over time, and if so, what are the factors that lead to these shifts? And, further, how do shifts in commitment change the potential for longevity and impact of participatory governance institutions?

Given the relative newness of participatory governance in Brazil, previous literature on participatory governance institutions in the country does not generally address questions of longevity. As these institutions age, however, we should be concerned about whether participatory governance will stand the test of time. As the initial enthusiasm for participation wears off, CSOs (civil society organizations) and government officials may come to see the process of deliberation as cumbersome. CSOs may revert to bilateral negotiations or protest as a means of securing benefits and policy change, and government officials may limit the power of the institution as a space for policy making and program implementation. Conversely, both sides may see increasing benefits to participatory governance if CSO demands are increasingly met and the administration sees results in terms of popularity and efficiency in policy making. Both sides are likely to continue their commitment to participatory governance if they feel the needs of the population are being well served by investing in the institution.

Though the federal system mandates the creation of a municipal housing council and fund to manage federal resources, municipal governments may still decide whether they want to participate in the federal system and receive federal funding. Since the implementation of housing policy is left to the discretion of municipal governments in Brazil, the continuation of municipal housing councils is subject to the will of each new municipal administration. In a report led by Brazilian scholar Marta Arretche on the operation of government institutions supporting housing policy across Brazil, a team of researchers found that approximately 6% of municipal housing councils ceased to exist when a new municipal administration came to power.[2] The researchers found that municipal housing councils in the Northeast and Center-West of the country were somewhat more likely to "die" than those in the South, Southeast, and Northern regions of the country. Beyond this statistical association, however, the research team did not attempt to uncover why region matters to institutional longevity. It appears that even with the federal rules in place, the decision to operate a municipal housing council is still subject to local political will. Failure to operate a housing council should result in a loss of federal transfers.

Municipal housing councils, though, may still be more popular with local mayors than other types of institutions. Compared to housing agencies, researchers found that municipal housing councils were much more likely to remain in place under a new administration. Arretche et al. write, "The data could indicate that, once created, the councils give rise to social actors that fight for their preservation, while the costs of closing other housing policy institutions are lower."[3] Participatory governance institutions are different from other government agencies in that civil society becomes invested in the process, and if they foresee future returns on this investment, they are likely to fight for the preservation of that investment. Other types of government agencies without direct citizen participation are not subject to the same level of involvement and may more easily close their doors without protest. While the study conducted by Arretche et al. provides an important evaluation of the current housing institutions in Brazil, it leaves many unanswered questions regarding the reasons behind the longevity of participatory governance institutions and their relationship to the broader institutional environment. The research hints at the importance of location and the administration in power to the continuation of municipal housing councils, but does not systematically assess how participatory governance institutions change over time or the factors that lead to their longevity. Though the researchers speculate that commitment of social actors is important to longevity in participatory institutions, they do not thoroughly investigate this proposition.

Arretche et al.'s study on the continuance of municipal housing councils, though, does correspond to previous studies that find commitment from the administration in power is key to the effectiveness of participatory governance institutions.[4] I argue that continued commitment also relies on how actors view the effectiveness of the institution. Presumably, commitment of the administration should play an important role in explaining the longevity of these institutions. But as I described in the last chapter, civil society commitment may be equally important in ensuring these institutions are used as effective spaces for policy formation. The relationship between government actors and civil society changes over time, across administrations, and through the inevitable highs and lows of housing program implementation. The question, then, is that given inevitable shifts in policy makers and their relationship to civil society, what can we realistically expect for the effectiveness of participatory governance institutions over time?

Clearly we have seen the longevity of some participatory institutions, such as the New England town meetings, even as we have witnessed the demise of other attempts to engage citizens in planning and budgeting exercises.[5] I argue that the commitment of civil society to the participatory process prolongs the life of these institutions, though a number of factors, including the ideology of the administration in power, federal transfers, the role of the private sector, and changing needs, also determine shifts in actors, agendas, and outcomes.

In this chapter I review the case of the Municipal Council for Housing (Conselho Municipal de Habitação [CMH]) in São Paulo. The combative nature of the CMH in São Paulo may make it exceptional as a case study, but given the level of conflict within the council it also serves as an example of how participatory institutions weather the worst of storms. Given the scale of housing needs in the city, São Paulo is also somewhat unique in that it does not have a choice of whether or not to receive federal funds.[6] The housing council in São Paulo, though, began operating in 2002, as a result of civil society pressure and the ideological support of a PT (Worker's Party) administration, many years before the federal mandate went into effect. As such, in the summer of 2012, I returned to the city to meet with civil society, private sector, and government leaders to assess how the council has changed over the course of its 10-year existence. This chapter draws on my interviews with relevant actors as well as documents from the council and news reports. In 2011–2012, civil society leaders challenged the legality of council elections, leading to a disruption in the council's activities and a debate over the legitimacy of the institution. Given news of this conflict, before embarking on this portion of the study I was pessimistic that commitment to the process would remain strong among civil society leaders and government officials. On the ground, however, I observed a tired, but persistent, effort by civil society leaders to press the government to comply with what they perceived as the role of the state to promote broad participation and transparency in the elections. I found that while *social movements* maintained their commitment to the participatory process, the current administration and many other civil society actors largely did not. The following analysis describes the role of all sides and the factors shaping the agenda and policy outcomes.

In this chapter I first review changes in the agenda and actors in the CMH over the course of 10 years. I present the details of the CMH in conflict regarding the 2011–2012 elections as an example of how participatory institutions withstand crisis. I then review a number of factors that led to shifts in the CMH and conclude with a discussion of how these factors have shaped commitment over time. In the end, I argue that the longevity of participatory governance institutions relies on commitment of all actors to the process but also a realistic expectation that the process will not be smooth over time and will require significant investments in time and patience as well as a recognition of the incentives needed to keep all actors engaged.

TEN YEARS IN THE MAKING: THE MUNICIPAL COUNCIL FOR HOUSING IN SÃO PAULO

São Paulo represents a case where civil society fought hard for the creation of the housing council and was highly energized to participate from the beginning. As mentioned in Chapter 5, the initial idea for a housing council in São Paulo surfaced in the late 1980s under the administration of Luiza Erundina from the PT. At the time, however, more conservative forces controlled the city's legislature, and the idea to create the council stalled. Under the leadership of PT mayor Marta Suplicy (2000–2004), the idea again gained political force and this time the PT also controlled the city's legislature. The law to create the council passed the legislature in 2002, establishing the CMH under the direction of the secretariat for housing. According to the regulations accompanying the law to create the council, "The Municipal Council for Housing has deliberative, oversight and consultative powers with the basic objectives of establishing, monitoring, controlling and evaluating municipal housing policy."[7]

Unlike many housing councils, which have equal representation from government and civil society, the CMH in São Paulo has a tripartite division of members in which one-third come from the municipal and state governments, one-third come from civil society, and one-third are elected from social movements. The CMH has 48 regular members, 16 from government, 16 from civil society, and 16 from social movements. For each of these seats, there is also an alternate representative, meaning that the total membership of the CMH is close to 100 people.

THE ACTORS

Depending on to whom you pose the question, the membership of the council has either remained stagnant or varied tremendously over time. In terms of government representation, members of the council certainly change with each new administration. Since the creation of the housing council, three separate administrations have directed the city. Following the Suplicy administration, José Serra (PSDB [Partido da Social Democracia Brasileira]) was elected mayor, but only served for a brief time before resigning to run for governor of São Paulo state. Serra's deputy mayor, Gilberto Kassab (PSD [Partido Social Democrático]), took over the administration and was then elected on his own as mayor in 2008.[8] The term for all council members is two years and the head of the council is always the secretary for housing. Under the Suplicy government, the secretary for housing was Paulo Teixeira, a long-standing member of the PT. The secretary for housing under Kassab, Ricardo Pereira Leite, worked primarily in the civil construction sector before joining the government.

As a rule, the secretary for housing always has the "vota minerva," or final vote, on all matters. Though in practice this vote is seldom exercised, members say they are more likely to compromise with the government on council decisions because they know the secretary really has the final say. The orientation of the secretary for housing should then matter for the direction of the CMH. The orientation of the superintendent for social housing, who directly manages the CMH, also changed significantly under each administration. Under Suplicy, Superintendent Gisela Mori, with a background in social service and strongly affiliated with the PT, was well-known among the city's social movements. The superintendent under Kassab, Elisabete França, is an architect and urban planner who takes an academic approach to redesigning the slums.

According to social movements, changes in the council's membership have been dramatic. Under Suplicy, the majority of members from social movements supported the PT. For example, the União dos Movimentos da Moradia, which has always been linked to the PT, held six seats on the council. Two members from the Central dos Movimentos Populares, also aligned with the PT, held official liaison positions between the movements and the government. Under the Serra government, the position of liaison was eliminated. The movements that served under the Suplicy administration from 2003 to 2005 charged that the Serra administration conspired to elect movements allied with their own party for the 2005–2007 term. In 2007, therefore, the PT-allied movements launched a strong campaign to win their seats back and again largely controlled the council from 2007 to 2009. In the elections for social movement members in 2009, the PT-oriented movements once again lost a number of seats in an election many NGOs (nongovernmental organizations) and movements claimed was unfairly controlled by the Kassab administration. According to government officials, however, though the individual members have changed over time, their organizational representation has not changed much nor have individual movements been privileged over others.

Finally, membership from civil society has not drastically changed, but their numbers have dwindled over the course of 10 years.[9] With 16 seats, civil society members, who come from universities, labor unions, private sector associations, policy-related NGOs, and social and legal services NGOs, are selected in an open meeting. In the first term, all 16 seats were occupied. By the 2009–2011 term, however, 6 seats remained empty. Union leaders, for whom several seats are reserved, have never strongly participated in the council. In the current selection for the 2011–2013 term, 8 seats are currently unoccupied, including those for the unions, universities, and a social service NGO. Representatives from these organizations failed to register in time for the elections, either for lack of interest or for lack of information regarding the timing of the process.

Many of the actors in the CMH change as a result of turnover in the municipal administration. What is important to note is the variation in social movement membership based on alliances with political parties and the waning interest of CSOs over time. In the following analysis I seek to understand how these changes are shaped by various factors outside of administrative turnover to create evolving relationships among actors.

THE AGENDA

The CMH has a long list of responsibilities, including approving the budget and allocating money for the Municipal Housing Fund; participating in the development of social housing plans and programs; defining the criteria by which housing needs are prioritized; and contributing to the plans for using funds from the federal and state levels as well as international donors. While social movements and other CSOs may disagree on the extent to which the CMH has successfully incorporated their voices into the policy-making process, all seem to agree that there have been substantial changes in the agenda over the course of the council's 10-year existence.

The nature of programs, budgets, and policies shifts over time, and the way in which members debate and negotiate items on the agenda has also changed. Due to the size of the council and the complex nature of many of the issues with which the council deals, actors I spoke with agreed that smaller working groups have become the primary site for negotiating rules and regulations. In reality, rather than engaging in larger policy debates, the CMH often decides the details of program implementation. For each responsibility assigned to the council, subtle and significant shifts to the agenda emerge over time.

Approving the Budget and Allocating Money from the Municipal Housing Fund

Throughout the CMH's existence, civil society and social movement members claim there has not been enough money in the Municipal Housing Fund to have a substantial impact on the extreme need for social housing in the city. Nonetheless, placing resource decisions in the hands of nongovernmental actors represented a significant departure from the past in which decisions were always made behind closed doors. Conflicts over how to spend the money that does exist in the fund have been constant in the CMH, and are exacerbated by the complexity of financing. In the first term of the CMH, Gisela Mori, then superintendent for social housing, stated that "controversial issues over funding had to be moved to smaller working groups because there were few people within the administration and outside of it who had a firm understanding of financial questions regarding the Fund for Housing."[10] With time there has been substantial learning among all actors, but particularly among those who have been there from the beginning.

The presence of a public-private entity set up to promote social housing in São Paulo, COHAB (Companhia Metropolitana de Habitação) intensifies the complexity of the financial issues for housing under debate in the CMH. While the secretariat for housing establishes housing policy and programs, COHAB works with the private sector to invest and finance social housing. In addition, COHAB manages public housing projects in the city and is responsible for collecting payments from residents. The fund for housing falls under COHAB's responsibility, and as such COHAB representatives are active in the budgeting process within the CMH.

According to current housing council members, in the beginning of the council's existence, the fund had less money than it does currently, but the money it did have represented a greater share of the overall housing budget. Under the Kassab administration, social movement and other civil society actors have complained that the government withholds all but a small portion of the housing budget for the council's control. According to a member of the council from SECOVI, the largest real estate association in the country, the government wants to keep control over social housing programs, and therefore the CMH does not have the force that it should.

Specifically, several budgetary issues have shaped the agenda throughout the council's existence. First, the issue of mutirões, cooperative self-build projects, has always been a point of strong contention. During the first term of the CMH, social movements pressed for funding for mutirão projects and many were built. Many of the social movements favor mutirões as community-building mechanisms in which residents contribute money and sweat equity during the building process. During the Serra and Kassab administrations, however, the council did not approve any new mutirão projects. Both government officials and the private sector associations represented on the council criticize the mutirões for the quality of the construction and high costs. The question now is what to do with the remaining unfinished projects: some have people living in them, some have been removed, and for some, the people who paid into these homes and helped to build them want to come back to finish construction. The job of the CMH is then to decide which projects to fund. On this issue, allocation of money from the Municipal Housing Fund has shifted from creating new projects to debating the criteria by which old projects should be completed or abandoned. Deciding these issues brings out tensions among social movements of various ideologies and the government officials and private sector representatives who do not see the value in these types of projects.

Other budgetary issues have to do with expropriation and the role of the municipality as landlord. In the beginning of the council's existence, the Locação Social program sought to build public housing units in the city's central areas. Today, however, many of these buildings have become run-down, and the council must decide what to do about the debts to COHAB resulting from nonpayment of residents and how much to invest in maintaining the buildings. Building new units from scratch, such as under the Locação Social program, in which the government manages the upkeep and payments in the buildings, creates conflict between government officials, who do not want the task of managing properties, and many social movement representatives, who demand more affordable housing units to address the large housing deficit.

From the start, social movements also demanded the expropriation and renovation of buildings in the city center rather than strictly new construction. For many years the debate centered on one building, São Vito, which had been abandoned and then occupied by the poor in search of shelter in the city's center. São Vito is often referred to as a "vertical favela" because of its enormous size and capacity to house a large number of families. In the end, the council agreed to the demolition of the building with the promise of assistance for the people living there and new affordable housing units in the center of the city. Today, the debate about the city center has expanded as more abandoned buildings are occupied by the poor. The CMH recently approved funds to expropriate 52 buildings in the city center, which should generate 5,000–10,000 units in partnership with the federally funded Minha Casa Minha Vida program and other state-funded programs.

Programs

Changes in programs over time can be seen in the preceding detail regarding budget decisions, but the CMH also has a say in the type of housing programs adopted and the regulations by which programs are implemented. In the beginning, according to Gisela Mori, many programs had already been created in partnership with social movements before the CMH was established. The council then played a role in discussing regulations to implement existing programs. For instance, the program to support mutirões had existed previously, but the council worked to renew and grow the program. The Locação Social program had already been in development for two years, but the CMH had to decide not only questions regarding funding, but also prioritization of who would receive the new units. In addition, under the Suplicy administration, the CMH developed a program to assist residents living in cortiços (tenements), which was a major achievement for social movements, demanding that the government take action against slum landlords.

During the Kassab administration, focus shifted away from social housing in the center of the city to urbanization of favelas.[11] Instead of removing and relocating residents, this administration invested in urbanization, involving upgrading infrastructure and keeping people where they are. In addition, a working group of the council has been assigned the task of regulating regularization of land titles to promote security of tenure. Recently, however, the administration has returned focus to the center with the promise to expropriate over 50 buildings to renovate units for social housing, as mentioned earlier. Social movements on the council and throughout the city argue that the progress to renovate these buildings has been extremely slow, and in the meantime residents occupying the buildings have been forced out without sufficient planning for where they will be relocated.

Current program priorities should be defined by the city's recently developed Plan for Social Housing. Under the national housing system (Sistema Nacional de Habitação de Interesse Social [SNHIS]), all municipalities receiving federal funds are supposed to develop a plan for housing in addition to creating a fund for housing and a municipal housing council. Developing a plan to meet the scale of São Paulo's needs and actors' demands seemed a tall feat. While many social movements deem the now agreed upon plan inadequate, government officials do claim that creating the plan generated substantial debate, which led to an increase in understanding and an exchange of information across parties. According to Ana Maria Maluf, staff for the CMH, participation in debates within the council led to substantial changes to the housing plan.

Prioritizing Housing Needs

Like many cities in Brazil, São Paulo has a registry of people who are in need of housing assistance. Within the council, however, the question of who should be attended to first frequently comes up for debate. For instance, movements often request priority assistance for residents occupying abandoned buildings (i.e., squatting). Generally these occupations are led and supported by one of the main housing movements. In addition, since many projects are funded through neighborhood associations, movements help associations to put together project proposals and then advocate for the priority of those particular neighborhood proposals. During the Suplicy administration, given the close ties between social movements and the government, and their inclination to support the demand for mutirão projects, project proposals by neighborhood associations often received priority over the formal registry. Government officials in the Kassab administration, however, formally state that priority should be given to those who have been waiting on the list the longest and to those living in areas of environmental risk.[12] During their administration officials have, in fact, worked to relocate people from informal settlements in the Guarapiranga region, where they were living on or near waterways. These types of projects have for the most part fallen outside of the council's control, perhaps due to the contentious debate over their prioritization.

Despite the Kassab administration's statement that the registry receive priority, special working groups for programs within the council still decide on the criteria for who should receive priority, indicating that the matter is still up for debate. For example, recently a special working group established criteria for who should have priority in benefiting from the Minha Casa Minha Vida program. According to government officials, the working group invited community members, academics, and NGOs to participate in the development of these criteria. In the end, neither the government nor social movements have complete control over the criteria for prioritization of beneficiaries. Government officials remove some special programs from the council's control when they want to design the criteria themselves. And, while social movements have some control through the council's working groups, they are still forced to negotiate with other civil society and government officials to define prioritization of benefit distribution.

Planning for the Use of Federal and State Funds

The federal government has invested increasing resources into housing since the early 2000s. In part the increase is in recognition of the enormous housing challenges facing Brazil and in part due to a growing national economy. Changes in the planning for the use of federal and state funds within the CMH are mainly a result of the increasing amounts of money available. Still, as noted previously, the amount of money allocated for approval by the CMH remains a critical issue. The secretary for housing decides which portion of state and federal transfers will go through the CMH. Social movement leaders charge that the current secretary provides very little money to be decided by the CMH, preferring to direct projects using federal and state funds without civil society input.

As an official from the state housing agency who has also served on the CMH noted, in 2003 there was a paradigm shift in resource allocation for housing. Before 2003 each unit of government had its own money, but since 2003 resources have been combined in order to strengthen programming. Municipal-level officials are still deciding how to distribute these resources in a way that enables them to preserve their own political agenda. The tension within the CMH is over whose hands should receive the money. As detailed previously, social movements affiliated with the PT still want money for mutirões, while the Kassab administration would prefer to invest in public-private partnerships and urbanization of favelas. Social movements want money from the federal level given directly to neighborhood associations for construction, while the current administration would like to direct the money through private construction companies producing for the low-income sector. Planning for the use of state and federal funds, therefore, follows the same line of debate as program implementation.

COUNCIL IN DISPUTE: 2011–2012 ELECTIONS

Though far from ideal, the CMH has become an important space for policy formulation and implementation as well as a means for promoting transparency and accountability in local governance. But in the latter part of 2011 into 2012, conflict over elections of council members brought the work of the council to a standstill. By the law that created the CMH, elections of social movement members are to be open to all citizens of the city who would like to vote.[13] In each successive election for members, an increasing number of citizens have participated. In 2003, approximately 31,000 residents voted, while by 2009, 47,000 people voted. Over 100,000 people registered to vote in the 2011–2012 elections.

In the fall of 2011, the Electoral Commission of the CMH met to define the rules and timeline for elections of members for a new two-year term (2011–2013). In the 2009 elections, the Electoral Commission decided by consensus that members would be elected by "chapa" (candidate list or ticket). Seats for each list were distributed according to the proportion of votes received. In the 2011 elections, however, the commission proposed a return to an "all or nothing" system in which only one candidate list would win seats on the council.

Social movements to the left charged that the administration was attempting to manipulate the elections in favor of their allies.[14] Two candidate lists registered for the 2011 election: "Habitação no Rumo Certo" (Housing on Track) and "Unidade na Luta" (United in the Struggle). The first were supporters of Mayor Kassab and his administration, and the latter were mainly social movements oriented toward the PT or other leftist parties. In the preceding election in 2009, movements to the left charged that the administration assisted the "Habitação no Rumo Certo" ticket by passing out its campaign materials in government offices, such as health clinics. They also alleged that the government changed polling places at the last minute, falsely told people who did arrive to vote that they had already voted, and failed to provide privacy for the voting machines.[15] When the government-allied ticket won the majority of seats in the 2009 election, movements to the left were resentful of a process they believed violated the principles of transparency on which the council is based.[16] After the government initiated the change to an "all or nothing" vote by candidate list, movements to the left again felt that the administration aimed to influence the election in their favor and ensure that only their allies were represented on the council.

In November 2011, a group of PT legislators from the Legislative Assembly for the State of São Paulo filed an action with the Ministério Público (Public Ministry) regarding the elections set to be held on December 4, 2011. The action called for judicial intervention in the elections to resolve several issues. First, the movements argued, the "all or nothing" voting by candidate list would effectively disenfranchise minorities from the participatory policy-making process. Second, the new rules stated that all voters must preregister for the election through the municipal government's website. Social movements argued that many citizens living in poor communities do not have access to the Internet and this requirement would take away their right to vote. Third, though São Paulo has 33 subdistricts in which elections are generally held, the administration stated that only 22 polling stations would be opened. Movements charged that the long commute to the polling stations would limit the number of citizens from participating. Finally, the movements claimed that the housing secretariat had done little to publicize the elections. At one point the link to the election website was missing. In response to several judicial actions, the election was cancelled twice.

In an interview, a government official responsible for the CMH expressed her opinion that the movements to the left sought to stop the elections not because of procedural issues but because they did not think they could win an "all or nothing" vote. The movements, of course, dispute this view as the arrogance of the current administration. Juliana Avanci, an attorney for the Gaspar Garcia Center for Human Rights, which holds a seat on the CMH, explained that the movements wanted the elections to happen, but not with just any set of rules. In a radio interview, Avanci stated, "The CMH has a fundamental role to play in construction, implementation, monitoring, evaluation, and the management of resources, which are critical in this area of public policy. So the criteria for the election have to re-discussed and re-evaluated. The outcome will be very important for the legitimacy of the next council."[17] In her view the council is too important to housing policy for the elections to be compromised by undemocratic rules.

The legitimacy of the council is certainly at stake in these controversial elections. The future commitment of all actors depends on the resolution of the electoral rules and the perception that all sides are willing to play fairly. Movements to the left are calling for the government to reopen the registration and generate more publicity for the elections. In addition, they want to hold the elections without preregistration and return to the election of candidate lists according to rules of proportionality rather than an "all or nothing" system.

A group studying the CMH from the University of Campinas, just outside of the city of São Paulo, summed up the importance of this electoral crisis: "These elections for the CMH demonstrate the growing importance of institutions of participatory democracy in Brazil, while at the same time they show their vulnerability to the tendency to control by government officials."[18] In this group's opinion, and in the opinion of social movement leaders I interviewed, the municipal administration is using the election to consolidate the representation of their allies on the council. While if true this represents a disturbing antidemocratic use of the council, at the same time it verifies the significance of this participatory governance institution in redistributive politics in the city. That the government feels the need to control the council suggests that it wields some degree of power in housing policies and programs.

The hope among the parties involved is that the democratic institutions used to mediate the issues over the election will come up with legitimate solutions by which both sides can move forward. Following the judge's ruling, which cancelled the elections for the second time, the movements involved signed a statement celebrating the court's decision as a victory to stop a process that is "arbitrary and antidemocratic."[19] According to Juliana Avanci, the movements hope that with judicial and legislative support they will be able to gain more cooperation from the administration. This speaks to another lesson in this controversy, which is the importance of representative institutions of democracy as complement to participatory institutions. Without the force of the courts and the legislature to enforce the laws of the CMH, the government would have the ability to negate the participatory process without penalty.

WHAT VARIABLES INFLUENCE CHANGES IN THE COUNCIL OVER TIME?

Over 10 years of existence, actors, and issues on the agenda in the CMH have shifted in various ways. In the following analysis I identify a number of variables responsible for these changes beginning with the most apparent factor: the administration in power. In addition to the administration, I identify the role of the private sector, the nature of the problems, and federal transfers as variables in this ever-changing participatory institution.

The Administration

The preceding analysis clearly shows the importance of the administration in power to changes in the actors and agenda of participatory governance institutions. It is impossible to talk about changes in the council without mentioning the differences across administrations. As I discussed in previous chapters, the dynamic between CSOs and the government is highly dependent on the political party of the administration. While fights likely erupt among actors regardless of party alignment, there is a certain expectation that conflicts will be resolved when party and CSO interests align. The policy-making process should be less contentious when interests among parties coincide.

Under the administration of Suplicy, the PT was still learning how to be a party in power rather than an opposition party. From the time of the first PT mayor in the city in the late 1980s to the 2000 election of Suplicy, social movements involved with housing had time to mature. They had learned how to negotiate the institutions of representative democracy during the first decade of the new democracy in Brazil. Still, political alliances did not always signal smooth relationships. Leaders in the housing secretariat had to get used to the idea that the movements would still protest and fight with government officials even when they were from the same party. According to Gisela Mori, they had to "accept that protests meant something had gone wrong with the process or that they were asking for something that was beyond our capacity to provide."[20] The government also had to understand the job of social movements is to protest and make demands. Social movement leaders and government officials were still allies, but the dynamic between them shifted when the movements won the right to participate in the policy-making process, but their friends in the government sometimes had to say no to their demands. Formally involving movements in policy making provided greater transparency and accountability in the process, but did not mean that the movements were satisfied with the breadth of the municipal government's actions.

Shifts in the council also demonstrate that when the administration clashes ideologically with the most vocal social movements, a lack of trust on both sides interrupts the participatory process. During the Kassab administration this lack of trust led housing officials to seek more control over resources and elections. In a time when the housing budget increased due to an influx of federal transfers, by taking certain projects out of the council's agenda and limiting the money the council controls, the Kassab administration may have provoked more conflict among members and between movements and the government, particularly because there was a sense that the government had money but was not allowing popular control or oversight of these new funds. By appearing to support one candidate list in council elections and raising the barriers to voting, the administration further strained relations with the left.

As I found in the previous chapter, the commitment of the administration to the process is important for how participatory governance institutions function. When the administration and the strongest CSOs clash, conflict arises. Over time, however, administrations and CSOs undoubtedly change and the participatory process shifts along with them. Whether the institution remains active over time, then, may be a matter of how actors manage conflict and the value they place on maintaining the participatory process.

The Private Sector

The profit motive in the private sector for housing remains fairly constant over time. The margins for profit and the means to achieve profit, however, do change. According to representatives from SECOVI, private sector construction and real estate associations are motivated to participate in the council by the desire to improve conditions in the city. Though private sector actors may have altruistic motives to improve the lives of their fellow city residents, a growing city also means higher real estate prices, more construction, and therefore more profit. Private sector actors are motivated to participate in the council and in social housing policy more broadly, because they want to know about upcoming construction contracts and have a voice in the location of future projects.

The price of land in the city has risen steadily alongside overall economic growth in Brazil. At the same time, federal resources for social housing construction have steadily grown. Rising real estate prices generate interest in reserving parts of the city for high-price housing units, while an influx of federal investment for social housing means more and bigger contracts for building. Because of the rise in real estate prices, many housing projects end up in the less desirable periphery of the city. Still, the private sector is motivated to build social housing in the center of the city if the government is willing to invest more money in projects.

So how does the private sector affect changes in actors and agendas in the CMH? First, connections to the administration in power may privilege private sector interests. The private sector does not change the actors on the council per se, but their relationships with the government change significantly under different administrations. The current secretary for housing was previously the head of SECOVI and therefore understands its interests in the council quite well. Compared to the previous administration in which housing secretariat leaders came from political or social service backgrounds, the private sector appears to be more closely aligned with this government. On votes within the council, the private sector and government officials generally agree. In effect, they are able to form a stronger voting block.

Second, the private sector has always favored projects involving large-scale construction rather than other means to satisfy demands for secure and affordable housing, such as regularization. Particularly when its interests align with the government's, the private sector can sway the agenda toward projects that will ultimately benefit business. Under the Suplicy administration, private sector members of the council fought the development of public housing in the city center and projects and legislation to assist residents living in tenement houses. According to housing movement leader Evaniza Rodrigues, the private sector members rejected these initiatives because there was nothing in it for them. Resolutions to assist residents in tenement houses passed the council with the combined support of social movements and the leftist government at the time.

Under the Kassab administration, the agenda shifted toward provision of social housing through private market mechanisms rather than through mutirões. This was in direct response to both the business background of leaders in the housing secretariat as well as their alignment with private sector actors within the council. As Abelardo Campoy, SECOVI representative on the CMH, told me, "It matters who is in control."[21] The increase in funds from the federal level largely went to building units in the periphery, which could then be sold through the federal government's bank (Caixa Econômica Federal). Still, Campoy critiques the municipal administration's reticence to provide enough money for the council to control. He says the amount the council has available to allocate for new building is insufficient to permit any building or renovation in the city center. According to Campoy, with the money the municipal government will invest, private companies cannot make enough profit in the city center to make it worthwhile for them. Instead the government relies on partnerships with the state and federal levels for new construction.

Nature of the Problems

Reducing the housing deficit in the city of São Paulo is always the top priority for the CMH. The means by which public policy and programs seek to reduce the deficit clearly changes over time. In addition, the perception among social movements, civil society, and the government as to the most pressing problems changes depending on where the greatest need lies, what programs are already in place, and outside events. In the early years of the CMH, housing in the city center was a priority due to the issues with tenements and abandoned buildings occupied by various movements. In response, the CMH allocated funding to the Locação Social program. Mutirões were also seen as a mechanism to rejuvenate communities of favela residents in the periphery of the city. In the beginning of the Kassab administration, the needs did not so much change as the perception of how best to address the challenges of favelas shifted toward urbanization.

Now, however, focus has come back to the city center due to a number of factors. First, the center of the city is undergoing a large-scale renovation project, funded by a partnership between all three levels of government and private sector developers. In this process, residents occupying abandoned buildings are being forced to move—sometimes compensated by rental subsidies or relocation to public housing units—and social movements are fighting for the inclusion of low-income housing within the city center's redevelopment plans. In combination with increasing commuting costs in the city and problems with infrastructure in the periphery, the city center provides an important space in which the poor can safely afford to live and work. At the same time, the municipal government claims they are less able to expropriate land within the city's center due to rising real estate prices. This tension between need for social housing in the city's center and the increasing value of land in the city is playing out in the CMH as social movements demand more funds allocated to expropriation and renovation of existing buildings. Due to the electoral conflict in the CMH, however, much of the negotiation over the city center development is going on outside of this public space. Social movements claim they are being shut out of the redevelopment process, and deals are being made in a nontransparent manner. The need for social housing is as great as ever, but the emphasis on where to address the needs of the poor changes over time along with broader processes of development in the city.

Federal Transfers

As mentioned earlier, the availability of federal funds for specific types of projects has drastically changed the agenda of the CMH. In the beginning of the Lula administration, when the CMH first began, there was little funding for housing programs flowing down to the municipal level. Social movements claim that the federal government before Lula did not have a national housing policy. By all accounts, when Lula took office in early 2003, he made housing and urban development a priority of his administration. The Lula administration created the Ministry for Cities and the National System for Housing in the Social Interest. In the mid- to late 2000s, two important programs reached the municipal level: PAC (Program for Accelerated Growth), which focused on building infrastructure for urbanization, and Credito Solidario, which enabled housing associations to apply for funding to construct new units. These available sources of funding changed the task of the council. Federal transfers largely dictate the parameters of housing programs even though the choice of program adoption and program details are left to municipalities.

Further, the federal-level Minha Casa Minha Vida (MCMV) program has also recently changed the focus of the CMH. According to the executive secretary for the CMH, Ana Maria Maluf, "Minha Casa Minha Vida has been a big advance for housing in São Paulo because some projects that the municipality would like to have done were not possible without the sharing of costs from the federal level."[22] For example, in 2011, the council approved an agreement between the Caixa Econômica Federal and COHAB to contribute R\$15 million from the Municipal Housing Fund to produce 3,000 housing units. The municipality's contribution to each of the 3,000 units is R\$5,000. Since the MCMV limit for spending per housing unit in São Paulo is R\$80,000, this means they could construct units for \$85,000. Brazilian scholar Marta Arretche points out that the municipal government of São Paulo takes a great deal of credit for their rather small contribution. Nonetheless, the resources available through MCMV have changed the direction of policy making within the CMH. Instead of focusing on urbanization, regularization, or mutirão projects, the council approved funding for this project, which will bring new construction to the city.

THE IMPACT OF CHANGING ACTORS AND AGENDAS ON COMMITMENT AND LONGEVITY

The commitment of civil society and government actors is critical for the participatory process to succeed in shaping policy discussions and outcomes. Without commitment from both sides the council cannot be a space for transparency, accountability, and responsiveness. So how do changes in actors and agenda affect this commitment? I expect that commitment of actors increases in moments of perceived victory and wanes in moments of conflict and frustration. Given the path of the CMH in São Paulo and the current electoral crisis, what then is the future for the council? And, further, what are the lessons for longevity of participatory institutions more broadly?

Commitment of the Government

As the preceding analysis shows, the commitment of government officials has changed markedly over the course of the CMH's 10-year existence. In the Suplicy administration, the PT government came in with the intention of creating the housing council and pleased their electoral base—low-income residents and social movements—by ensuring the council made a difference in housing policy. However, though the government displayed great commitment to the participatory process, the council's impact was hampered by lack of funds from the federal level. In general, the council functioned relatively smoothly throughout its early years under the PT administration because social movements and government officials often formed a voting block within the council. As a united front they were able to fund mutirão projects, support public housing in the city center, and put forward regulations for tenement housing. The actors involved in the council largely aligned around a distinct housing agenda and were mostly pleased with the outcomes. In turn, shared success enhanced commitment of both government and social movement actors.

Despite current government representatives' stated commitment to the participatory process in the housing council, their inability to quickly resolve the current electoral crisis may indicate otherwise. The civil servants tasked with managing the daily operation of the housing council have little stake in its continuation while the political appointees in the housing secretariat have never expressed much admiration for the work of the council. The current administration has until now fulfilled their obligation to maintain the council's operation, but they have also withheld large portions of the budget from the control of the council.

What does the story of decreasing commitment of government actors to the participatory process in São Paulo mean for the continuation of the CMH in the city and for the longevity of participatory governance institutions more broadly? The most obvious answer seems to be that the future of the council in São Paulo will depend on the politics of the next administration. I might expect that if the PT wins the upcoming mayoral election in the fall of 2012, the CMH will receive greater priority in attention and resources. The PT in São Paulo has a history of supporting the CMH, and a new PT mayor would be likely to continue this tradition if he wants to maintain strong relationships with social movements and their supporters in the city.

But to promote continuity in policy making, the longevity of participatory governance institutions should not be solely dependent on the electoral fortunes of one party. Regardless of the party in power, government officials need to believe that the participatory process serves their interests in making effective policy that responds to the needs of the poor. CSOs in São Paulo have an enormous capacity for understanding policy making—many past and current CMH members have served within the municipal, state, and federal governments themselves—but they also have long-standing feuds with each other and strong partisan tendencies. In order for the government to *want* to reengage with CSOs through the CMH, civil society members may need to become better partners in compromise and negotiation.

Government officials need to trust the ability of CSOs to transmit the needs of citizens in order for the council to engender responsiveness. Though, if the allegations by social movements are true, the government needs to stop playing politics in the elections for the CMH and allow fair representation of citizens' needs, and CSOs also need to take some responsibility in making the deliberative process less contentious to incentivize greater cooperation.

In sum, government commitment to the participatory process will undoubtedly ebb and flow as actors and agendas shift. Participatory governance institutions are meant to make policy making more effective in that the input from civil society should allow the government to more accurately respond to the needs of citizens. The incentive of government officials to participate relies on the transmission of information regarding need and the collective will to come up with solutions that match the problems. But more responsive programs and policies come at the cost of a sometimes slow and laborious deliberative process. The government's commitment to the process over the long haul may in part depend on how civil society conducts itself within the institution. For the process to be worthwhile from the perspective of government officials, they need to see cooperation from CSOs in order to rely on them as effective partners in policy making.

Commitment of Civil Society

What then motivates CSOs to continue to participate in participatory governance institutions and what might turn them away? Over the course of very different administrations in São Paulo, the commitment of social movements has not changed substantially, but other CSOs, including unions, professional associations, universities, and NGOs, have displayed decreasing interest in the CMH. For these CSOs, the problem may be that the process requires large investments in time and patience without direct personal benefit. This problem of generating ongoing participation is not unique to participatory governance institutions, but occurs in many volunteer positions. Initial enthusiasm is replaced by fatigue, and attention is diverted elsewhere. Social movement representatives often live within poor communities themselves, or if they do not, they have staked their careers as lawyers or activists on improving the housing conditions for the poor. The CSOs that did not register candidates for the 2011–2013 term—unions, a social service organization, and universities—all have diverse interests outside of housing policy and programs. The composition of membership, then, is important for the overall commitment of civil society to the process. The law creating the CMH in São Paulo specifies the inclusion of these categories of members. In designing participatory governance institutions for longevity, planners should consider the incentives to participate across membership categories.

For social movements, too, energies may be diverted outside of the participatory institution, especially if the process is not working as efficiently as they would like. Most recently, social movements have regained momentum with protests while at the same time increasingly relying on the courts to prevent evictions of residents occupying abandoned buildings in the city center. Leaders from housing movements say these actions are necessary because the current administration is not providing enough new housing options for the very poor. With the city center redevelopment, which has its own participatory council, participation is also refocused elsewhere.

Social movements, particularly those affiliated with the PT, do continue to call for the resolution of the electoral crisis, but as the conflict remains unresolved, their commitment to the process is at risk. At this point the council needs members who understand the participatory process and are willing to make demands on behalf of civil society. As Gisela Mori stated, "It is very important to have people who are prepared and not co-opted, who know what they want, who have a position, and know how to negotiate as well, because if you have people who don't know how to negotiate it's also difficult."[23] Social movements fighting for a fair election know this to be the case, but their commitment to ensure elections are held and the results of those elections will be important for the future longevity of the institution.

Social movements for housing in São Paulo have been around for several decades at this point, and they understand the benefits of transparency provided by the council, which never existed in the past. Though the CMH may never be a perfect site for civil society to impact policy making, the fact that nongovernmental actors now have access to budgetary documents and internal regulations means civil society has the information at hand to see where improvements can be made and make demands for change.

In the end, participatory governance institutions cannot influence policy outcomes without commitment of actors to the process. Without commitment, participatory governance institutions become hollow spaces for policy making, with real decisions being made outside of civil society–government consultation. Collaboration to ensure policies and programs are responsive to real citizen needs, institutional rules to make sure those with the most at stake direct the process, and government compliance with the established institutional rules are all important factors to ensure commitment on all sides and longevity in participatory governance institutions.

CONCLUSIONS: LESSONS IN LONGEVITY FROM THE SÃO PAULO MUNICIPAL COUNCIL FOR HOUSING

Participatory governance institutions do promote positive changes to pro-poor policies. But maintaining the commitment to participation, which is more costly and slower than the government alone making decisions, may be an ongoing struggle for both civil society organizations and government administrators.

The shifts in actors and agendas within São Paulo's CMH provide insight into the potential for long-term impact of housing councils and other types of participatory governance institutions. First, the case shows that the administration in power largely determines the actors involved in the process, but forces controlling the agenda, including the perception of need and federal transfers, often lie outside of the administration's direct control. When private sector interests intervene, ideological divides emerge over the direction of social policy. CSOs question the allegiance of the state, which in turn creates greater conflict within participatory institutions. In addition, changes in the rules for selection of members interrupt the policy-making process and lead to questioning of motives on all sides. For long-term stability, institutional rules should be established and maintained.

In terms of generating long-term commitment, both sides have a role in creating incentives for participation. Government officials need to feel that civil society provides honest information to allow programs to be more responsive to all citizens' needs. In turn, the government should be more willing to cede control over a larger share of resources. Civil society requires transparency from the government to ensure they are treated as partners in policy making and program implementation. Now that CSOs have seen the benefits of transparency, it would be difficult to go back to an environment lacking information and a public space in which to voice their demands. Recognition of the importance of transparency continues to motivate CSOs to make sure the government maintains their responsibility to operate participatory governance institutions. If both sides see that the participatory process can have a positive impact on responding to the needs of citizens and improving the quality of life for the poor, these institutions have the potential for great longevity.

As the newness of participatory governance institutions wears off, actors change, agendas become complicated, and fatigue settles in, incentives for continued coordination need to be clear on all sides. The problems related to poverty and development that municipal housing councils and other participatory governance institutions address require long-term engagement by policy makers and citizens. As such, it is critical that these institutions, which I show in this book make a difference in the adoption of social programs that benefit the poor, survive over time to continue to provide policy direction.

8 Conclusion
Can Democracy Remedy Social Challenges? Findings on the Effect of Participatory Governance Institutions

Participatory governance institutions do matter. I started this project with a healthy dose of skepticism that participatory governance institutions could be the panacea to marginalization of the poor that many scholars, donors, and activists suggest. Could these forums really lead to policy change, or were governments merely paying lip service to the idea of civil society incorporation in policy making? Though scholars had thoroughly documented the benefits of participatory budgeting in Porto Alegre, Brazil, I was not convinced that participatory institutions in other contexts would have similar effects. But, after several years of studying Brazil's municipal housing councils, talking to numerous government officials and civil society leaders, and conducting quantitative analysis controlling for other effects, I can say with some certainty that participatory governance institutions do matter for policy outcomes. Like any blanket statement, however, this one comes with a number of caveats. Not all participatory governance institutions produce the same effects. Context, influenced by civil society–state dynamics, institutional rules, and commitment of actors, matters for the direction and strength of impact. In addition, housing policy is determined by factors outside of council control. Though municipal councils for housing have an effect on policy outcomes, they will never be the only determining factor of housing policy. No participatory governance institution will ever be the only site for policy making in a particular issue area. Politics, economics, and institutional constraints will always also matter to policy making.

SUMMARY OF FINDINGS

In this book I sought to contribute to our understanding of whether a new type of democratic institution could generate greater responsiveness and accountability to the poor. Previous literature on democracy and development suggests that democratic institutions and civil society lead to responsiveness and accountability of government officials. But given continuing problems of poverty and inequality in the developing world, traditional institutions of democracy do not appear to be enough to remedy social challenges. This led me to test whether one type of participatory governance institution is associated with an increase in social program adoption across contexts. In addition, I sought to address *when* and *how* participatory governance institutions lead to policy change. By focusing on housing policy, I hoped to expand the social policy literature to an issue of great concern in developing countries. Here I review the evidence presented related to these objectives.

Chapter 2 first addressed the importance of housing policy for democracy and development. The scale of housing needs, including physical shelter, property rights, and community improvements, is vast and growing along with urban populations. The benefits of tackling housing challenges, however, are also great. The provision of housing is an internationally recognized human right, and housing contributes to reducing poverty and inequality while improving security and environmental sustainability. Moreover, governments tend to prioritize housing programs because they are politically popular and relatively inexpensive, tangible symbols of progress. Large civil societies oriented toward housing in the developing world keep housing in the public's eye. Housing policy in Brazil and in other developing countries has largely shifted from state-managed complexes to market-based mechanisms, including contracting out projects to private firms and mortgage financing and rental subsidies for citizens. The state, however, continues to play a large role in creating these market incentives and continuing to provide property rights and some direct program implementation. In addition, the state manages the decentralization of resources and the participatory process. The state, then, is not absent from housing policy. Despite the role of housing policy as a central component of social benefits or welfare policies, particularly in developing countries, political science scholars have shied away from including housing in their analysis of governmental provision of benefits. This analysis remedied that gap by providing evidence of policy influences for housing across Brazil.

To address the main question of this book regarding participatory governance institutions, I first sought to determine if municipal housing councils are associated with social housing program adoption. In Chapter 3 I conducted statistical analysis to assess whether participatory governance institutions increase the likelihood of provision of social benefits to the poor. More specifically, I developed several statistical models to measure whether municipal housing councils are associated with a greater probability of social housing program adoption. I found that municipal housing councils are associated with adoption of each type of housing program and a housing index, measuring the number of programs adopted by the municipality. This provides evidence to suggest that in fact participatory governance institutions do promote adoption of social benefits to the poor. Though mainstream political science literature has tended to focus on the institutions of representative democracy as keys to accountability, this study provides confirmation that participatory institutions contribute to social policy, particularly in a relatively new democracy where social challenges persist even in the face of fast-paced economic growth. In addition, scholars of participatory governance institutions have generally relied on case studies and focused on the nature of deliberation within these institutions without systematically comparing policy outcomes across contexts. By conducting an analysis across municipalities within one country, I was able to control for a number of factors to discern the independent effect of municipal housing councils.

Having established that participatory governance institutions do matter for policy outcomes I set out to assess *when* and *how* these institutions make a difference. In Chapter 4 I evaluated whether the density of civil society matters for the effect of participatory governance institutions. Using Brazilian government data on the number of nonprofits and foundations per capita as a proxy for the depth of civil society, I found that the density of civil society does not matter on its own or for the effectiveness of municipal housing councils. This contradicts common expectations regarding the need for a strong civil society to hold governments accountable and existing literature citing the importance of civil society density for participatory governance impact. It appears that municipal housing councils may level the playing field for access to government officials. The depth of civil society is not critical for the functioning of the institution. Again, by reviewing evidence across municipalities instead of through single cases, I was able to evaluate the importance of the density of civil society across diverse municipalities. Though a strong civil society may still be key for the effectiveness of participatory governance institutions in many instances, across the universe of cases in Brazil, the density of civil society does not significantly alter the impact of participatory governance. This finding is promising for new participatory governance institutions created in Brazil and in other countries without strong histories of associationalism.

In Chapter 5, I looked further into case studies to determine how exactly participatory governance institutions do influence policy outcomes. Here I aimed to identify the factors shaping the relationship between civil society and the state, which may contribute to how civil society uses participatory governance institutions and the eventual impact they are able to have on policy. From case study research in São Paulo, Santo André, and Salvador, I argued that the party in power significantly determined whether alliances between civil society and the state facilitated the smooth functioning of the municipal housing council. I also found that because housing policy is largely connected to the real estate sector, the relationship between civil society, the municipal government, and the private sector also matters for the effect of municipal housing councils. The private sector is often left out of analysis of social policies and participatory governance, but I found through the case studies that the role of the private sector in social housing policy made a significant difference in the policy process and outcomes. Finally, the extent to which civil society adopts more contentious or cooperative strategies influences how governments respond and use the council as a space for deliberation and decision making. In the end, from the case studies I found that the party in power, whether it be the Worker's Party (PT) or a more conservative party, mattered the most for the dynamics between civil society and the municipal government. These relationships, in turn, appeared to strongly determine whether and how the council was used for policy making.

Across the larger universe of cases, I sought to understand how the party in power affects the outcomes of participatory governance institutions. Since the PT in Brazil traditionally champions participatory governance as part of its party platform and the presence of the PT appeared to affect the civil society–state dynamic in the case studies, I hypothesized that where a PT mayor held office, the municipal council for housing would be more likely to bring about adoption of social housing programs across cases. However, while in the case studies the party in power appeared to largely determine the nature of the policy process in municipal housing councils, across the larger universe of cases the party did not make a substantial difference.

Contrary to the case studies, from the statistical analysis I found that the institutional rules actually make a significant difference for the effect of municipal housing councils. In particular, the type of responsibility afforded to the councils appears to shape whether they lead to increasing likelihood of housing program adoption. Specifically, those councils with oversight responsibilities written into the council's mandate were the most strongly associated with housing program adoption across municipalities. This analysis is important for identifying institutional rules as key to outcomes, but it also contributes to our understanding of how case studies and quantitative methods complement one another. Though the case studies pointed to the importance of the party in power, in the aggregate the institutional rules mattered more for policy outcomes. I speculate that party may be a weak predictor of administrative behavior at the local level across Brazil, while the power to increase transparency through oversight responsibilities more closely affects the impact of these institutions across contexts.

Chapter 6 then continued the search for determining when participatory governance institutions are effective mechanisms for promoting adoption of social benefits. Here I examined the effect of bottom-up versus top-down creation of participatory governance institutions. The cases of Recife and Curitiba, where governments adopted municipal housing councils in response to the federal mandate, provide comparison to São Paulo, Santo André, and Salvador. When governments created municipal councils for housing in response to the federal mandate rather than in response to civil society demands or ideological conviction of the municipal administration, I found that both local government officials and civil society exhibit less commitment to the participatory process. Using statistical analysis, I confirmed that commitment matters: municipalities with housing councils created before the federal mandate were more likely to adopt social housing programs than those that created housing councils after the mandate. These results imply that participatory governance institutions imposed from the federal to the municipal level may not have the same effects across municipalities.

Finally, in Chapter 7 I reviewed the case of São Paulo's Municipal Council for Housing over its 10-year existence. The case presents an opportunity to reflect on how participatory governance institutions change over time and what these changes mean for longevity. I found significant shifts in actors and agendas and identify several factors influencing these shifts: the administration in power, the role of the private sector, perception of needs, and federal resource transfers. In order to generate greater commitment to the process, both CSOs (civil society organizations) and government officials need to see the benefits of cooperation in terms of more responsive programs and increasing transparency. Changes within participatory governance institutions are inevitable, but continuous reflection on the purpose and worth of participatory processes ensures the long-term relevance of the institutions.

In sum, I found that participatory governance institutions do generate responsiveness and accountability of governments to provide social benefits to the poor. Municipal housing councils are innovative democratic mechanisms to involve civil society in decision making and cement their role as "co-governors" with the state. But the effectiveness of participatory governance institutions is not guaranteed. Though a dense civil society may not be needed for these institutions to shift policy making, the dynamics between civil society and the state change over time and may shift the ways in which the councils are used for policy making and respected as credible institutions. In addition, across cases the legal responsibilities afforded to councils matter for the effect they have on policy outcomes. Actors concerned with the influence of participatory governance institutions should take institutional design into account during creation. In fact, the reason for creation may be critical for the influence of participatory governance institutions. Government officials and civil society leaders may not be committed to the process if these institutions are mandated from the federal level rather than initiated in response to local demand. But recognition of the mutual benefits participatory governance institutions can provide should motivate commitment in the long term.

This analysis demonstrated that participatory governance institutions, which complement representative democratic institutions and incorporate civil society into decision making, should be taken seriously by scholars and policy makers as institutions to promote adoption of social benefits for the poor. Further, civil society can hold the government accountable for addressing social challenges when they are invited to the table to present their demands, solicit information from government officials, and maintain a dialogue with government officials over time.

I would be remiss if I did not mention that while the findings in this book strongly contribute to our understanding of how participatory governance institutions affect policy outcomes, the study also comes with several limitations. First, though municipal housing councils are representative of one type of institution charged with deciding the distribution of resources and programmatic details, not all participatory governance institutions are given these responsibilities, and I cannot generalize to every type of participatory approach. Second, though I try to address issues of longevity in Chapter 7, a longer time horizon for the quantitative analysis would uncover how the effect of participatory governance changes over time and across political administrations, as these institutions age and become routine mechanisms for policy making. Third, though I believe Brazil to be representative of a developing country facing challenges to democracy and development, it is also unique in many ways. For instance, Brazil has had a leftist administration in charge at the federal level for almost a decade, it is a fast-growing economy with some international prestige, and it is wealthier as a whole than most developing countries in the world. Moreover, Brazil now has over two decades of experience with participatory institutions. All of these factors may contribute to both a greater willingness to invest in social benefits and a recognition of the importance of participatory governance.

Finally, because of data limitations and the fact that municipal housing councils are relatively new institutions, I was not able to connect municipal housing councils to changes in living conditions within Brazilian municipalities. Future research connecting the presence of these institutions with decreases in the quantitative and qualitative housing deficits would increase our understanding of how participatory governance institutions impact the lives of the poor. Scholars are now moving toward assessing the impact of participatory governance institutions on quality of life indicators.[1] Though this study contributed to this new research trend by assessing the impact of municipal housing councils on social program adoption, future research should show the relevance of these institutions for improving the quality of residents' lives.

FINAL CONCLUSIONS

As local and national governments struggle to confront social challenges on a grand scale, scholars, donors, policy makers, and activists need to understand what works in promoting adoption of social benefits for the poor. Severe inequalities, marginalization, and clientelism often limit the effectiveness of democratic institutions, leaving the poor without a voice in policy making. Civil society organizations that represent the poor aim to provide that voice by accessing government officials to make demands and elicit promises for action. Participatory governance institutions should ensure that CSOs have equal access to government officials to negotiate responses to citizen needs. Further, CSOs should gain information about government activities, which they can then pass along to their members and the community at large. By analyzing the effect of municipal housing councils on social housing program adoption, this study has contributed to the debate about whether participatory governance institutions actually achieve these goals. Creation of participatory governance institutions to encourage prioritization of social benefits is sound advice, but should also come with the caveats regarding civil society–state dynamics, institutional design, and commitment of actors. As many developing countries enjoy increasing prosperity and deepening of democratic institutions, participatory governance may solidify the contribution of civil society to addressing key social challenges into the future.

This study provides evidence that subnational institutional design can promote better outcomes. Moreover, democratic institutions created with the intent of helping the poor can have a positive impact on persuading governments to address their needs.

Appendices

Appendix A Percentage of Municipalities with Existing Housing Programs by Region and Population

Region	Number of Municipalities	2005					2008						
		Construction of New Units	Construction Materials	Plots of Land	Regularization	Other Programs	Construction of New Units	Construction Materials	Plots of Land	Regularization	Acquire Units	Improve Units	Urbanization
In all of Brazil	5563	48%	35%	19%	9%	25%	61%	36%	25%	20%	16%	46%	14%
North	449	35%	30%	32%	11%	14%	53%	34%	43%	29%	14%	37%	22%
Northeast	1793	50%	38%	20%	6%	27%	66%	36%	27%	15%	17%	51%	15%
Center West	466	57%	42%	29%	12%	29%	70%	44%	36%	32%	14%	49%	17%
South	1187	53%	33%	16%	12%	27%	65%	34%	21%	21%	17%	49%	11%
Southeast	1668	45%	32%	13%	10%	22%	51%	35%	16%	20%	13%	42%	11%

Population	Number of Municipalities	2005					2008						
		Construction of New Units	Construction Materials	Plots of Land	Regularization	Other Programs	Construction of New Units	Construction Materials	Plots of Land	Regularization	Acquire Units	Improve Units	Urbanization
Under 20,000	3965	45%	34%	18%	5%	21%	57%	35%	24%	14%	14%	46%	8%
20,001 to 50,000	1026	49%	36%	19%	12%	27%	66%	37%	25%	27%	17%	48%	18%
50,001 to 100,000	313	62%	35%	23%	25%	37%	75%	40%	31%	42%	25%	47%	32%
100,001 to 500,000	220	76%	36%	26%	43%	55%	80%	34%	30%	65%	26%	47%	50%
500,001 and up	39	74%	41%	38%	64%	67%	95%	38%	33%	85%	41%	64%	82%

Appendix B Negative Binomial Results for Influences on the Housing Program Index, 2005 and 2008*

	2005		2008	
	Program Index	Program Index	Program Index	Program Index
Municipal Housing Council	0.23*** (0.04)	0.82*** (0.27)	0.19*** (0.03)	0.28 (0.19)
Municipal Housing Fund	0.28*** (0.04)	0.28*** (0.04)	0.13*** (0.03)	0.13*** (0.03)
Population (log)	0.22*** (0.02)	0.23*** (0.02)	0.15*** (0.02)	0.15*** (0.02)
Percent Urban Population (log)	0.16*** (0.04)	0.16*** (0.04)	0.14*** (0.03)	0.14*** (0.03)
Municipal Budget per Capita (log)	0.43*** (0.04)	0.43*** (0.04)	0.28*** (0.04)	0.28*** (0.04)
PT Mayor	−0.03 (0.05)	−0.03 (0.05)	0.06 (0.04)	0.06 (0.04)
Gini Coefficient	0.61** (0.28)	0.59** (0.28)	0.83*** (0.22)	0.82*** (0.22)
Income per Capita (log)	−0.17*** (0.06)	−0.17*** (0.06)	−0.02 (0.04)	−0.02 (0.04)
Nonprofits and Foundations per Capita (log)	0.05** (0.02)	0.03 (0.03)	−0.01 (0.02)	−0.01 (0.02)
Existence of Favelas	−0.01 (0.04)	−0.01 (0.04)	0.06** (0.03)	0.06** (0.03)
Housing Council × Nonprofits and Foundations per Capita (log)		0.10** (0.04)		0.01 (0.03)
Constant	−4.05*** (0.46)	−4.25*** (0.47)	−3.30*** (0.38)	−3.35*** (0.39)
Observations	3877	3877	4093	4093

* State dummies also included in models.
Standard errors in parentheses. *** $p < 0.01$, ** $p < 0.05$, * $p < 0.1$.

Notes

NOTES TO CHAPTER 1

1. Sen 1999, 155.
2. Putnam 1993.
3. The Ministério Público is an independent branch of government charged by the Brazilian Constitution with defending "diffuse and collective interests." Housing rights organizations often use the Ministério Público to fight evictions.
4. Boone 1996; Bueno de Mesquita et al. 2003; Dasgupta 1993; Franco, Alvarez-Dardet, and Ruiz 2004; Lake and Baum 2001; J. McGuire 2001; Moon and Dixon 1985; Przeworski et al. 2000; Sen 1981, 1999; Siegle, Weinstein, and Halperin 2004; Zweifel and Navia 2000.
5. Avelino, Brown, and Hunter 2005; Brown and Hunter 2004; Gerring, Thacker, and Alfaro 2012; Kaufman and Segura-Ubiergo 2001; Lake and Baum 2001; J. McGuire 2006; Przeworski et al. 2000; Stasavage 2005; Tavares and Wacziarg 2001.
6. Haber 2007; Mares and Carnes 2009.
7. Sen 1981, 1999.
8. Sen 1981, 1999.
9. Haggard and Kaufman 2008; Mares and Carnes 2009.
10. Deacon 2009; Lake and Baum 2001; M. McGuire and Olson 1996; Niskanen 1997.
11. Manin, Przeworski, and Stokes 1999.
12. See, for example, Banting 1987; Immergut 1992; Skocpol 1992; Weir, Orloff, and Skocpol 1988.
13. Tsebelis 2002.
14. Mainwaring and Welna 2003; O'Donnell et al. 1999; Peruzzotti and Smulovitz 2006.
15. Tendler 1997, 144.
16. For example, Ackerman 2004; Adhikari, Di Falco, and Lovett 2004; Crook 2003; Ostrom 2005; Steiner 2007.
17. For example, Asante and Ayee 2008; Blair 2000; Crook and Manor 1998; Crook and Sverrisson 2001; Manor 1999.
18. Tocqueville 1835.
19. Putnam 1993.
20. Gaventa 2006, 14.
21. For example, McAdam, Tarrow, and Tilly 2001.
22. Giugni, McAdam, and Tilly 1999.
23. Tarrow 1998.

24. H. J. Kwon 2002; S. Kwon 2002.
25. Though I argue that the literature on the policy impact of CSOs is limited, a number of authors do provide important contributions on the subject, including Fioramonti and Heinrich 2007; Fung and Wright 2003; Giugni 1998.
26. Ackerman 2004; Carothers 1999; Gaventa 2006.
27. Avritzer 2002; Fung and Wright 2003.
28. Malena 2009.
29. Selee and Peruzzotti 2009.
30. Fishkin 1991.
31. Baiocchi, Heller, and Silva 2011.
32. World Bank 1994.
33. Huther and Shah 1998.
34. Abers 2003.
35. Baiocchi 2001; Houtzager 2003; Abers 2003.
36. Fukuyama 1996; Inglehart 1989; Lipset 1959.
37. Andersson and van Laerhoven 2007.
38. World Bank 1996; Fiszbein 1997; Blair 2000.
39. Gaventa 2006; Goldfrank 2007.
40. Ackerman 2004.
41. Hardjono and Teggemann 2003.
42. Wampler and McNulty (2011) summarize research on impact in the following areas: individual-level capabilities, civil society publics, state reform, democracy (interest mediation, representation, deliberation), social well-being, and public policy outcomes.
43. Abers 2001; Avritzer 2002; Baiocchi 2005.
44. For example, Baiocchi 2003; UNDP 2002.
45. Baiocchi, Heller, and Silva 2011; McNulty 2011; Wampler 2007b.
46. Sandbrook et al. 2007.
47. World Bank 2012.
48. IBGE 2009.
49. Fiszbein and Schady 2009.
50. IBGE 2010.
51. Ibid.
52. Baiocchi, Heller, and Silva 2011.
53. IBGE 2010.
54. Baiocchi, Heller, and Silva 2011.
55. Mainwaring 1999.
56. Ames 2001.
57. UNDP 2008.
58. Schattschneider 1960.
59. Keck 1992; McAdam, McCarthy, and Zald 1996.
60. Mainwaring 1986.
61. Benedito Barbosa, in discussions with the author, São Paulo, Brazil, June 2008.
62. Keck 1992.
63. Abers 1998, 1996; Baiocchi 2003.
64. Nylen 2000.
65. Holston 2008.
66. As McNulty and Wampler point out in their review of current literature on participatory governance, Brazil is not unique in the embedding of participatory requirements in the Constitution. The constitutions of Kenya, Peru, and Uganda, among others, also require or allow participation in decentralized institutions (Wampler and McNulty 2011).
67. Coelho, Pozzoni, and Cifuentes 2005, 174.
68. Jacobi 1999, 7.

69. World Bank 2008.
70. Wampler 2007b.
71. Abers 1998; Baiocchi 2005; Heller, Baiocchi, and Silva 2011; Wampler 2007a.
72. Wampler and Avritzer 2005.
73. Avritzer 2009; Cornwall and Coelho 2007.
74. Though, see Wampler 2007b and Andersson and van Laerhoven 2007.
75. Favela is generally translated to the English word "slum." As Janice Perlman notes, however, this translation does not adequately capture the vitality of favelas in which residents often build very permanent structures, receive land titles, and settle for generations (2010). The UN defines slums by their deficits in infrastructure, personal space, and secure housing, which Perlman argues does not adequately reflect the conditions in which many favela residents live. In Brazil favelas are now often referred to as "communities" or the more technical "subnormal agglomerations."
76. IBGE 2010.
77. Centro Gaspar Garcia 2012.
78. The FNRU also includes unions, architects, engineers, and other actors involved in urban policy and planning. In total there are about 20 organizations that work with the FNRU.
79. For example, the União Nacional dos Movimentos da Moradia Popular and Rede Jubileu Sul Brasil.
80. Duquette et al. 2005.
81. IBGE 2008.
82. Lieberman 2005.
83. IBGE 2005, 2008.
84. As described further in Chapters 3 and 4, I use the Brazilian government's FASFIL (Fundações Privadas e Associações Sem Fins Lucrativos) survey of foundations and nonprofits to compile an indicator of civil society density. Because I wanted cities from diverse regions of the country, I based the characterization of "high" and "low" civil society on the comparison of the city's civil society density score to the regional average. In general, the South and Southeast regions of the country have the highest average civil society density scores.
85. Cymbalista and Santoro 2008, 148.
86. Avritzer 2006; Houtzager and Moore 2003.
87. Avritzer 2006.
88. Baiocchi 2003.
89. Cooke and Kothari 2001.
90. Avritzer 2002, 2009; Baiocchi 2005; Wampler 2007a.
91. Baiocchi, Heller, and Silva 2008.
92. Grugel 1999.
93. Edwards 2004.
94. Avritzer 2009.
95. Wampler 2007b.
96. Agrawal and Gupta 2005; Fagatto and Fung 2006; Kumar 2002; Ostrom 1996.
97. Ackerman 2004; Baiocchi, Heller, and Silva 2011; Fagatto and Fung 2006; Kumar 2002; Ostrom 1996.
98. Sen 1999.

NOTES TO CHAPTER 2

1. Raquel Rolnik, in discussions with the author, São Paulo, Brazil, December 2008.

2. Moradia is often translated as "dwelling" in English, but this does not really capture the meaning as used by CSOs in Brazil.
3. UN Habitat 2003.
4. UN Habitat 2008.
5. Ibid.
6. Mitlin 2007.
7. Mitlin and Satterthwaite 2004, 5.
8. UN Habitat 2008.
9. UN Habitat 2003
10. UN Habitat 2008.
11. Mitlin 2007.
12. Ministério das Cidades 2011.
13. Fundação João Pinheiro 2009. President Getúlio Vargas established the minimum salary (e.g., minimum wage) for Brazil in 1936. Today, the amount needed to "attend to the basic necessities of workers and their families, including housing, food, education, health, leisure, hygiene, transportation, and social welfare" as guaranteed by the Constitution equals approximately four to five times the minimum salary (Departamento Intersindical de Estatística e Estudos Socioeconômicos [DIESSE] 2005, http://www.dieese.org.br/).
14. Fundação João Pinheiro 2009.
15. Ministério das Cidades 2011.
16. Mitlin 2007.
17. Cavalcanti, Marques, and Costa 2004.
18. OHCHR 1991.
19. Frente de la Luta Moradia 2010.
20. *O Globo* 2010.
21. FNRU 2010.
22. de Soto 2000.
23. de la Fuente and Estache 2004.
24. Caixa Econômica Federal 2012.
25. For example, Arias 2006; Caldeira 2001; Perlman 2010.
26. Henry-Lee 2005; Lall, Suri, and Deichmann 2006.
27. Perlman 2010.
28. UN Habitat 2008.
29. Rosero-Bixby 2006.
30. Holston 2008.
31. For example, a local hospital has reported a 50% reduction in the number of gunshot victims brought to the emergency room since the Pacification Program began (Cunha 2012).
32. UN Habitat 2008.
33. UN 2012.
34. Gilbert 2002; Castells 1983.
35. Baumann 2007; Boonyabancha 2005; Satyanarayana 2007; Rodrigues and Rolnik 2007; World Bank 2004.
36. Buckley and Kalarickal 2005.
37. For example, Perlman 2004 and 2010 on Rio de Janeiro.
38. Buckley and Kalarickal 2005; Jenkins, Smith, and Wang 2007.
39. Galasso and Ravallion 2000.
40. Jenkins, Smith, and Wang 2007, 253.
41. Huchzermeyer 2004.
42. Mitlin 2007.
43. Ibid.
44. IADB 2012.
45. Mitlin 2007, 165.
46. Jenkins, Smith, and Wang 2007.

47. UN Habitat 2008.
48. Mitlin 2007.
49. Benedito Barbosa, in discussions with the author, São Paulo, Brazil, June 2008.
50. Angela Gordilho Souza, in discussions with the author, Salvador, Brazil, November 2008.
51. Cavalcanti, Marques, and Costa 2004.
52. Eaton 2004.
53. Benedito Barbosa, in discussions with the author, São Paulo, Brazil, June 2008.
54. Cardoso 2008.
55. Ministério das Cidades 2009b.
56. Office of the President 2009.
57. Marta Arretche, in discussions with the author, São Paulo, Brazil, June 2008.
58. Cardoso 2008.
59. Raquel Rolnik, in discussions with the author, São Paulo, Brazil, December 2008.
60. Ministério das Cidades 2009a.
61. Ibid.
62. Ministério das Cidades 2009c.
63. FNRU 2009.
64. Caixa Econômica Federal 2012.
65. UNMP 2010.
66. Cymbalista and Santoro 2008.
67. IBGE 2008.

NOTES TO CHAPTER 3

1. In discussions with the author, Salvador, Brazil, November 2008.
2. Sections of this chapter and Chapter 4 first appeared in Donaghy, Maureen. "Do Participatory Governance Institutions Matter? An Analysis of Municipal Councils and Social Housing Programs in Brazil," *Journal of Comparative Politics* 44 (October 2011): 83–102.
3. The number of council members and the mix of civil society and government official membership varies by type of council and by the rules established by the municipal government. In general, civil society members may come from professional nongovernmental organizations, local social movements, and neighborhood associations. They are elected either in an open public forum or by a formal public election. The majority of government members are appointed by the relevant municipal agency, though seats are also reserved for state and federal government representatives.
4. Afonso and de Mello 2000.
5. Pessanha, Compagnac, and Matos 2006.
6. Coelho, Pozzoni, and Cifuentes 2005.
7. Gomes 2007.
8. Cymbalista et al. 2007.
9. IBGE 2008, 2005.
10. IBGE 2008.
11. Cymbalista et al. 2007; Draibe 2007.
12. Huchzermeyer 2004.
13. This argument draws on decentralization literature, in which scholars find that decentralization of responsibilities and resources to local officials often leads to improved responsiveness and accountability of local governments to

citizens' concerns. See, for example, World Bank 1996; Fiszbein 1997; Blair 2000. Participatory governance institutions formally involve civil society in the process of decentralization.

14. Ackerman 2004; Schneider 1999; Wampler 2007b.
15. Grindle 2007.
16. Avritzer 2002; Fung and Wright 2003.
17. Bardhan and Mookerjee 2006.
18. Ackerman 2004.
19. Grindle 2007.
20. Olson 1965.
21. Dagnino, Olvera, and Panfichi 2006; Hagopian 1996; Nunes 1997; Wampler 2007a.
22. In discussions with the author, Recife, Brazil, November 2008.
23. Instead of pooling the data across years, I use the two years as separate data points because the level of federal investment, flowing down to the municipal level, increased dramatically over these years.
24. Holston 2008.
25. IBGE 2002.
26. The data follow the internationally recognized classifications of the *Handbook on Nonprofit Institutions in the System of National Accounts* distributed by the UN in collaboration with Johns Hopkins University. The nonprofit sector is characterized by Johns Hopkins University collaborator Anheier as "the social infrastructure of civil society, creating as well as facilitating a sense of trust and social inclusion that is seen as essential for the functioning of modern societies." Anheier 2004, 5.
27. Esping-Andersen 1990; Huber and Stephens 2001.
28. The existence of municipal housing councils and funds are correlated at .53 in 2005 and .69 in 2008. In 2005, 456 municipalities out of 979 had a housing council but no fund. In 2008, there were 374 municipalities out of 1,709 that had housing councils but no fund.
29. Bardhan and Mookerjee 2006.
30. Jacobi 1999.
31. Though an ordered probit model would also seem appropriate to assess the probability of a municipality adopting multiple programs, after performing a Brant test of the parallel regression assumption, I discovered that the ordered probit model violated the assumption of equal proportional odds between categories. A negative binomial regression model is appropriate to use instead for extradispersed data. Rather than predicting probabilities, the negative binomial model predicts expected counts.
32. The one exception is programs for offering construction materials in 2005, for which municipal housing councils are not statistically significant in the model.
33. Though there are 5,564 municipalities in Brazil, the number of observations in the model is primarily limited by missing data for the municipal budget variable. The data include 4,117 observations for municipalities reporting budgetary totals for 2005.
34. The number of housing units produced or the budget amount spent on housing across municipalities may also be good measures of the commitment of municipal governments to addressing housing needs. However, these numbers were not readily available in 2009 to include in this analysis. The number of different types of programs adopted provides a measure of the government's willingness to attend to multiple demands and address diverse housing needs.
35. Scholars have long documented the effects of locating poor residents on the peripheries of cities. For example, see Perlman1976 and Roy and Al Sayyad 2004.

36. Raquel Rolnik, in discussions with the author, São Paulo, Brazil, December 2008.
37. Leader from the Movimento dos Trabalhadores Rurais Sem Terra (MST), in discussions with the author, São Paulo, Brazil, June 2008.

NOTES TO CHAPTER 4

1. Maria das Graças, in discussions with the author, Curitiba, Brazil, October 2008.
2. Avritzer 2006, 2008; Wampler 2007b.
3. Avritzer 2006; Houtzager and Moore 2003; Putnam 1993.
4. Avritzer 2006.
5. Avritzer 2009; Cooke and Kothari 2001.
6. Navarro 2003.
7. Carneiro 2002; Carvalho 1998; Santos, Ribeiro, and Azevedo 2007.
8. IBGE 2005.
9. Holston 2008.
10. Edwards 2004, 15.
11. Waisman 2006.
12. Putnam 1993.

NOTES TO CHAPTER 5

1. Benedito Barbosa, in discussions with the author, June 2008.
2. Selee and Peruzzotti 2009; (1) Avritzer 2002, (2) Bebbington 2005, (3) Fung and Wright 2003; Avritzer 2002.
3. Agrawal and Gupta 2005; Avritzer 2009; Fagatto and Fung 2006; Kumar 2002; Ostrom 1996.
4. Avritzer 2009; Wampler 2007b.
5. Agrawal and Gupta 2005; Avritzer 2009; Fagatto and Fung 2006; Kumar 2002.
6. Bates 1984; North 1990; Ostrom 1990.
7. MUNIC survey conducted by IBGE in 2008. Municipal-level government officials who may or may not be directly involved with the management of the housing council fill out these surveys.
8. IBGE 2008.
9. Ibid.
10. Avritzer 2009; Wampler 2007b.
11. Putnam 1993.
12. Avritzer 2009; Wampler 2007b.
13. For arguments related to the effect of the party in power, see Avritzer 2009; Baiocchi 2005; Lavalle, Acharya, and Houtzager 2005; Selee and Peruzzotti 2009; Tatagiba and Teixeira 2008; Cornwall and Coelho 2007; Wampler 2007b. For arguments related to the strategies of civil society, see Mahmud 2007; Wampler 2007b.
14. The data do not show a significant correlation between the PT and the existence of municipal housing councils. Further, the statistical analysis in Chapter 3 does not show a significant relationship between the PT and the adoption of social housing programs. Administration by a PT government does not appear to be endogenous either to the existence of participatory governance institutions or to social housing policies.

15. Avritzer 2002.
16. Wampler 2007b.
17. Secretaria de Habitação 2008.
18. Benedito Barbosa, in discussions with the author, São Paulo, Brazil, June 2008.
19. After the research on Santo André was completed, the PT actually lost control of the municipal administration. Since 2009, Mayor Aidan Ravin from the PTB (Partido Trabalhista Brasileiro) has led the city administration.
20. The label "ABC region" is formed by the initials of Santo André, São Bernardo do Campo, and São Caetano do Sul.
21. Dr. Newton da Costa Brandão from the PSDB (Partido da Social Democracia Brasileira) was mayor from 1993 to 1997.
22. IPEA 2000.
23. Prefeitura de Santo André 2006.
24. Ibid.
25. IPEA 2000.
26. Secretaria Municipal de Habitação 2008.
27. Mayor João Henrique Carneiros left the PDT in 2007 to affiliate with the PMDB (O Partido do Movimento Democrático Brasileiro), the largest political party in Brazil.
28. Avritzer 2002; Hagopian 1996.
29. Mayor Gilberto Kassab started his administration as a member of the DEM party (Partido Democrático), but in 2011, during his second administration, he switched his party affiliation to the PSD (Partido Social Democrático).
30. SEHAB-SP 2008. Chapter 8 further explores the tensions of elections for social movement representatives on São Paulo's housing council.
31. The four main national movements for housing are the União Nacional dos Movimentos da Moradia Popular, the Central dos Movimentos Populares, CONAM (Confederação Nacional dos Associações da Moradia), and the Frente da Luta de Moradia Popular.
32. Elisabete França, in discussions with the author, São Paulo, Brazil, December 2008.
33. Evaniza Rodrigues, in discussions with the author, São Paulo, Brazil, September 2008.
34. Municipal government official, in discussions with the author, Santo André, Brazil, October 2008.
35. SECOVI representative, in discussions with the author, São Paulo, Brazil, December 2008.
36. Abers 2001; Baiocchi 2003.
37. I include this measure in the statistical analysis here as a control variable because the make-up of the legislature appeared to be relevant to housing policies and programs in the case studies. However, as demonstrated in the results in Tables 5.6, 5.7, and 5.8, the percentage of seats in the municipal legislature held by PT party members is not significantly related to housing program adoption. Therefore, I did not revise the previous models to include this variable.
38. Dantas 2006.
39. Avritzer 2007 acknowledges regional differences while arguing that participation is not homogeneous within regions. For example, the city of Recife, Brazil, in the Northeast is also known for civil society engagement.
40. A negative binomial model is appropriate for this analysis because the proportional odds between categories cannot be assumed to be equal and the data is extra-dispersed. The negative binomial model predicts expected counts rather than probabilities.

41. Angela Gordilho Souza, in discussions with the author, Salvador, Brazil, November 2008.

NOTES TO CHAPTER 6

1. Gisela Mori, in discussions with the author, São Paulo, Brazil, September 2008.
2. For example, Abers 2003; Andersson and van Laerhoven 2007; Wampler 2008.
3. Montero and Samuels 2004.
4. Wampler and McNulty 2011.
5. Ibid.
6. Avritzer 2009, 17.
7. Kauneckis and Andersson 2009; Wampler 2008.
8. Morrison and Singer 2007.
9. Andersson and van Laerhoven 2007.
10. Baiocchi, Heller, and Silva 2008.
11. Cornwall 2007.
12. Luiz Herlain, in discussions with the author, Curitiba, Brazil, October 2008.
13. Rev. Marcos Cosmo, in discussions with the author, Recife, Brazil, November 2008.
14. Leonardo Avritzer, in discussions with the author, Rio de Janeiro, Brazil, June 2009.
15. The position of those I interviewed in each city varied. In Recife I interviewed the secretary for housing and several of her advisors. In Salvador, I interviewed the previous secretary for housing and several current officials in the secretariat. In Curitiba, which does not have a housing secretariat, I interviewed several managers from COHAB responsible for program decisions and the housing council. In São Paulo I interviewed the superintendent for social housing, managers from COHAB, and several other housing secretariat officials involved with the housing council. Finally, in Santo André I interviewed municipal government members of the housing council.
16. Elisabete França, in discussions with the author, São Paulo, Brazil, December 2008.
17. Angela Gordilho Souza, in discussions with the author, Salvador, Brazil, November 2008.
18. Curitiba municipal government official, in discussions with the author, Curitiba, Brazil, October 2008.
19. Rev. Marcos Cosmo, in discussions with the author, Recife, Brazil, November 2008.
20. FASE advocate, in discussions with the author, Recife, Brazil, November 2008.
21. Though time series analysis comparing 2005 to 2008 would seem appropriate to assess the differences in council effects, I believe the effect of federal-level programs increasing between the three years may bias the estimates.
22. I also ran these models with regional dummies included. The inclusion of regional dummies did not alter the findings regarding council creation. For the sake of simplicity, therefore, I do not show the results of models including regional dummies since I am not presenting an argument for the importance of region in this chapter.

NOTES TO CHAPTER 7

1. Municipal government official, in discussions with the author, São Paulo, Brazil, September 2008.
2. Arretche et al. 2012.
3. Arretche et al. 2012, 96.
4. See, for example, Baiocchi, Heller, and Silva 2011.
5. See, for example, Weir, Rongerude, and Ansell 2009.
6. According to Brazilian scholar Marta Arretche, some smaller municipalities may actually continue to receive federal funds without having a municipal housing council because the current federal government has not made it a priority to penalize these municipalities for noncompliance with the federal system. As the largest city in the country, however, São Paulo could not operate under the radar of federal-level enforcement.
7. Translated from the following: "O Conselho Municipal de Habitação tem caráter deliberativo, fiscalizador e consultivo e como objetivos básicos o estabelecimento, acompanhamento, controle e avaliação da política municipal de habitação." LEI N°. 13.425, de 02 de setembro de 2002.
8. At the time he became mayor Gilberto Kassab was part of the DEM (Democratas) party. In 2011, he started the PSD and changed his affiliation.
9. In this chapter I differentiate between civil society and social movements simply because that is how membership is divided within the city's CMH. In the rest of the book, except where noted, I include social movements within the definition of civil society.
10. Gisela Mori, in discussions with the author, São Paulo, Brazil, September 2008.
11. Cymbalista and Santoro 2008.
12. Elisabete França, in discussions with the author, São Paulo, Brazil, December 2008.
13. As opposed to elections for federal, state, and municipal executives and legislators, voting in the elections for the CMH is not obligatory.
14. NEPAC-UNICAMP 2011.
15. Tatagiba and Blikstad 2011.
16. Juliana Avanci, in discussions with the author, São Paulo, Brazil, May 2012.
17. Juliana Avanci, radio interview, 2012.
18. NEPAC-UNICAMP 2011.
19. CMP 2012.
20. Gisela Mori, in discussions with the author, São Paulo, Brazil, September 2008.
21. Abelardo Campoy, in discussions with the author, São Paulo, Brazil, May 2012.
22. Ana Maria Maluf, in discussions with the author, São Paulo, Brazil, May 2012.
23. Gisela Mori, in discussions with the author, São Paulo, Brazil, September 2008.

NOTES TO CHAPTER 8

1. Wampler and McNulty (2011) refer to this trend as the "third generation" in research on participatory institutions.

References

Abers, Rebecca Neaera. "Reflections on What Makes Empowered Participatory Governance Happen." In *Deepening Democracy: Institutional Innovations in Empowered Participatory Governance*, edited by Archon Fung and Erik Olin Wright, 200–207. London: Verso Press, 2003.

———. *Inventing Local Democracy: Grassroots Politics in Brazil*. Boulder, CO: Lynne Reiner, 2001.

———. "From Clientelism to Cooperation: Participatory Policy and Civic Organizing in Porto Alegre, Brazil." *Politics and Society* 26, no. 4 (1998): 511–37.

———. "From Ideas to Practice: The Partido dos Trabalhadores and Participatory Governance in Brazil." *Latin American Perspectives* 23, no. 4 (1996): 35–53.

Ackerman, John. "Co-Governance for Accountability: Beyond 'Exit' and 'Voice.'" *World Development* 32, no. 3 (2004): 447–63.

Adhikari, Bhim, Salvatore Di Falco, and Jon C. Lovett. "Household Characteristics and Forest Dependency: Evidence from Common Property Forest Management in Nepal." *Ecological Economics* 48, no. 2 (2004): 245–57.

Afonso, Jose Roberto R., and Luiz de Mello. "Brazil: An Evolving Federation." Prepared for the IMF/FAD Seminar on Decentralization, Washington, DC, 2000.

Agrawal, Arun, and Krishna Gupta. "Decentralization and Participation: The Governance of Common Pool Resources in Nepal's Terai." *World Development* 33, no. 7 (2005): 1101–14.

Ames, Barry. *The Deadlock of Democracy in Brazil*. Ann Arbor: University of Michigan Press, 2001.

Andersson, Krister, and Frank van Laerhoven. "From Local Strongman to Facilitator: Institutional Incentives for Participatory Municipal Governance in Latin America." *Comparative Political Studies* 40 (2007): 1085–1111.

Anheier, Helmut K. *Civil Society: Measurement, Evaluation, Policy*. London: Earthscan, 2004.

Arias, Enrique Desmond. *Drugs and Democracy in Rio de Janeiro: Trafficking, Social Networks, and Public Security*. Chapel Hill: University of North Carolina Press, 2006.

Arretche, Marta, Berenice de Souza Cordeiro, Edgard Fusaro, Edney Cielici, and Mariana Bittar. *Capacidades administrativas dos municípios Brasileiros para a política habitacional*. São Paulo, Brazil: Secretaria Nacional de Habitação/Ministério das Cidades e do Centro de Estudos da Metrópole/Cebrap, 2012.

Asante, F. and J. Ayee. "Decentralisation, Poverty Reduction, and the Ghana Poverty Reduction Strategy." In *Poverty Reduction Strategies in Action: Perspectives and Lessons from Ghana*, edited by Joe Amoako-Tuffour and Bartholomew Armah, 183–204. Lanham, MD: Lexington Books, 2008.

Avanci, Juliana. "Eleição do Conselho Municipal de Habitação e suspense por cercear participação popular." *BrasilAtual,* February 4, 2012. Accessed April 2, 2012, http://www.redebrasilatual.com.br/radio/programas/jornal-brasil-atual/elei cao-do-conselho-municipal-de-habitacao-e-suspensa-por-cercear-participacao-popular/view.

Avelino George, David S. Brown, and Wendy Hunter. "The Effects of Capital Mobility, Trade Openness and Democracy on Social Spending in Latin America 1980–1999." *American Journal of Political Science* 49, no. 3 (2005): 625–41.

Avritzer, Leonardo. *Participatory Institutions in Democratic Brazil.* Washington, DC: Woodrow Wilson Center Press, 2009.

———. "Democratization and Citizenship in Latin America: The Emergence of Institutional Forms of Participation." *Latin American Research Review* 43, no. 2 (2008): 282–89.

———. *A participação social no nordeste.* Belo Horizonte: Editora UFMG, 2007.

———. "New Public Spheres in Brazil: Local Democracy and Deliberative Politics." *International Journal of Urban and Regional Research* 30 (2006): 623–37.

———. *Democracy and the Public Space in Latin America.* Princeton, NJ: Princeton University Press, 2002.

———. *Militants and Citizens: The Politics of Participatory Democracy in Porto Alegre.* Palo Alto, CA: Stanford University Press, 2005.

———. "Participation, Activism, and Politics: The Porto Alegre Experiment." In *Deepening Democracy: Institutional Innovations in Empowered Participatory Governance,* edited by Archon Fung and Erik Olin Wright, 45–76. New York: Verso, 2003.

———. "Participation, Activism, and Politics: The Porto Alegre Experiment and Deliberative Democratic Theory." *Politics & Society* 29 (2001): 43–72.

Baiocchi, Gianpaolo, Patrick Heller, and Marcelo Kunrath Silva. *Bootstrapping Democracy: Transforming Local Governance and Civil Society in Brazil.* Stanford, CA: Stanford University Press, 2011.

———. "Making Space for Civil Society: Local Democracy in Brazil." *Social Forces* 86, no. 3 (2008): 911–35.

Banting, Keith G. *The Welfare State and Canadian Federalism.* Montreal: McGill-Queen's University Press, 1987.

Bardhan, Pranab, and Dilip Mookherjee, eds. *Decentralization to Local Governments in Developing Countries: A Comparative Perspective.* Cambridge, MA: MIT Press, 2006.

Bates, Robert. *Markets and States in Tropical Africa: The Political Basis of Agricultural Policies.* Berkeley: California University Press, 1984.

Baumann, T. "Shelter Finance Strategies for the Poor: South Africa." Background paper for meeting of the Rockefeller Foundation/CSUD Urban Summit, 2007.

Bebbington, Anthony. "Comunidades indígenas, desarrollo local y concertación local en América Latina." Working paper. Arlington, VA: Inter-American Foundation, 2005.

Blair, Harry. "Participation and Accountability at the Periphery: Democratic Local Governance in Six Countries." *World Development* 28, no. 1 (2000): 21–39.

Boone, Peter. "Politics and the Effectiveness of Foreign Aid." *European Economic Review* 40, no. 2 (1996): 289–329.

Boonyabancha, S. "Baan Mankong: Going to Scale with 'Slum' and Squatter Upgrading in Thailand." *Environment and Urbanization* 17, no. 1 (2005): 21–46.

Brown, David, and Wendy Hunter. "Democracy and Human Capital Formation." *Comparative Political Studies* 37, no. 7 (2004): 842–64.

Buckley, Robert M., and Jerry Kalarickal. "Housing Policy in Developing Countries: Conjectures and Refutations." *World Bank Research Observer* 20, no. 2 (2005): 233–57.

Bueno de Mesquita, Bruce, Alistair Smith, Randolph M. Siverson, and James D. Morrow. *The Logic of Political Survival*. Cambridge, MA: MIT Press, 2003.

Caixa Econômica Federal. "Dois milhões de casas para os Brasileiros." 2012. Accessed June 28, 2012, http://www.caixa.gov.br/habitacao/mcmv/index.asp.

Caldeira, Teresa. *City of Walls: Crime, Segregation, and Citizenship in São Paulo*. Berkeley: University of California Press, 2001.

Cardoso, Patrícia. "Sistema nacional de habitação de interesse social à luz do novo marco legal urbanistico: Subsidios para implementação nos estados e municípios: Lei federal no. 11.124/05." São Paulo: Instituto Pólis, 2008.

Carneiro, Carla Bronzo Ladeira. "Conselho de políticas públicas: institucionalização." *Revista de Administração Pública* 36 (2002): 277–92.

Carothers, Thomas. *Aiding Democracy Abroad: The Learning Curve*. Washington, DC: Carnegie Endowment for International Peace, 1999.

Carvalho, Maria do Carmen Albuquerque. "Participação Social no Brasil Hoje." Pólis Integras, 2, 1998. Accessed June 9, 2009, http://www.polis.org.br/publi cacoes_lista.asp?cd_serie=18.

Castells, Manuel. *The City and the Grassroots: A Cross-Cultural Theory of Urban Social Movements*. Berkeley: University of California Press, 1983.

Cavalcanti, Débora, Olinda Marques, and Teresa Hilda Costa. "Municipal Programme for the Reform and Extension of Homes: Casa Melhor/PAAC Cearah Periferia, Brazil." In *Empowering Squatter Citizen: Local Government, Civil Society and Urban Poverty Reduction*, edited by Diana Mitlin and David Satterthwaite, 165–92. London: Earthscan, 2004.

Central dos Movimentos Populares (CMP). Email to author from the Forum Centro Vivo listserv, April 1, 2012.

Centro Gaspar Garcia de Direitos Humanos. *Moradia é Central: Lutas, desafios, e estratégias*. São Paulo, Brazil: Centro Gaspar Garcia, 2012.

Coelho, Vera Schattan P., Barbara Pozzoni, and Mariana Cifuentes. 2005. "Participation and Public Policies in Brazil." In *The Deliberative Democracy Handbook: Strategies for Effective Citizen Engagement in the Twenty-First Century*, edited by John Gastil and Peter Levine, 174–84. New York: Jossey-Bass, 2005.

Cooke, Bill, and Uma Kothari, eds. *Participation: The New Tyranny?* London: Zed Books, 2001.

Cornwall, Andrea. "Deliberating Democracy: Scenes from a Brazilian Municipal Health Council." IDS Working Paper 292. Brighton: Institute of Development Studies at the University of Sussex, 2007.

Cornwall, Andrea, and Vera Schattan Coelho, eds. *Spaces for Change? The Politics of Citizen Participation in New Democratic Arenas*. New York: Zed Books, 2007.

Crook, Richard C. "Decentralisation and Poverty Reduction in Africa: The Politics of Local-Central Relations." *Public Administration and Development* 23, no. 1 (2003): 77–88.

Crook, Richard C., and James Manor. *Democracy and Decentralisation in South Asia and West Africa*. Cambridge: Cambridge University Press, 1998.

Crook, Richard C., and Alan Sturla Sverrisson. "Decentralisation and Poverty-Alleviation in Developing Countries: A Comparative Analysis or, Is West Bengal Unique?" IDS Working Paper 130. Brighton: Institute of Development Studies at the University of Sussex, 2001.

Cunha, Vania. "Pacificação libera até 70 vagas por mês no Hospital Getúlio Vargas." *O Dia*, July 2, 2012. Accessed August 20, 2012, http://odia.ig.com.br/portal/rio/ pacifica%C3%A7%C3%A3o-libera-at%C3%A9-70-vagas-por-m%C3%AAs-no-hospital-get%C3%BAlio-vargas-1.458438.

Cymbalista, Renato, and Paula Freire Santoro. "Housing—Evaluation of the Municipal Policy (2005–2006)." In *The Challenges of Democratic Management in Brazil: Participation*, edited by Ana Claudia Teixeira, 147–81. São Paulo: Instituto Pólis, 2008.

Cymbalista, Renato, Paula Freire Santoro, Luciana Tatagiba, and Ana Cláudia Chaves Teixeira. *Habitação: Controle Social e Política Pública*. Caderno 31. São Paulo: Instituto Pólis, 2007.

Dagnino, Evelina, Alberto J. Olvera, and Aldo Panfichi. *A disputa pela construção democrática na América Latina*. São Paulo: Paz e Terra, 2006.

Dantas, Paulo Fábio Neto. *Tradição, autocracia, e carisma: A política de António Carlos Magalhães na modernização da Bahia (1954–1974)*. Belo Horizonte: Editora da UFMG, 2006.

Dasgupta, Partha. *An Inquiry into Well-Being and Destitution*. New York: Oxford University Press, 1993.

Deacon, Robert. "Public Good Provision under Dictatorship and Democracy." *Public Choice* 139, nos. 1–2 (2009): 241–62.

de la Fuente, Angel, and Antonio Estache. "Infrastructure Productivity and Growth: A Quick Survey." Washington DC, World Bank IGF, mimeo, 2004.

Departamento Intersindical de Estatística e Estudos Socioeconômicos. "Nota técnica: Salário mínimo constitucional." October 2005, Accessed October 10, 2012, http://www.dieese.org.br/notatecnica/notatecSMC.pdf.

de Soto, Hernando. *The Mystery of Capital: Why Capitalism Triumphs in the West and Fails Everywhere Else*. New York: Basic Books, 2000.

Donaghy, Maureen. "Do Participatory Governance Institutions Matter? An Analysis of Municipal Councils and Social Housing Programs in Brazil." *Journal of Comparative Politics* 44 (2011): 83–102.

Draibe, Sonia M. "The Brazilian Developmental Welfare State: Rise, Decline, Perspectives." In *Latin America: A New Developmental Welfare State Model in the Making?* edited by Manuel Riesco, 239–81. Houndmills, UK: Palgrave, 2007.

Duquette, Michel, Maurilio Galdino, Charmain Levy, Berengere Marques-Pereira, and Florence Raes. *Collective Action and Radicalism in Brazil: Women, Urban Housing, and Rural Movements*. Toronto: University of Toronto Press, 2005.

Eaton, Kent. *Politics beyond the Capital: The Design of Subnational Institutions in South America*. Stanford, CA: Stanford University Press, 2004.

Edwards, Michael. *Civil Society*. Cambridge: Polity Press, 2004.

Esping-Andersen, Gösta. *The Three Worlds of Welfare Capitalism*. Princeton, NJ: Princeton University Press, 1990.

Fagatto, Elena, and Archon Fung. "Empowered Participation in Urban Governance: The Minneapolis Neighborhood Revitalization Program." *International Journal of Urban and Regional Research* 30, no. 3 (2006): 638–55.

Fioramonti, Lorenzo, and V. Finn Heinrich. "How Civil Society Influences Policy: A Comparative Analysis of the CIVICUS Civil Society Index in Post-Communist Europe." Overseas Development Institute and CIVICUS, 2007. Published online April 8, 2011. Accessed August 15, 2012, https://civicus.org/fr/actualites-et-res sources/rapports-et-publications/246-how-civil-society-influences-policy-a-com parative-analysis-of-the-civicus-civil-society-index-in-post-communist-europe.

Fishkin, James. *Democracy and Deliberation: New Directions for Democratic Reform*. New Haven, CT: Yale University Press, 1991.

Fiszbein, Ariel. "The Emergence of Local Capacity: Lessons from Colombia." *World Development* 25 (1997): 1029–43.

Fiszbein, Ariel, and Norbert Schady. *Conditional Cash Transfers: Reducing Present and Future Poverty*. Washington, DC: The World Bank, 2009.

Forum Nacional de Reforma Urbana (FNRU). "Documento final do FUM considera Declaração do Fórum Nacional de Reforma Urbana." 2010. Accessed October 10, 2012, http://www.unmp.org.br/index.php?option=com_content&view=article& id=377:documento-final-do-fum-considera-declaracao-do-forum-nacional-de-reforma-urbana&catid=36:noticias&Itemid=61.

————."Boletin FNRU: A Reforma Urbana e o Pacote Habitacional." 2009. Accessed March 19, 2009, http://www.abong.org.br/final/noticia/php?faq=19483.

Franco, Álvaro, Carlos Alvarez-Dardet, and Maria Teresa Ruiz. "Effect of Democracy on Health: Ecological Study." *BMJ* 329, no. 7480 (2004): 1421–23.

Frente de la Luta Moradia, email to the author from the Forum Centro Vivo Listserv, April 26, 2010.

Fukuyama, Francis. "The Primacy of Culture." *Journal of Democracy* 6, no. 1 (1996): 7–14.

Fundação João Pinheiro. "Déficit habitacional no Brasil." 2009. Accessed October 10, 2012, http://www.fjp.gov.br/index.php/indicadores-sociais/deficit-habitacional-no-brasil.

Fung, Archon, and Erik Olin Wright. *Deepening Democracy: Institutional Innovations in Empowered Participatory Governance*. New York: Verso, 2003.

Galasso, Emanuela, and Martin Ravallion. "Distributional Outcomes of a Decentralized Welfare Program." Policy Research Working Paper Series 2316, the World Bank, 2000.

Gaventa, John. "Triumph, Deficit or Contestation? Deepening the 'Deepening Democracy' Debate." IDS Working Paper 264. Brighton: Institute of Development Studies at the University of Sussex, 2006.

Gerring, John, Strom C. Thacker, and Rodrigo Alfaro. 2005. "Democracy and Human Development." *Journal of Politics* 74, no. 1 (2012): 1–17.

Gilbert, Alan. "Power, Ideology and the Washington Consensus: The Development and Spread of Chilean Housing Policy." *Housing Studies* 17, no. 2 (2002): 305–24.

Giugni, Marco. "Was It Worth the Effort? The Outcomes and Consequences of Social Movements." *Annual Review of Sociology* 24 (1998): 371–93.

Giugni, Marco, Doug McAdam, and Charles Tilly, eds. *How Social Movements Matter*. Minneapolis: University of Minnesota Press, 1999.

Goldfrank, Benjamin. "The Politics of Deepening Local Democracy: Decentralization, Party Institutionalization, and Participation." *Comparative Politics* 39, no. 2 (2007): 147–68.

Gomes, Patrícia. "Conselho municipal de habitação: Uma experiência de participação popular na cidade de Goiânia Macedo." Conference paper delivered to the Conference on Social Movements, Participation and Democracy, UFSC, Florianopolis, Brazil, 2007.

Grindle, Merilee. *Going Local: Decentralization, Democratization and the Promise of Good Government*. Princeton, NJ: Princeton University Press, 2007.

Grugel, Jean, ed. *Democracy without Borders: Transnationalization and Conditionality in New Democracies*. London: Routledge, 1999.

Haber, Stephen. "Authoritarian Government." In *The Oxford Handbook of Political Economy*, edited by Barry Weingast and Donald Wittmans, 688–711. New York: Oxford University Press, 2007.

Haggard, Stephen, and Robert Kaufman. *Democracy, Development, and Welfare States: Latin America, East Asia, and Eastern Europe*. Princeton, NJ: Princeton University Press, 2008.

Hagopian, Frances. *Traditional Politics and Regime Change in Brazil*. New York: Cambridge University Press, 1996.

Hardjono, Ratih, and Stefanie Teggemann, eds. "The Poor Speak Up—17 Stories of Corruption." The Partnership for Government Reform, Washington, DC: The World Bank, 2003.

Henry-Lee, Aldrie. "The Nature of Poverty in the Garrison Constituencies of Jamaica." *Environment and Urbanization* 17, no. 2 (2005): 83–99.

Holston, James. *Insurgent Citizenship: Disjunctions of Democracy and Modernity in Brazil*. Princeton, NJ: Princeton University Press, 2008.

Houtzager, Peter. *Changing Paths: International Development and the New Left of Inclusion*. Ann Arbor: University of Michigan Press, 2003.

Houtzager, Peter, and Mick Moore, eds. *Changing Paths: International Development and the New Politics of Inclusion.* Ann Arbor: University of Michigan Press, 2003.

Huber, Evelyn, and John D. Stephens. *Development and Crisis of the Welfare State: Parties and Policies in Global Markets.* Chicago: University Chicago Press, 2001.

Huchzermeyer, Marie. *Unlawful Occupation: Informal Settlements and Urban Policy in South Africa and Brazil.* Trenton, NJ: Africa World Press, 2004.

Huther, Jeff, and Anwar Shah. "Applying a Simple Measure of Good Governance to the Debate on Fiscal Decentralization." Washington, DC, World Bank, 1998. Accessed October 17, 2010, http://web.worldbank.org/WBSITE/EXTERNAL/WBI/EXTWBIGOVANTCOR/0,,contentMDK:20789820~isCURL:Y~pagePK:641684 45~piPK:64168309~theSitePK:1740530,00.html.

Immergut, Ellen. *Health Politics: Interests and Institutions in Western Europe.* Cambridge: Cambridge University Press, 1992.

Inglehart, Ronald. *Culture Shift in Advanced Industrial Countries.* Princeton, NJ: Princeton University Press, 1989.

Instituto Brasileiro de Geografia e Estatística (IBGE). "2010 Population Censuses." 2010. Accessed June 20, 2012, http://www.ibge.gov.br/english/estatistica/popu lacao/censo2010/default.shtm.

———. "SIS 2009: In Ten Years, Percentage of Families Living on Up to Half a Minimum Wage per Capita Decreases from 32.4% to 22.6%." October 2009. Accessed June 20, 2012, http://www.ibge.gov.br/english/presidencia/noticias/no ticia_visualiza.php?id_noticia=1476&id_pagina=1.

———. "Pesquisa de Informações Básicas Municipais: Perfil dos Municípios Brasileiros, Gestão Publica (MUNIC)." 2005 and 2008. Accessed May 2008, http://www.ibge.gov.br/.

———. "Fundações Privadas e Associações sem Fins Lucrativos no Brasil (FAS-FIL)." Cadastro Central de Empresas. 2002. Accessed May 2008, http://www.ibge.gov.br/.

Instituto de Pesquisa Económica Aplicada (IPEA). Databank on regional and social indicators. 2000. Accessed May 2008, http://www.ipeadata.gov.br/.

Inter-American Development Bank (IADB). *Room for Development: Housing Markets in Latin America and the Caribbean.* Edited by César Patricio Bouillon. New York: Palgrave Macmillan, 2012.

Jacobi, Pedro. "Challenging Traditional Participation in Brazil: The Goals of Participatory Budgeting." Number 32, Washington, DC: Woodrow Wilson Center for Scholars, 1999.

Jenkins, Paul, Harry Smith, and Ya Ping Wang. *Planning and Housing in the Rapidly Urbanising World.* London: Routledge, 2007.

Kaufman, Robert R., and Alex Segura-Ubiergo. "Globalization, Domestic Politics, and Social Spending in Latin America." *World Politics* 53, no. 4 (2001): 553–87.

Kauneckis, Derek, and Krister Andersson. "Making Decentralization Work: A Cross-National Examination of Local Governments and Natural Resource Governance in Latin America." *Studies in Comparative International Development* 44 (2009): 23–46.

Keck, Margaret. *The Worker's Party and Democratization in Brazil.* New Haven, CT: Yale University Press, 1992.

Kumar, Sanjay. 2002. "Does 'Participation' in Common Pool Resource Management Help the Poor? A Social Cost-Benefit Analysis of Joint Forest Management in Jharkhand, India." *World Development* 30, no. 5 (2002): 763–82.

Kwon, Huck-ju. "Advocacy Coalitions and the Politics of Welfare in Korea." *Policy and Politics* 31, no. 1 (2002): 69–82.

Kwon, Soonman. "Achieving Health Insurance for All: Lessons from the Republic of Korea." Working Paper ESS1. Seoul, Korea: Social Security Policy and Development Branch, International Labor Office, 2002.

Lake, David A., and Matthew Baum. "The Invisible Hand of Democracy: Political Control and the Provision of Public Services." *Comparative Political Studies* 34, no. 6 (2001): 587–621.

Lall, Samik V., Ajay Suri, and Uwe Deichmann. "Housing Savings and Residential Mobility in Informal Settlements in Bhopal, India." *Urban Studies* 43, no. 7 (2006): 1025–39.

Lavalle, Adrian Gurza, Arnab Acharya, and Peter P. Houtzager. 2005. "Beyond Comparative Anecdotalism: Lessons on Civil Society and Participation from Sao Paulo, Brazil." *World Development* 33, no. 6 (2005): 951–64.

Lieberman, Evan S. "Nested Analysis as a Mixed-Method Strategy for Comparative Research." *American Political Science Review* 99, no. 3 (2005): 435–52.

Lipset, Seymour. M. "Some Social Requisites of Democracy: Economic Development and Political Legitimacy." *American Political Science Review* 53, no. 1 (1959): 69–105.

Mahmud, Simeen. "Spaces for Participation in Health Systems in Rural Bangladesh: The Experience of Stakeholder Community Groups." In *Spaces for Change? The Politics of Citizen Participation in New Democratic Arenas*, edited by Andrea Cornwall and Vera Schattan Coelho, 55–75. New York: Zed Books, 2007.

Mainwaring, Scott. *Rethinking Party Systems in the Third Wave of Democratization: The Case of Brazil*. Stanford, CA: Stanford University Press, 1999.

———. *The Catholic Church and Politics in Brazil, 1916–1985*. Stanford, CA: Stanford University Press, 1986.

Mainwaring, Scott, and Christopher Welna, eds. *Democratic Accountability in Latin America*. Oxford: Oxford University Press, 2003.

Malena, Carmen. "Building Political Will for Participatory Governance: An Introduction." In *From Political Won't to Political Will: Building Support for Participatory Governance*, edited by Carmen Malena, 3–30. Sterling, VA: Kumarian Press, 2009.

Manin, Bernard, Adam Przeworski, and Susan C. Stokes. *Democracy, Accountability and Representation*. Cambridge: Cambridge University Press, 1999.

Manor, James. *The Political Economy of Democratic Decentralisation*. Directions in Development Series. Washington, DC: The World Bank, 1999.

Mares, Isabela, and Matthew E. Carnes. "Social Policy in Developing Countries." *Annual Review of Political Science* 12 (2009): 93–113.

McAdam, Doug, Sidney Tarrow, and Charles Tilly. *Dynamics of Contention*. Cambridge: Cambridge University Press, 2001.

McAdam, Doug, John McCarthy, and Mayer Zald, eds. *Comparative Perspectives on Social Movements: Political Opportunities, Mobilizing Structures, and Cultural Framings*. New York: Cambridge University Press, 1996.

McGuire, J. W. "Democracy, Basic Service Utilization, and Under-5 Mortality: A Cross-National Study of Developing States." *World Development* 34, no. 3 (2006): 405–25.

———. "Social Policy and Mortality Decline in East Asia and Latin America." *World Development* 29, no. 10 (2001): 1673–97.

McGuire, M. C., and M. Olson. "The Economics of Autocracy and Majority Rule: The Invisible Hand and the Use of Force." *Journal of Economic Literature* 34, no. 1 (1996): 72–96.

McNulty, Stephanie. *Voice and Vote: Decentralization and Participation in Post Fujimori Peru*. Stanford, CA: Stanford University Press, 2011.

Ministerio das Cidades. *Déficit habitacional no Brasil 2008*. Brasília: Ministério das Cidades, 2011.

———. "PAC—Urbanização de favelas." 2009a. Accessed February 16, 2009, http://www.brasil.gov.br/pac.

————. "SNHIS/FNHIS." 2009b. Accessed February 16, 2009, http://www.cidades. gov.br/index.php/sistema-nacional-de-habitacao-de-interesse-social-snhis.

————. "Programa Crédito Solidário." 2009c. Accessed February 16, 2009, http://www. cidades.gov.br/index.php/programas-e-acoes/519-programa-credito-solidario.

Mitlin, Diana. "New Directions in Housing Policy." In *Global Urban Poverty: Setting the Agenda*, edited by Allison Garland, Mejgan Massoumi, and Blair Ruble, 151–80. Washington, DC: Woodrow Wilson Center, 2007.

Mitlin, Diana, and David Satterthwaite. *Empowering Squatter Citizen: Local Government, Civil Society, and Urban Poverty Reduction.* London: Earthscan, 2004.

Montero, Alfred P., and David J. Samuels. *Decentralization and Democracy in Latin America.* Notre Dame, IN: University of Notre Dame Press, 2004.

Moon, Bruce E., and William J. Dixon. "Politics, the State, and Basic Human Needs: A Cross-National Study." *American Journal of Political Science* 29, no. 4 (1985): 661–94.

Morrison, Kevin M., and Matthew M. Singer. "Inequality and Deliberative Development: Revisiting Bolivia's Experience with the PRSP." *Development Policy Review* 25, no. 6 (2007): 721–40.

Navarro, Zander. "O Orcamento Participativo de Porto Alegre (1989–2002): Um conciso comentário crítico." In *A inovação democratica no Brasil*, edited by Leonardo Avritzer and Zander Navarro, 89–128. São Paulo: Cortez, 2003.

Niskanen, William A. 1997. "Autocratic, Democratic, and Optimal Government." *Economic Inquiry* 35, no. 3 (1997): 464–79.

North, Douglass C. *Institutions, Institutional Change and Economic Performance.* Cambridge: Cambridge University Press, 1990.

Núcleo de Pesquisa em Participação, Movimentos Sociais, e Ação Coletiva, Universidade de Campinas (NEPAC-UNICAMP). "Em defesa do conselho Municipal de Habitação de São Paulo." *Le Monde Diplomatique Brasil* 5, no. 53 (2011): 34–35.

Nunes, Victor. *Coronelismo, enxada e voto: O município e o regime representativo no Brasil.* São Paulo: Editora Nova Fronteira, 1997.

Nylen, William. "The Making of a Loyal Opposition: The Workers' Party (PT) and the Consolidation of Democracy in Brazil." In *Democratic Brazil: Actors, Institutions, and Processes*, edited by Peter Kingstone and Timothy J. Power, 126–43. Pittsburgh: University of Pittsburgh Press, 2000.

O'Donnell, Guillermo, Andreas Schedler, Larry Diamond, and Marc F. Plattner, eds. *The Self-Restraining State: Power and Accountability in New Democracies.* Boulder, CO: Lynne Rienner, 1999.

Office of the High Commissioner for Human Rights (OHCHR). 1991. "The Right to Adequate Housing (Art. 11 (1)): 13/12/91. CESCR General Comment 4." 1991. Accessed March 29, 2010, http://www.unhchr.ch/tbs/doc.nsf/0/469f4d91a93782 21c12563ed0053547e?Opendocument.

Office of the President of the Republic of Brazil. "Highlights: Actions and Programmes of the Federal Government." Brasilia: Secretariat for Social Communication, 2009.

O Globo. "Sem-teto querem ir ao MP denunciar violação dos direitos humanos." April 27, 2010. Accessed April 28, 2010, http://g1.globo.com/sao-paulo/noti cia/2010/04/sem-teto-querem-ir-ao-mp-denunciar-violacao-dos-direitos-huma nos.html.

Olson, Mancur. *Logic of Collective Action: Public Goods and the Theory of Groups.* Cambridge, MA: Harvard University Press, 1965.

Ostrom, Elinor. *Understanding Institutional Diversity.* New York: Cambridge University Press, 2005.

————. "Crossing the Great Divide: Coproduction, Synergy, and Development." *World Development* 24, no. 6 (1996): 1073–87.

————. *Governing the Commons: The Evolution of Institutions for Collective Action*. New York: Cambridge University Press, 1990.

Perlman, Janice. *Favela: Four Decades of Living on the Edge in Rio de Janeiro*. Oxford: Oxford University Press, 2010.

————. "The Metamorphasis of Marginality in Rio de Janeiro." *Latin American Research Review* 39, no. 1 (2004): 183.

————. *The Myth of Marginality: Urban Poverty and Politics in Rio de Janeiro*. Berkeley: University of California Press, 1976.

Peruzzotti, Enrique, and Catalina Smulovitz, eds. *Enforcing the Rule of Law: Social Accountability in Latin America*. Pittsburgh: Pittsburgh University Press, 2006.

Pessanha, Lavínia, Vanessa Campagnac, and Denise Ferreira Matos. "Panorama Brasileiro dos conselhos municipais de políticas setoriais." Presented at the 30th Encontro Nacional da ANPOCS, Caxambu, Brazil, 2006.

Prefeitura de Santo André. *Habitação: Prefeitura de Santo Andre*. Santo André: Prefeitura de Santo André, 2006.

Przeworski, Adam, Michael E. Alvarez, Jose Antonio Cheibub, and Fernando Limongi. *Democracy and Development: Political Institutions and Well-Being in the World, 1950–1990*. New York: Cambridge University Press, 2000.

Putnam, Robert D. *Making Democracy Work: Civic Traditions in Modern Italy*. Princeton, NJ: Princeton University Press, 1993.

Rodrigues, Evaniza, and Raquel Rolnik. "Shelter Finance Strategies for the Poor: Brazil." Background paper for meeting of the Rockefeller Foundation/CSUD Urban Summit, 2007.

Rosero-Bixby, Luis. "Social Capital, Urban Settings and Demographic Behavior in Latin America." *Population Review* 45, no. 2 (2006): 24–43.

Roy, Ananya, and Nezar Al Sayyad, eds. *Urban Informality: Transnational Perspectives from the Middle East, Latin America, and South Asia*. New York: Lexington Books, 2004.

Sandbrook, Richard, Marc Edelman, Patrick Heller, and Judith Teichman. *Social Democracy in the Global Periphery: Origins, Challenges, Prospects*. Cambridge: Cambridge University Press, 2007.

Santos, Orlando Alves dos, Luiz César de Queiroz Ribeiro, and Sergio De Azevedo. *Governança democrática e poder local: A experiência dos conselhos municipais*. Rio de Janeiro: FASE, 2007.

Satyanarayana, S. "Shelter Finance Strategies for the Poor: India." Background paper for meeting of the Rockefeller Foundation/CSUD Urban Summit, 2007.

Schattschneider, Elmer E. *The Semisovereign People*. New York: Holt, Rinehart and Winston, 1960.

Schneider, Hartmut. "Participatory Governance for Poverty Reduction." *Journal of International Development* 11 (1999): 521–34.

Secretaria de Habitação. *Urbanização de favelas: A experiência de São Paulo*. São Paulo: Prefeitura da Cidade de São Paulo, 2008.

Secretaria de Habitação (SEHAB-SP). "Conselho Municipal de Habitação." 2008. Accessed June 2008, http://www.prefeitura.sp.gov.br/cidade/secretarias/habitacao/organizacao/cmh/.

Secretaria Municipal de Habitação. *Plano Municipal de Habitação de Salvador 2008–2025*. Salvador: Prefeitura Municipal do Salvador, 2008.

Selee, Andrew, and Enrique Peruzzotti, eds. *Participatory Innovation and Representative Democracy in Latin America*. Washington, DC: Woodrow Wilson Center Press, 2009.

Sen, Amartya. *Development as Freedom*. New York: Alfred A. Knopf, 1999.

————. *Poverty and Famines: An Essay on Entitlement and Deprivation*. New York: Oxford University Press, 1981.

Siegle, J. T., M. W. Weinstein, and M. H. Halperin. "Why Democracies Excel." *Foreign Affairs* 83, no. 5 (2004): 57–71.

Skocpol, Theda. *Protecting Soldiers and Mothers: The Political Origins of Social Policy in the United States*. Cambridge, MA: Harvard University Press, 1992.

Stasavage, David. "Democracy and Education Spending in Africa." *American Journal of Political Science* 49, no. 2 (2005): 343–58.

Steiner, Susan. "Decentralisation and Poverty: Conceptual Framework and Application to Uganda." *Public Administration and Development* 27 (2007): 175–85.

Tarrow, Sidney. *Power in Movement: Social Movements and Contentious Politics*. New York: Cambridge University Press, 1998.

Tatagiba, Luciana, and K. Blikstad. "Como se fosse uma eleição para vereador: Dinâmicas participativas e disputas partidárias na cidade de São Paulo." *Lua Nova*. Universidade de Campinas, São Paulo, Brazil, 2011.

Tatagiba, Luciana, and Ana Cláudia Chaves Teixeira. "The Role of the Housing Council of the Municipality of São Paulo in the City's Housing Policy." In *The Challenges of Democratic Management in Brazil: Participation*, edited by Ana Claudia Teixeira, 183–218. São Paulo: Instituto Pólis, 2008.

Tavares, Jose, and Romain Wacziarg. "How Democracy Affects Growth." *European Economic Review* 45, no. 8 (2001): 1341–78.

Tendler, Judith. *Good Government in the Tropics*. Baltimore: Johns Hopkins University Press, 1997.

Tocqueville, Alexis de. *Democracy in America*. New York: Vintage. (Original work published in 1835, reprinted here in 1945.)

Tsebelis, George. *Veto Players: How Political Institutions Work*. Princeton, NJ: Princeton University Press, 2002.

União Nacional de Moradia Popular (UNMP). "Programa de Produção Social de Moradia." 2010. Accessed November 29, 2012, http://www.unmp.org.br/index.php?option=com_content&view=category&id=66:programa-de-producao-social-de-moradia-fnhis&Itemid=98&layout=default.

United Nations. "Outcome of the Conference." Final document for the Rio +20 United Nations Conference on Sustainable Development. Document No. A/CONF.216/L.1, 2012. Accessed June 28, 2012, http://www.uncsd2012.org/thefuturewewant.html.

United Nations Development Program (UNDP). *Human Development Report 2007/2008. Fighting Climate Change: Human Solidarity in a Divided World*. New York: United Nations, 2008.

———. *Human Development Report 2002*. New York: Oxford University Press, 2002.

United Nations Habitat Program. *State of the World's Cities 2008/9 Harmonious Cities*. London: Earthscan, 2008.

———. *The Challenge of Slums: Global Report on Human Settlements 2003*. Nairobi: UN Habitat, 2003.

Waisman, Carlos H. "Autonomy, Self-Regulation and Democracy: Tocquevillian-Gellnerian Perspectives on Civil Society and the Bifurcated State." In *Civil Society and Democracy in Latin America*, edited by Richard Feinberg, Carlos H. Waisman, and Leon Zamosc, 17–34. New York: Palgrave Macmillan, 2006.

Wampler, Brian. "When Does Participatory Democracy Deepen the Quality of Democracy? Lessons from Brazil." *Journal of Comparative Politics* 41, no. 1 (2008): 61–81.

———. "Can Participatory Institutions Promote Pluralism? Mobilizing Low-Income Citizens in Brazil." *Studies in Comparative International Development* 41 (2007a): 57–78.

———. *Participatory Budgeting in Brazil: Contestation, Cooperation, and Accountability*. University Park: Pennsylvania State University Press, 2007b.

Wampler, Brian, and Leonardo Avritzer. "The Spread of Participatory Budgeting in Brazil: From Radical Democracy to Participatory Good Government." *Journal of Latin American Urban Studies* 7 (2005): 37–52.

Wampler, Brian, and Stephanie McNulty. "Does Participatory Governance Matter? Exploring the Nature and Impact of Participatory Reforms." Washington, DC: The Woodrow Wilson Center, 2011. Accessed June 19, 2012, http://www.wilsoncenter.org/program-publications/Comparative%20Urban%20Studies%20Project.

Weir, Margaret, Jane Rongerude, and Christopher K. Ansell. 2009. "Collaboration Is Not Enough: Virtuous Cycles of Reform in Transportation Policy." *Urban Affairs Review* 44, no. 4 (2009): 455–89.

Weir, Margaret, Ann Shola Orloff, and Theda Skocpol, eds. *The Politics of Social Policy in the United States*. Princeton, NJ: Princeton University Press, 1988.

World Bank. "Data: Brazil." 2012. Accessed June 20, 2012, http://data.worldbank.org/country/brazil.

———. "Brazil: Toward a More Inclusive and Effective Participatory Budget in Porto Alegre. Volume 1." Washington, DC: The World Bank, 2008. Accessed June 20, 2012, http://internationalbudget.org/ibp_publication_categories/public-participation/?pagenum=2&attest=true.

———. *World Development Report: Making Services Work for Poor People*. Washington, DC: The World Bank, 2004.

———. *The World Bank Participation Sourcebook*. Washington, DC: The World Bank, 1996.

———. "Governance, The World Bank's Experience." Washington, DC: The World Bank, 1994.

Zweifel, Thomas D., and Patricio Navia. "Democracy, Dictatorship, and Infant Mortality." *Journal of Democracy* 11, no. 2 (2000): 99–114.

Index

For Product Safety Concerns and Information please contact our EU
representative GPSR@taylorandfrancis.com
Taylor & Francis Verlag GmbH, Kaufingerstraße 24, 80331 München, Germany

www.ingramcontent.com/pod-product-compliance
Lightning Source LLC
Chambersburg PA
CBHW070419270326
41926CB00014B/2853